MORE PRAISE FOR CAROLE FUNGAROLI'S

TRADITIONAL DEGREES

for

NONTRADITIONAL STUDENTS

"For our cyber-besotted age this book is a reminder and a reaffirmation of the matchless treasures still to be found in 'brick-and-mortar' institutions. Fungaroli offers both a testimonial to traditional higher education and a guidebook for the growing numbers of 'nontraditional students,' the older people whose return for degrees is the best news in American higher education today."

—Scott Rice, Professor of English,
San Jose State University

"Offers a refreshing pep talk for students who have dropped out, fallen away, or lurked on the margins of higher education after a disappointing high school experience. It gives new credibility to the proposition that a true education, on a *real* campus, is much more a matter of changing one's life than of getting a job certificate."

—Mary Burgan, General Secretary,
American Association of University Professors

"What makes this such a valuable book is its rousing, optimistic call to claim your own education, to imagine the very richest experience possible, and then, how to build a sensible strategy for giving yourself that unmatchable gift—a powerful education at a first-rate institution.

I have taught and advised hundreds of adult women students in the Frances Perkins Program at Mount Holyoke College. We *do* welcome them, appreciate their maturity and intensity, treasure their

hunger to learn, and wonder at their bountiful energy and gifted-
ness."   —Penny Gill, Mary Lyon Professor of Humanities
                    and Professor of Politics, Mount Holyoke College

"With honesty and insight, Carole Fungaroli lays it all out: from
overcoming the bad feelings of not having a college degree to finding
financial aid and managing time for family, job, and classes. She's
dead-on right that if you've been thinking of dropping back into college, then you're ready. She's also dead-on right that the best professors will welcome the maturity and real-life knowledge that you
bring into the classroom."
            —Julie Tetel Andresen, Associate Professor, Duke University

About the Author

CAROLE SARGENT FUNGAROLI earned her bachelor's degree at age thirty while working full-time. She has a doctorate in English literature from the University of Virginia and teaches at Georgetown University in Washington, D.C.

ALSO BY CAROLE S. FUNGAROLI

The Slam and Scream (and Other Powerful Strategies and Great Career Moves for Secretaries, Assistants, and Anyone Else Who Has Had Enough)

TRADITIONAL
DEGREES

 for

NONTRADITIONAL
STUDENTS

How to Earn a Top Diploma
from America's Great Colleges
at Any Age

Carole S. Fungaroli

FARRAR, STRAUS AND GIROUX
NEW YORK

Farrar, Straus and Giroux
19 Union Square West, New York 10003

Copyright © 2000 by Carole S. Fungaroli
Distributed in Canada by Douglas & McIntyre Ltd.
Printed in the United States of America
Designed by Thomas Frank
First Edition, 2000

Library of Congress Cataloging-in-Publication Data
Fungaroli, Carole S.
Traditional degrees for non-traditional students : how to
earn a top diploma from America's great colleges at any age /
Carole S. Fungaroli.—1st ed.
p.   cm.
ISBN 0-374-29989-7 (alk. paper)
1. Adult college students—United States.   2. College student
orientation—United States.   3. Degrees, Academic—United States.
I. Title.

LB2343.32.F86 2000
378.2'4'0973—dc21   99-026745

Grateful acknowledgment is made to the following:

Excerpt from "My Wives Club" by Dana Milbank. Copyright © 1997 by
The New Republic, Inc. Reprinted by permission of The New Republic.

Excerpt from "The Great Sorting" by Nicholas Lemann. Copyright © 1995
by The Atlantic Monthly, Inc. Reprinted by permission of The Atlantic
Monthly.

Excerpt from "An Insider's War Stories" copyright © 1998 by Newsweek,
Inc. Reprinted by permission of Newsweek.

Contents

5. Paying for It:
The Simple Math of Financial Aid   87

6. The Inevitable Application Process   122

Introduction: The Dropout Who Dropped Back In Again

A rumor circulates through the corridors and cubicles of professional America. Men and women in business suits whisper it to one another as though it were the Truth, carved on an altar in the holiest of temples:

Psssssst! Dropouts never drop back in again. *Pass it on.*

If you leave college, or if you don't go at all, these helpful souls feel obliged to remind you of this every chance they get. They'll stop you in the elevator. They'll reinforce it at the coffee machine. Whenever you eye a promotion or a transfer that involves more education and experience than you have, someone will take the golden opportunity to cross-stitch it on the throw pillow of your heart.

But is it true? *Do* dropouts really never drop back in again? If you didn't finish college at age twenty-two, does that mean it's too late now?

Absolutely not.

I spent the past four years interviewing scores of students who returned to college, sometimes many decades after their so-called only chance. For their big return, they went back to top universities and colleges, and earned traditional degrees. They didn't limit themselves to weekend college or distance learning. Instead, they enjoyed the great American college campus—ivy walls, a cappella choral groups, football, mascots, caps and gowns, Professor Kingsfield, Mr. Chips, and all—and had the time of their lives. Most of them earned high grades, or even honors. Many went on to graduate school and excelled there as well.

They proved what I learned through my own back-to-college experience: adults make the best college students. We work harder, get more out of our classes, grow more, and have more fun. We're ready to enjoy and appreciate all of the riches of the American undergraduate experience that traditional-age students often party away. If you are over age twenty-two and thinking about returning to college now, you are *far* better suited to the task than you were at eighteen.

This book will tell you what you need to know to earn a traditional bachelor's degree at a top college or university, no matter what your age. Beyond that, it will introduce you to some remarkable adults all over the United States who have successfully completed their degrees, or who are finishing them now.

Single moms will tell you about finishing college—with honors—while caring for three or four kids. Retirees will discuss earning a first bachelor's degree at age sixty-five. Abused spouses will tell you how they went back to college and soon realized just how unacceptable their domestic lives really were. People with various disabilities who could no longer work in their chosen careers will explain how college helped them earn a living despite physical challenges. There are stories here from men and women who dropped out of high school and went to work, or who started families in their teens. You will read about veterans who finished college after life in the military. You will find stories of addiction and recovery, bankruptcy, poverty, middle-class ennui, and rich-kid-*itis*. These students each started out differently, but they all ended the same way: in triumph.

They make my academic achievements seem modest by comparison. Before writing this book. I thought I was hot stuff. Defying predictions, I finished college with great grades at age thirty, got into a competitive graduate program, and earned a master's degree and Ph.D. a little less than four years later. Every time I remembered that long climb through my twenties out of the typing pool and into college, I'd swell up with pride. I'd recall certain Washington, D.C., lawyers who dished out verbal abuse, and I'd think, "Buddy, if you could only see me now."

Now that I've met these wonderful students, though, my so-called struggle seems like a pirouette in the primroses compared to their challenging lives. If they can do it, then so can you.

Before I introduce you to these adult students and their stories, you may want to know more about mine. After all, what does an English professor know about struggle? How can I presume to tell others how to get up the nerve—and the money—to go back?

I can do it because I lived it. Here's the story of how I finished college.

When I was in grade school, many of my teachers said that I was slothful, stubborn, and hopelessly distracted. I stared out of the window at interesting shapes in the treetops instead of paying attention to the math lesson. I drew pictures of the children from the Healthtex advertisements over and over in the margins of my notebook instead of finishing my spelling assignment. My desk was an organizational disaster. My mind wandered no matter how hard I tried to focus on the blackboard, or on the droning monotony of the school day. Teachers shouted at me, sent me to the principal's office, pleaded with me, and once an infuriated teacher even shook me in front of the entire second-grade class until I peed on her shoes in fear.

Elementary school was a daily battleground to which I trudged, a quiet, obedient, but reluctant soldier. The school system wanted me to present myself front and center and say, "I need help," or else no one would help me. But my confusion and growing isolation prevented me from asking for help.

By the third grade, I was having serious and consistent problems with mathematics, but instead of trying to figure out why, my teacher simply moved on to the brighter pupils who would represent her successes. She spent the rest of the time with the stragglers who misbehaved, and therefore "asked for" the kind of help she could offer. I languished in the corner, quiet, daydreaming, and missing out on important years of education.

My parents tried to help me, but neither of them knew how. My mother had been a top student in all subjects, and was even the salutatorian of her Oklahoma high school class. She turned down a full scholarship to the Oklahoma State Teachers College for the more exciting prospect of working to support the war effort. Then she met and married my father. Like most wives during World War II, she quickly became a mother and forgot about college for good. Mom's advice was to "stick with it," for she was certain that my setbacks were only temporary.

My father's grades had been all over the map. He showed genius with engineering and anything involving spatial relationships. Electricity made perfect sense to him, and he could reason his way through the complicated mathematics required of military pilots. But when he tried to write, it came out all tangled. Nobody ever diagnosed his dyslexia. Instead, his childhood school system tried to label him slow or even stupid, even though he could effortlessly solve problems that stumped his superiors. Dad gave me the 1960s suburban equivalent of "Don't let the bastards get you down," which was comforting but not particularly helpful when it came to long division.

Between them, there wasn't much they could do with my third-grade math woes. Most days I hid my troubles out of embarrassment and frustration. Whenever I did something right, my teachers ignored it as a fluke, and they became heavily invested in viewing me as an amiable mediocrity. And when I did something wrong, it went into my file. Soon that manila envelope bulged with comments about my missteps and general unworthiness for a bright academic future.

Novelist David Guterson, a home-schooling advocate, once described kids in American public schools as "inmates in an institution." That's certainly how I felt. Occasionally a teacher would take an interest in me, but mostly they let me lag far, far behind the others. After the sixth grade, many of my friends went on to programs for the gifted and talented and earned foil stars in every color. Meanwhile, I trudged alone to a prisonlike junior high and watched my grades crawl farther down the scale.

The school system could not have invented a more effective way to make children hate learning than the typical American junior high school. Mine was so dominated by bullies that it's a wonder I made it through every day without getting beaten up. Some of my friends *did* get beaten up. I managed to fly under the radar of the nastiest characters by keeping quiet and reading a lot. Now and then, one particular loud, obnoxious blond girl would single me out for insults or taunts, and I'd wonder what I had done to deserve such cruelty.

Our teachers didn't see the worst of the abuse, because it wore two faces. The meanest kids were also some of the best students and the top athletes. Since our principal didn't know how to investigate conflicts or ask important questions, he took their word that all was well in his little fiefdom. Meanwhile, many of us languished intellectually. Every day was an exercise in basic survival. In this environment, learning was next to impossible.

By then our files had followed us from elementary school, and all of my teachers presumed that my work would not shine. Now and then, I would try harder for my favorite teachers, just for the fun of it. But the 1970s school system had already identified me as part of a slow group, so my successes were treated like aberrations.

After junior high, I drifted into a big regional high school, where I was tracked away from college goals. As at most schools, my teachers were a random mixture of the dedicated, the indifferent, and the malevolent, but it hardly mattered. By this time I deeply believed in my own lack of academic intelligence, and almost any flame that I had for learning had been systematically extinguished. Even a year in private school didn't help.

I worked for a year after high school, clerking in a record store. Then I started college at age nineteen. Even though no reputable school accepted me on the first try, I wrote an eloquent letter to the dean of admissions at the University of North Carolina at Greensboro, and much to my surprise, he let me in on probation. My study skills hadn't improved, however, and I struggled, dropping out for good in the first semester of my junior year.

Dropping out of college seemed terrifying before I did it. But the act itself wasn't really all that painful. I simply walked back to my dorm room, loaded up my 1974 pea-green Chevy Nova, and drove away. In the manner of all lost souls in good country songs, I went south. The long, all-night drive felt like a run for the border. I fled to my parents' home and stayed there for six months, until I got back on my feet.

During that time I worked as a hostess at a coastal resort restaurant. Every day I put on a bright dress—hibiscus patterns were my favorite—feeling like a character in a Jimmy Buffett song. The money from the restaurant never seemed like enough, so I took a second job as a manicurist in an upscale hair salon near the beach. There I met clients from the Church of Scientology, who tried to convert me while I collected their stories for my notebook of Characters I Have Known. I befriended surfers, pot smokers, drug runners, divorcées starting a new life, gamblers, and drifters of various descriptions. I wrote songs, worked out at the YMCA, and perfected an allover hazelnut-brown tan.

That year, Tom Selleck was still on television as Magnum, P.I., cruising around Hawaii in a red Ferrari. He made a beach-bum existence seem smart and fashionable. My sunset adventures were the envy of my friends, so I didn't question my life. It was sunny and warm every day. I lost enough weight to wear a knit brown bikini. I met famous baseball players from the spring training camps. Relationships came and went easily, without rancor or even tears.

After that rejuvenating winter in Margaritaville, the hotter months drove me away from the Sun Coast. I moved back to Washington, D.C., and accepted a temporary job for the summer. Although I vaguely considered returning to school, college seemed like a distant, unclear memory. Dropping out felt like the smartest thing that I had ever done. Rather than an isolated failure, it simply seemed to be the logical culmination of years of feeling lost in public and private schools.

Despite my lack of interest in college, if you had told me that it would be six years before I returned and eight years before I graduated, I would have considered you daft and pessimistic. Until that fall, college had always been a given. Everyone went, didn't they?

Of course they didn't. Today I know that only 20 percent of working adults have a bachelor's degree or higher, but back then I mistakenly assumed that most people did go to college. When I found out that the opposite was true, and that there was no pressure for me to *ever* return, I slowly forgot about the miseries of the academic system. Many of my co-workers didn't have diplomas. A few lied about it, but most people simply did their jobs, even without college. They accepted the lower pay and usually did not consider the possibility of returning later in life.

Over the next few years, I worked, saved money, traveled around Europe, and bought an apartment. Along the way I had many interesting jobs. I bagged groceries at a food warehouse, where workers took me into the back room and scared me into joining the union. I worked as a salesclerk at an upscale clothing store and cringed as young teenagers waving their parents' credit cards treated me like a servant. For a while I tried to learn catering at a now-defunct gourmet delicatessen run by a couple who left— on the lam—without paying any of their employees. I stayed briefly at a rural Virginia commune. I worked for lawyers in Washington who verbally harassed me and the other members of the clerical staff, and I collected stories for my first book, *The Slam and Scream.*

During those years, I learned that there is a professional and even a social chasm between those who have bachelor's degrees and those who lack them. No matter how competent I was at any job, I couldn't earn a promotion without a diploma. Even though I produced a stock market directory and wrote well, I couldn't move beyond entry level.

I also encountered the basic lack of respect that most executives have for members of the clerical staff. Higher education becomes a mark of personal worth in the business world. Most employers— whether they admit it or not—believe that the college-educated are smarter and more deserving of recognition. The more prestigious the campus, in their minds, the more worthy the worker. For two years I tried to deny the obvious, but finally a manager at the stock exchange sat me down to explain it.

"Graduate," he said, "and show me a decent transcript, or I can't promote you. I want to, but until you have a piece of paper, there's nothing I can do."

He was the first person who told me the truth. Thanks to him, I took one night class in English poetry at a local university, and startled myself when I earned an A.

The grade was terrifying. It stared back at me from that report card like a mocking, shrill mistake. Although I was proud of the grade, it also confused me.

If I could earn an A so simply, then why had I suffered in the school system? If college was so doable, why had high school been such a mystery? Why did I feel sick with fear the night before a math test in elementary school? Why had I spent years hiding my books and then scrambling to do my homework on the bus before class? What did all those years of humiliation and defeat mean, if I could earn an A?

I didn't return to college right away because I needed time to think about what an A meant. The class hadn't been a "gut course." My fellow students hadn't all earned A's. The professor seemed shocked when I asked him to sign the form that would remove me from academic probation so that I could take more classes at the university. He said, "*You?*" when I handed it to him, as if he couldn't reconcile one of his best students with this embarrassing piece of paper.

I didn't yet understand what a difference a little maturity makes. Even a short time working in "the real world" will give you the skills you need to succeed in college. Had I understood this, I might have gone back to college immediately.

Instead, I went back to work as though nothing had happened, but actually something profound had taken place. Now I remembered that I had, in fact, done well on aptitude tests in the past. I recalled earning one quarter's worth of A's in junior high school, and then having an administrator question my only B. My grades plummeted again after that. I remembered taking a course in art history at Greensboro and earning my only A at that university. The professor didn't know about my poor academic record, and he had treated me well. That's how I first learned that there are three levels of treatment in the school system: an engaged and encouraging one for the top students, a polite but indifferent one for the masses in the middle, and a bored or even surly one for the bottom-dwellers.

Bit by bit, these new or recollected images warmed up my frozen intellect, and I began to think of myself as a potential student. Oh, I still didn't think that I could be an actual scholar. High achievement was for *really* smart people, I thought, not for plodders like me. But I gradually became more comfortable with the idea of at least finishing college. When I re-enrolled as a full-time student two years later—at age twenty-eight—I believed that college was a possibility.

My first full semester of A grades felt like hitting the slots in Vegas. Quarters poured into my lap, sirens blared, lights flashed, and a crowd gathered. Straight A's? Again, impossible! I knew that I had worked hard, but still, who was I to expect such riches? I fought with feelings of imposterdom and images of naked emperors, but I kept going to class, and the grades kept coming. Now and then I faltered. But most of my grades were high, and I always earned top marks in English, my major. By the time I graduated, one month before my thirtieth birthday, I felt like a scholar after all.

Academic accomplishment is personally quite rewarding. But the world won't stop and notice you just because you finish college, any more than it slowed its revolutions to honor me. You'll still have to struggle, and life's challenges will be as daunting as they ever were. *With* college, however, you'll stand a chance at getting what you want. If you excel at your studies, you will also join a small, exclusive group of adults who enjoy the self-confidence that comes with high achievement, and who have the necessary credentials to get ahead. Whether fairly or not, many people will treat you better once you finish your studies at a college or a university.

In this book you'll read anecdotes from many students who have even more exciting tales to tell than mine. The only changes I have made are to names, when requested to do so, and to pertinent facts such as city, state, or campus when an individual expressed a strong wish not to be identified. Except for these minor alterations to preserve anonymity, the testimonials you are about to read are true.

Enjoy the book, and please don't feel too intimidated by all these success stories. As you read, remind yourself that this would be, should be, and *could* be you, if you go slowly and give yourself time to adjust. Many of these students started out taking just one course in a subject they loved in order to adapt to college life. Some of them earned their degrees over a period of many years. Others dove in, changed their lives, and returned to college full-time, even in their forties, fifties, and sixties. Their stories may sound daunting now, but they all started out with the same things you have: basic intelligence, a hunger to finish college, and the determination to keep going even when it becomes difficult.

If you are a distance learner now, then you may want to think about switching to on-campus education. You'll have a wonderful time getting to know professors in person and making new friends among your fellow students. In addition, your distance learning experience will help make your transition to the traditional campus that much easier.

I hope this book will inspire you to earn your bachelor's degree. If it does, and if you have a story to tell about returning to college, I would love to hear it and congratulate you. Send E-mail to carole@traditionaldegrees.com, or visit www.traditionaldegrees.com, and tell me your story. You may not think that your tale is all that unique, but it might be just what a reader in another part of the country needs. Good luck!

Traditional Degrees
for
Nontraditional Students

WHY COLLEGE . . . AND
WHY NOW?

You may have any of a variety of reasons for thinking about college now. Perhaps you want a better job. A diploma from one of America's great colleges or universities will certainly help you find a rewarding one. Or maybe not having a degree has created a yearning for "something more." Perhaps you always knew that you could have been a good student, if only you could have focused. Now, years or even decades later, you may feel ready.

Ads in newspapers and on the radio often talk about adults as if all we think about are jobs, promotions, and dry-as-dust responsibility. For many nontraditional students, however, college isn't just a path to a job. It also involves discovering a love of the arts, politics, history, public service, technology, the sciences, and the glories of a life of the mind. You don't have to have any reason for returning to college aside from an interest in seeing what fascinating information might be waiting for you in various classes.

Whatever your reasons for going back to college now, you'll have lots of company. According to the Department of Education, nearly half of the enrolled college students in the United States are twenty-four or older. Over one-third are at least thirty-five! That means that over four million of the ten million students sitting in college classrooms today are adults just like you. Although you may initially feel like the World's Oldest Living Undergraduate—as I jokingly dubbed myself when I returned to college—you'll soon find that nontraditional is becoming the norm.

No matter who you are or why you're going, finishing college is a great idea. Not only will it give you an important credential for employment, it will change how you feel about yourself and your abilities. Many of the adults we'll meet in this book started college thinking it would simply help them get a job. Eventually, however, most of them discovered the joy of learning for its own sake. They stopped thinking of themselves solely as parents, spouses, partners, employees, and "busy adults," and started thinking of themselves as scholars, too.

For them, and for you, finishing college isn't just about adding a line to your résumé or snagging a promotion. It will help with both of these, but there's much more. You'll learn new things about yourself, you'll make friends, you'll have opportunities to travel, and you'll be able to point proudly to the kinds of accomplishments that society not only recognizes, but also rewards. College *can* change your life. All you need to begin is the humility to start where you are, the patience to cut through some initial red tape, and the courage to walk onto a campus and ask for some of the best things that colleges and universities can offer.

What's the difference between a college and a university, anyway? The basic difference is the school's ability to grant various degrees. A college grants bachelor's degrees, and it may have limited opportunities for postgraduate study. It does not usually offer the master's or doctoral degrees. A university offers all of these. Colleges generally focus on the teaching abilities of their faculty. Universities engage in ongoing research and expect their faculty to do the same. Some faculty members at universities don't even have teaching responsibilities: they're just there to conduct research and to direct the occasional dissertation. When I use the word "college," I mean your bachelor's degree experience at either a college or a university. Depending upon your needs and the reputation of the school you select, you may attend either one.

In this chapter, you'll learn some surprising things about college degrees, beginning with just how uncommon they really are. As you read, try to place yourself in the mosaic of adults who have already returned to college. We all had a special reason for returning to college. But we all stayed for the same reason: college is easier in adulthood. What used to be a grind has now become a great deal of fun.

BELIEVE IT OR NOT, FOUR-YEAR DEGREES ARE STILL QUITE RARE

Given our society's emphasis on education, you'd think that college diplomas were as common as brown hair or right-handedness. They're not, however, since many traditional-age students drop out. When you finish college, you will join the *top 20 percent* of all working adults.

Does this statistic surprise you? Did you think that most working people had bachelor's degrees? They don't. Let's look at the numbers. Here is the educational attainment of 159 million American adults surveyed in the 1990 Census, according to the Department of Education and the journal *American Demographics:*

Eighth grade or less	10.4%
Some high school, no diploma	14.4%
High school diploma	30.0%
Some college, no degree	18.7%
Associate's degree	6.2%
Bachelor's degree	13.1%
Graduate or professional degree	7.2%

You probably already know that most supervisory and management positions go to college graduates. Therefore, just by finishing college, you will make yourself more promotable than almost 80 percent of the people around you.

And that's if you just squeak by. What if you do well, *really* well? And what if you are able to transfer into a more prestigious college or university because of that? *Top* college grads make up less than 5 percent of the working population. That small group often includes the most influential decision makers in the nation. It may seem like a distant prospect now, but you can join this group more easily than you might think, and this book will tell you exactly how.

COLLEGE GRADUATES EARN AS MUCH AS 70 PERCENT MORE THAN THOSE WITHOUT A DEGREE

If you graduate from college at age thirty, keep working full-time, and retire at age sixty-five, then you'll likely earn a career minimum of $350,000—over a third of a million dollars—more than your non-college-educated counterparts. And that's only at the lower levels. The top college graduates earn more than that, bringing your career bonanza closer to the half-million- or million-dollar range. That's a big return on the $20,000 or so that you are likely to spend in finishing college.

So why don't more adults take some risks and return to college? The first argument people usually offer is "I can't afford it." Yet college pays you much more than it costs. If a rich couple rode up in a limousine and offered you a trust fund of $500,000 or more for four years of work, would you take it? Most people would, but most people also claim that they can't afford college, or that they're too busy slogging away at a low-paying job to graduate.

In Chapter 5 we'll talk about the price tag on a college degree.

Then we'll see how it can cost less to earn a degree—even at one of America's top universities—than to buy a new midsize domestic automobile. If you can afford car payments, you can afford college. I'll also give you plenty of suggestions for earning your way through college without having to spend very much of your own money at all. And if you earn exceptional grades, universities could eventually pay *you* to go to school.

COLLEGE IS A RELIABLE ROAD TO THE GREAT PROFESSIONS AND CAREERS

Besides giving you the key to higher-paying jobs, college gives you access to different *types* of jobs. If your present work doesn't seem rewarding to you, then you probably have a job instead of a career. By far the most satisfied workers are those who labor in a field they love, and do so at a level that brings not just money, but recognition and personal satisfaction as well. Theo used college as a way of catching up on an important work requirement:

> The U.S. Immigration and Naturalization Service hired me as an inspector . . . and one of the prerequisites was that I speak fluent Spanish. I enrolled at Skyline College in San Bruno, California, and the teachers made the classes come alive. I was attending school because I wanted to, not because I had to, and learning became a pleasurable experience for me. I entered the door into a Spanish-speaking world, and shut it behind me. I graduated with highest honors from the community college one year later, and to this day I write and call to thank the teachers there who changed my life.

Theo is now in the University of Miami's Master of Arts in Liberal Studies (MALS) program, designed for adult learners. Without college, you will be limited to the clerical realms in business, or manual labor elsewhere, unless you develop top skills in a trade. College is the only acknowledged route to professions such as law, medicine, business, academia, and many others.

COLLEGE GRADUATES GET TO BE THE BOSS

Have you ever trained anyone to be your supervisor? Working adults often tell stories about having to teach a new, clueless middle manager how the department works. Sometimes these "instant bosses" are fresh out of college, with no more business sense than a stray dog. It can be terribly frustrating to watch younger men and women of average intelligence who don't know the company as well as you do earn the promotions every time.

So how did these managers get where they are in the first place? For many, simply possessing a prestigious bachelor's degree from one of America's great state or private universities made them automatically hireable at the management level. There's a poster on the walls of the business school at my university. It reads, LEARN WHAT A COMPANY IS LIKE BEFORE YOU SPEND THE FIRST SIX MONTHS MAKING COPIES. Translation? "As a college grad from a top university like this one, you shouldn't have to suffer the indignity of entry-level work."

And it's not just the business world that insists on a college education for its higher levels. Before Jan returned to college, she worked for years as the director of a children's education program at a Catholic parish. It was a rewarding job, but she struggled with low pay and insufficient recognition:

> I became painfully aware that the ideal educational level for
> the position I was already holding was a master's degree in
> either religious education or theology. Even though I had

trained two inexperienced pastoral ministers to perform the duties of director, I would never be offered that position myself, or the salary that came along with it, largely because I had no degree.

Also, I found that I was frequently taken advantage of, and that the work I did was not given the respect it deserved. I suspected that this was because I was viewed as a "glorified volunteer," somebody's mom who was helping out—and this was after twelve years of experience, a successful track record, and more hours spent in informal education than I could count.

Jan soon realized that she had both the intelligence and the experience to earn the degrees she needed. But without them, she would never be recognized for what she could contribute:

I had always given far more hours to my work than was healthy for myself and my family, and way beyond the hours for which I was paid. My motive in returning to school was partly to earn proper credentials, partly to earn some respect, partly to pull my salary range out of the teens (this was beginning to feel insulting), but mostly to fill a thirst and a desire to come closer to God through prayerful study. In the end, this has been the most important result.

Instead of sitting outside the parish door waiting for recognition, Jan earned her theology degree—with honors—from Aquinas College in Grand Rapids, Michigan. Today she is the Director of Religious Formation and Education in another Catholic parish. Earning her degree later in life was a challenge, but afterward promotions came easily: "I improved my salary by $4,000 a year without even trying very hard. I am nearing the end of my first year. It has held some challenges, but I have faced them with greater confidence and self-esteem."

Forget "foot in the door" jobs. With rare exceptions, you can't start out in the mailroom and advance to the boardroom. If you want to get ahead, or even land somewhere in the comfortable middle, you will need a bachelor's degree.

MAYBE YOU'RE THE FIRST IN YOUR FAMILY TO THINK ABOUT COLLEGE

Many people didn't go to college simply because no one ever expected them to. People in many regions of the United States place more value on physical labor and life-experience skills than on academia as it is traditionally defined. You may not have attended college because no one else in your family did. Some families would never even consider spending hard-earned money on such an endeavor.

Douglas's high school counselor discouraged him from his goal of attending the top university in his state, even though he was a strong student. Instead, she suggested that Douglas work in the local factory for a year, since most men in his region went directly to work for the same company after high school. Douglas did. Then he married and had children. He didn't go to college until his late thirties, even though college would have helped him and his family much earlier.

In rural regions there are generally colleges and universities that specialize in reaching out to a variety of students from nonacademic backgrounds. Jacquelyn, an administrator, writes glowingly of her typical adult returning student:

> Morehead State University serves the twenty-two poorest counties in the hills of eastern Kentucky, and several are the poorest in the state. Our students come at great sacrifice.

They are truly the most wonderful students. I count them as family.

She describes one woman who walked into her office with her hands covered in grease: "She had just changed a tire. She said, 'If I can change a tire without a tire tool, surely I can finish my degree!' "

You don't have to have a blue-collar background to have skipped higher education. Perhaps you grew up in a complicated household, and your college plans suffered because of it. A 1996 Cornell University study showed that only 14 percent of the children from divorced families were accepted into college, as compared with 24 percent of the children from two-parent households. Children from the divorced households also performed more poorly on standardized tests, partly because of stress and depression and partly because they didn't have parental support for their studies at home.

If this sounds like you back in your younger days, don't worry. You have plenty of company. Up to 40 percent of white children in the United States live with one parent, or even no parent, by high school age. In African-American families that statistic is nearly twice as high. According to studies published in *Black Issues in Higher Education* and in *Jet* magazine, this is one important reason why fewer minority students finish college.

If we look at the percentage of college-educated adults by race, it is evident that the bachelor's degree is rare enough in any ethnic group. But if you are black or Hispanic and you earn a bachelor's degree at an excellent university, you move yourself into an *even more* selective category than that of the average American. Take a look at the percentage of adults with a bachelor's degree or higher, by race, according to *The Chronicle of Higher Education*:

Asian	36.6%
White	21.6%
Black	11.3%
Hispanic	9.2%

If you are a member of a minority group, there may also be more financial assistance available to you, since not only colleges but many private donors as well have set up scholarships for minority students. When it comes time to look for a job, you'll also be more in demand, since many employers are motivated to find well-qualified candidates from a variety of demographic backgrounds.

YOUR HIGH SCHOOL COUNSELOR MAY HAVE MISJUDGED YOU

While collecting stories for this book, I was surprised to see how many academically successful adults had actually been steered away from college years earlier by their high school counselors. Although this had been my experience as well, I thought my story was unusual. Not at all. Many students who struggle in high school find that their counselors are noncommittal or even discouraging about college. Instead of encouraging bored, under-achieving high school students to take a year or two off to reassess their goals and work for a while, many counselors simply say, "Don't bother." Students believe them, and often spend the rest of their lives thinking that they're not college material.

Of course, many high school counselors are professionals who try hard to serve their students well. But a caseload of hundreds of students can overwhelm even the most dedicated counselor. The top students often get the best part of the counselor's time and attention, while the middle and bottom students languish.

In high school Mark had undiagnosed learning disabilities, and his grades and test scores were uneven. Instead of helping him figure out why he struggled, his guidance counselor said that he "shouldn't even consider" college, and encouraged him to enroll in auto mechanics training instead. He worked on cars for six years before realizing that college might be for him too. Today he's proud of his skills as a repairman, but he also has a bachelor's degree that he successfully earned in his later twenties. The degree doesn't stand for everything he knows. Instead, it represents the completion of a specific body of work that offers new and—for him—more useful opportunities.

Bev remembers her counselor as someone who was focused only on the academic stars, and who had little time for the rank-and-file pupils:

> He only "counseled" the elite of my class—those who were friends of his son—to go to college. It also seemed that he spent plenty of time addressing the armed-forces recruiters. I do believe that my school's apathy played a small part in my not going to college right after high school.

Bev found that the culture which discouraged her from going to college didn't have any better ideas for her, either. She couldn't earn the same living as her male counterparts in the technical fields or in a trade:

> Men can earn a livable wage through the trades, particularly via a technical college. But it is rare for women to be able to support a family with just a technical college or high school education. Women . . . need college degrees.

REASONS ADULTS RETURN TO COLLEGE (OR DECIDE TO GO FOR THE FIRST TIME)

In this section, we'll explore some of the stories of adults who have returned to college campuses—or who have started college for the first time.

RETURNING TO COLLEGE AFTER
TAKING TIME OFF TO GROW UP

After you've had a chance to work, college is a fine place to return
to in order to reorganize your priorities and to mature. Jorgiana,
now at the University of Arizona, was a top student in high school
and had been groomed for college. But youthful high spirits
caught up with her:

> Once in college, I found out how much fun it is to go out
> drinking and carousing every night. Needless to say, my
> grades soon suffered . . . I dropped out after talking with my
> parents, who gave me some real-world advice. They said that
> it was a waste of money for me to keep going, and that I
> should quit for a while and return once I was more focused.
> Still, that came as quite a blow, considering I had been
> pushed toward college for four years in high school.

Jorgiana dropped out of college and moved to Los Angeles, where
she worked in the entertainment industry and tried to make it on
her own. Unfortunately, she lost her job, and her life began to fall
apart.

> My dad (good ol' Dad) said, "Screw them. They don't know
> what they're doing. I'm coming out to get you and bring you
> home." This was quite shocking, since my life had been
> there for five years. I argued, but they insisted, and I'm glad
> they did now. Sure enough, I was back home in Dallas in two
> weeks, living with my parents at twenty-six. I thought, "Oh
> my God, what have I done?"
>   Once home, my parents pushed the college idea again. I
> wasn't working, so I figured I'd give it a try. Lo and behold,
> it was actually fun! Compared to working, it was a *piece of
> cake!* I excelled at school, got many A's (always good for

wounded self esteem) and knew all the answers (well, at least a lot of them). I told my parents this, and they said that is what real-world experience will do for you. After making honor roll at the local college, and after a semester of great grades, I transferred to my mother's alma mater, the University of Arizona! . . . Amazingly enough, those silly frat boys I once sat with now irritated the heck out of me with their incessant talking during lectures. That's when I truly knew I had changed.

Like Jorgiana, many traditional-age students drift away from school for a while, but return focused and ready to begin again. What happens in the meantime? What makes them such great candidates for academia? It's simple: they become adults.

Whether you're in your later twenties now or many decades beyond, you have grown up since the days when you were "supposed" to have been in college. What seemed difficult at age twenty will seem easy now. You'll be surprised how many of your daily life skills such as making lists, organizing your time, and focusing on the task at hand will translate into classroom success.

RETURNING TO COLLEGE BECAUSE OF FAMILY RESPONSIBILITY: IT MAY HAVE KEPT YOU OUT OF COLLEGE, BUT IT IS ALSO A GREAT REASON TO RETURN

Many people who drop out of or never start college do so because they need immediate jobs. Some of today's nontraditional students became parents at a young age, perhaps as early as high school or even before. Judy writes:

I got pregnant my senior year in high school. During those days, staying in school was out of the question. Shame on narrow-minded grown-ups! So I left in my final semester, just a few credits shy of graduation and a few months shy of delivering a baby, born in May.

My life took on new meaning when I brought this new life into the world. I had no problem giving up my childhood. I thoroughly fell in love with my son . . . I remained a single mom, living home with my family until my son turned four. At that time, I married my husband, and we welcomed our next child before our first anniversary.

Although Judy devoted herself to raising her children and keeping a happy home, she felt cheated by having missed out on the rest of her education. When she turned forty, instead of having a midlife crisis, Judy called a local admissions office:

Not having finished high school gnawed at me over the years. I don't know exactly what prompted me to make the call to our community education program at the time that I did, but I signed up for an art class and an English class. I tested out of a math class, and in a few short months I graduated and was awarded four free classes at an area business college. I took advantage of those classes, transferred to the community college, and then went on to finish at the college from which I graduated. At that time, we refinanced the house so I could quit my job and go full-time. My husband started working overtime, and I pulled 15 credits my first semester.

For Judy, college meant the difference between unsatisfying entry-level work and the job of her dreams. Today, ten years after she made that first phone call, she has a master's degree, of which she and her family are quite proud. She works in a college admissions office, making decisions about adult applicants who are just as nervous as she was a decade before. She is living proof that dropping out of high school doesn't have to mean giving up your education permanently.

Some high school seniors who planned to leave for college got married instead. For Barb, marriage meant more than just a goal or a commitment. It was also an escape: a way of finding the caring and security she had not known as a child:

> I was desperate for love and safety, so instead of waiting for the start of college, I got married at age nineteen to an abusive man: a real good trade-off. I divorced five years later and promptly married again. I worked full-time from the day after high school graduation in a variety of manual jobs until landing a job at a local hospital in the filing department.
>
> All during this time I was trying to follow the path my family expected of me: marry, work, have kids, buy a house . . . I had wanted to go to school, but had always found a reason not to go . . . no money, kids to raise, husband would feel intimidated since he did not have a degree . . . it was always something. But now, when I listened to my own wants and goals, I decided that a degree having to do with my passion— computers—was what would fill part of the void in me. I signed up for college courses toward a B.A. in technical writing.

For Barb, as for many of the students in this book, college was more than just a place to earn credits and get a degree that would lead to a job. It was a place to try out her own tastes, preferences, and talents, and discover a more dimensionally honest version of herself. Starting college at age thirty-six meant facing who she really was, rather than who society expected her to be. She ended up divorcing her second husband and meeting a life partner who supports her present interests and goals.

RETURNING TO COLLEGE
AFTER EARNING AN "M.R.S." DEGREE

Although many women, particularly those born before or during World War II, may have been encouraged to *attend* college, graduation hasn't always been the main goal. Instead, many were supposed to concentrate on dating and marrying college men who would earn a high salary someday. The term "coed" sprung up on campus to mean a young lady in a cashmere sweater set who spent more time eyeing that hunky senior in the second row of her sociology class than keeping her mind on her studies.

In 1970, 18 percent of college women surveyed by *Cosmopolitan* magazine said that they were there specifically to find a husband. That was almost as many as the 21 percent who cited "career preparation" as a reasonable goal. The remaining 61 percent were somewhere in the middle: pursuing a degree, but amenable to dropping out and getting married if the right man came along.

By 1980, according to *Cosmo*, that figure had changed dramatically. Only 1 percent of women reported their purpose for being on campus as simply marriage, without having any interest in a degree or a career. Today, women who came of age in the 1970s may feel caught between two conflicting eras: the 1950s, in which women were encouraged to earn diamond rings, and the new millennium, in which women are urged to have careers of their own and contribute to the family's income. Many of them are returning to college in their forties and fifties, and beyond.

When Angie started college directly after high school, she counted on earning good grades, as always. What she hadn't counted on was falling in love:

> I was so homesick and lovesick that I didn't attend classes, and as a result I failed every class. I remember calling home in tears just before Christmas break, begging my parents' forgiveness and asking if I could just come home.

After a second try at a college closer to home, Angie dropped out and married Kevin. At first she felt good about stopping school and raising a family, but soon she found that she felt left behind with just her high school diploma. She also worried that Kevin's long-distance trucking job kept him away from the family too much and that he was risking his life on the roads:

> Only as my friends were coming home with degrees and good jobs did I start questioning myself. I wondered if I was getting all that there was out of life. Maybe I was just fooling myself that I was as happy as anyone with a degree. I knew I didn't like earning minimum wage, and that I was worth more.

By earning a degree and getting a better job, Angie felt that she could give them all more choices:

> I returned to college in the fall of 1991 because of my son and my husband. Adam was eighteen months old at the time. I can remember rocking him one night, and as he looked at me with those shiny, bright blue eyes, I knew in an instant that I had to provide more for him than what a job at a discount store would pay . . . Being with Adam was great, but I needed to be with adults, too. By going back to school, I had the best of both worlds.

Today Angie is earning top grades in her nursing program at the University of Wisconsin–Eau Claire. She and Kevin have two more sons, yet she still manages to maintain a high grade-point average because she enjoys her studies so much. She hopes to work in the nursing profession for a while—to assist the family financially—and then eventually return for a master's degree and a Ph.D.

Like Angie, Colleen often felt as if something was missing without a bachelor's degree. Even though she had been taught to take pride in her children's accomplishments, that didn't quite satisfy her in the end:

> I guess it always bugged me, not having a degree, in spite of having a good job and all that goes with it. I had laughingly said to my children over the years that when the youngest went to college, I would have to go, so as not to be the only one without a degree.

Pay attention whenever you say something jokingly. Often there is some very real truth hiding underneath. In Colleen's case, the lighthearted attitude covered up the fact that she had ignored her own interests for the sake of her children. Going back to college gave her the fresh inspiration she needed after her years of successful parenting came to a natural conclusion.

Jo, who started college in her late forties, is now a top student at the University of Northern Iowa, earning a degree in public relations:

> I always felt I was missing out by not having a degree. It did not hold me back, but it was a goal I had not attained. I was sitting in the kitchen of a friend, a math tutor, in St. Louis. We discussed the old cliché "What will you be doing when you are fifty, anyway?" . . . Many women, wives of upper- and middle-management men, were returning to college. I was not the oldest person on campus at all. There were at least two women older—one in her seventies and the other in her fifties—and many my age.

Jo, like many wives of successful men, found that social events and civic duties just didn't take the place of her own intellectual achievement.

Mary, who was born in the early 1940s, writes about her own transition from know-it-all youngster to being a later-life bachelor's degree candidate: "I was nineteen . . . and I was positive that I knew more than almost anyone else about the world." She dropped out of the College of Notre Dame in Baltimore to get married.

By the 1990s, however—her Vietnam-era marriage ended, a second marriage come and gone—Mary felt the lack of a degree, which hadn't bothered her thirty years earlier. "I figured there must be something more for me. I loved being a mom, but I wanted more education . . . it was [too] easy for me to defer to my children and their accomplishments." Mary is now an Ada Comstock Scholar at Smith College in Northampton, Massachusetts.

RETURNING TO COLLEGE
AFTER A MILITARY CAREER

The armed forces recruit heavily in high school, and lots of young people—particularly those with marriage plans—sign up. In most cases, they plan to go to college later. Recruiters encourage this by showing young men and women how much money they can earn toward a college degree.

It doesn't always work out that way, though. Sometimes the military offers so much training for jobs that don't require a college degree that its veterans never go back to college. However, if you are a veteran, you should thoroughly explore the college benefits you may already have earned.

In the late 1960s, Jay had celebrated the Summer of Love by protesting the war and using psychedelic drugs. He attended college briefly, but dropped out in 1970 with low grades. To him, the Coast Guard seemed like a way to find some direction and grow up. While on active duty, he earned two associate's degrees—one in photography and another in Asian studies—through on-base programs. He rose in the ranks to become a chief warrant officer and says that he never missed having a regular bachelor's degree:

I can remember the day I decided to return [to college] very easily. I was going to retire in northwestern Wisconsin, which is a rural area. My fiancée and I were at the local high school, having her taxes done, when I happened upon the school superintendent. I asked him what the criteria were for substitute teaching. He informed me that a four-year degree was required. Also, all finance and business jobs required bachelor's degrees at a minimum. Janet asked me why I didn't return to school to get a degree.

The longer I thought about it, the more excited I became. I had the Vietnam-era GI Bill, which would help with the costs. I called the University of Wisconsin–Eau Claire, and went back to school full-time.

Jay's return to college gave him confidence and a new credential that even twenty-two years in the Coast Guard couldn't provide.

Marlo had a similar story about using the military as a basis for going to college. She wanted to be a nurse, but family tragedy caused her to seek escape rather than focus on college or her future:

I jokingly tell people that I majored in organic chemistry—drugs and alcohol—and gender studies—many boyfriends, most of whom were drug dealers.

I dropped out in the third semester of community college, when I had to withdraw from every course I was taking in order to not have F's on my record. I ended up joining the Navy a few months later because the recruiter was absolutely gorgeous.

After a stint in the military, Marlo eventually returned to college for a number of reasons, both personal and economic:

I felt that by not going to college I had let my father down. I grew up knowing that my younger sister and I would be the first females from his side of the family to graduate from college . . . I was encouraged to apply for the Medical Enlisted Commissioning Program, which would allow me to remain in the Navy while I went to nursing school full-time. I needed to pick up some more credits and drag my GPA out of the gutter, so I enrolled in a history course taught on base.

The Navy made good on its promise to help Marlo finish college and earn the nursing degree she had wanted since she was a little girl.

If you are in the military now, or if you are a veteran, you'll probably do well in college, since you'll already have the discipline you need to survive in the classroom. As Jay points out: "Since boot camp, I was always at the top of any classes I took." In Chapter 5 we'll discuss financial aid options for veterans from any branch of the armed forces.

RETURNING TO COLLEGE AS PART OF RECOVERY FROM SUBSTANCE ABUSE

For many traditional-age undergraduates, college can be one continuous party, with nothing on the other end to rescue them and help them organize their lives. For these eighteen-to-twenty-two-year-olds, schoolbooks and academics can end up being just a footnote to a demanding and exhausting social whirl.

Many students drop out of college because the party scene becomes too much for them. For nineteen-year-olds, starting the day with a bong hit and ending it by passing out while drinking may feel like freedom. Drug and alcohol use is often quite enslaving, however, when it culminates in physical problems and in dropping out, flunking out, or graduating with a dismal GPA. Sometimes these young party kids grow up quickly when they leave college without a degree, or with their "gentleman's C's," and try to earn a living. They often return to college later, with clearer goals in mind.

Susan describes her undergraduate experience as one of "parties, men, and sex, and not necessarily in that order!" Isaac remembers when acid tabs decorated with his favorite French cartoon character, Tintin, reappeared at his campus in the 1980s, just in time to help him flunk out of his pre-med program. Stacey drank her way through her freshman and sophomore years and dropped out in the first semester of her junior year when her parents pulled the plug on her funding.

Drugs and alcohol conquer many students, even (or perhaps especially) middle-class ones from sheltered backgrounds. They start out having what feels like a classic college experience, enjoying parties, late nights, and recreational pharmaceuticals. Often, however, the distinction between a party reptile and an addict isn't entirely clear. As Henry, now a student at Fordham University, put it:

> There's a fine line between doing it for fun, and looking at yourself in the mirror and thinking, "I'm a friggin' junkie."
> I started out with the romantic notion of experiencing all that the world has to offer. But it became old really fast.

Today Henry is in one of the top universities in the nation. Few of his fellow students would imagine that just a few years ago this affable, fashionably dressed man was living in his car on a Southern California beach.

Not every story of addiction and recovery is as clear-cut as Henry's, however. Cyndy dropped out of college in 1971. Then she became a professional hairdresser and salon owner in California: "Holding true to the hippie stereotype, I went to college for three semesters and only completed 7 1/2 units. I pretty much spent the next twenty years on a party." Cyndy's drug use was casual at first, but as personal problems increased, so did her need to escape. Soon she found herself turning to substances for solace and therapy. Things changed when she saw what her lifestyle was doing to her only child:

My nine-year-old son was beginning to make the wrong choices with his life, so I had to make some changes, and that is what I did. I had lost all of my clients, so I had to rebuild my life, financially, spiritually and physically. I began an adventure in the recovery meetings, and I found that I needed more to my life.

I went to American River College and took an assessment test. I had no idea what I wanted to do, so I ended up in Bonnie Miller's career-counseling class. She is not just a teacher, she is a guide. She put hope into what I thought was hopeless. She believed in me before I had a clue what I wanted to do. It is because of her that I continued on. I could only do about 6 or maybe 9 units at a time.

For Cyndy, as for many students whose education is part of their recovery, school soon became much more than something to do to get her life back together. The academic aspect of college became important for its own sake. She earned a place in an honor society, and her grades remained strong: "[My son and I] have discussed the possibility of us both graduating from Sacramento State with our bachelor's degrees at the same time."

Dave grew up in a seemingly quiet suburban household until violence erupted behind closed doors. His parents banded together to protect his addict brother, leaving Dave to raise himself and to become the focus of his brother's and parents' emotional abuse:

I had little sense of myself, and through a series of events I somehow came to believe that I was "not good enough." I eventually engaged in my own addiction. I relied upon the denials it brought, as well as acceptance within a somewhat "lost" culture, for a sense of self and belonging that eluded me in my family.

However, I was a functioning addict. I worked hard, saved money and was successful in my work environments . . . At age thirty, I was in a career that . . . didn't fulfill my inner needs.

I had just brought a house in a city that I did not feel a part of. It was about three days after I bought my house that I was sitting on my back porch and thought, "There has to be more than this."

Dave returned to college in California and earned a bachelor's degree in psychology. Then he completed a master's degree in gerontology. Today he is working on his Ph.D. For Dave, college wasn't just something to grab on to while he recovered from addictions. Instead, it was his basic tool for rethinking his whole life, from the foundations on up. He might have been fine without going back to college if his life's worth had been measured in material goods or sobriety alone. But he wasn't happy with the details of his days, and college gave him the framework to fundamentally change his circumstances.

RETURNING TO COLLEGE FOR
A FRESH START AFTER A SETBACK

Now I want to tell you about a different Dave who returned to college after an injury forced him to change careers. This Dave is a forty-four-year-old junior at the University of Massachusetts at Dartmouth, majoring in civil engineering. His son, a sophomore, attends the same university with him:

I went to Brown University in 1973 and lasted for one year. I dropped out because I did not know what I wanted to do with my life.

Not having a college degree did not bother me, because I started a small carpentry business. I decided to go back to college because my body was deteriorating. A few years ago, I broke my back in a car accident, and at times I would not be able to work because of the pain. My shoulders ached when I plastered houses, and my knees would become sore if I spent any length of time on them.

I was excited about the idea of returning to school. I was looking forward to the mental challenge of learning. At Brown, I dropped Chemistry and Calculus after three weeks, but these were the first courses that I would have to succeed at if I was to continue in my pursuit of an engineering degree . . . At Brown, my grades were average. I did not put much effort into preparing for classes. This has changed. I now spend a great deal of time doing homework, and my current GPA is 3.2.

For Dave, college represented a second chance to prove himself as a scholar. He found opportunities on campus to explore abilities beyond his obvious talents in carpentry. College didn't change who he was, but it enhanced his options. Although he says that he's the same guy he was the day he started school, his family has noticed a difference, and his wife claims that he has more self-esteem.

Like Dave, Debbie had to interrupt her thriving career because of a disability. She returned to the University of Wisconsin–Eau Claire and is double-majoring in American Indian studies and print journalism:

After having a career for two decades, I acquired an irreversible, bilateral overuse disability with my upper extremities. My limitations involve the entire structure from hands, arms, shoulders, and neck.

Since I began college in 1994, not only have I learned to use a computer, but I also use voice technology. This was only one of many challenges. It has been a long struggle since the beginning of my freshman year. I'm not prone to bragging, but I have worked extremely hard and have found success. I have two teenage sons at home, one of whom receives home schooling. I've been initiated into five honor societies, received three scholarships and a campus award.

Returning to College Even If
You Don't "Need" a Degree

There are many more reasons to return to college than just economic or logistic ones. Perhaps you want to go to college because you *belong* there. Emily decided to go back to college after her retirement at age sixty-five. She and her husband didn't need more money. He enjoyed a full-disability pension from the military, and their children were already independent. Personal satisfaction was Emily's only reason for returning to college.

Although Emily thought she'd enjoy a life of leisure, she was bored. She and her husband kept bumping into each other in their small house. He had taken over the cooking years earlier, and once she retired, they squabbled over whose responsibilities were whose:

> One day, when things in the kitchen heated up, I said to myself, "Well, I'll just find something else to do." And college seemed to fit the bill perfectly, so I went out to the University of Arkansas at Little Rock and registered for the spring term of 1990 . . .
>
> Frankly, I was a little disgruntled as I started out. Then, suddenly, I had a very real vision of myself crossing the stage in cap and gown, receiving my diploma. Over the crowd, I could hear the voice of my oldest son shouting, "Way to go, Sissy!" From that moment on, I never turned back.
>
> As soon as I parked the car on campus that morning in 1990, I felt as though I was home. I was not worried about whether I would succeed or not. I had my vision, after all. And I felt mentally up to the job. My earlier twenty academic hours had resulted in a 4.0 grade point average. I was excited. I almost felt like a girl again, although I was sixty-five years old!

Emily graduated summa cum laude, and her husband and children are her biggest fans. Today, at age seventy-five, she is continuing her studies toward a master's degree "as long as they let me drive the car out there."

Many people find that the structure and focus of a college degree can add a necessary layer of organization to an out-of-order life. College isn't a cure-all, but it can help when lack of direction or a vague sense of feeling lost in the world is part of the overall problem. If you feel depressed and frustrated from trying to live a life that seems purposeless, going to college may be a big part of your answer. Keri was like this. She found that her lack of direction translated into some later emotional difficulties:

> I decided to return to college when a friend repeatedly and regularly urged me to do so. I had been suffering with serious depression, and she suggested that I get myself back in school, that part of the problem was that I needed the stimulation. My friend happened to be friends with a director of the student center at a community college and *strongly* encouraged me to enroll in at least one course to get my feet wet. She even loaned me the money! I even paid it back!

If you struggle with depression, a college campus can be a supportive environment. You will make friends, and develop more skills and self-confidence. Also, most campuses include professional counseling services for students as part of tuition and fees. You could get the clinical help that you may need, while also taking important steps to refocus your life and set new goals.

Dan already had a college diploma, but it wasn't in a field that meant very much to him. After he lost his wife to lymphoma, he returned to college for a second bachelor's degree to give himself something meaningful to do:

> I had been in the office-furniture industry for twenty years after teaching high school math for two years right out of college. Eventually I talked to my wife about getting into marine biology, and she was supportive. Nature and marine

life have been longtime interests, but I'd never acted on them before.

After my wife passed away, I decided there was no better time to get into biology. My first year put me in a crowd of eighteen- and nineteen-year-olds, many of whom were taking biology only to satisfy a requirement. It was okay being in lecture and in lab with these younger people. I haven't been able to shake the constant thought that I am "the old guy," but I greatly enjoy being in the classes, especially biology.

Dan was surprised at what a better student he had become over the years. His professional discipline easily translated into classroom skills:

Early on, when I went to college I did well, but was quite typical, I think, mixing partying with time to study. But as an adult in my forties, I have been really driven to do well. I've noticed a B plus is hard to take, maybe because of the effort, even if the class was hard or the professor difficult or whatever. Overall, my grades now are A's.

I am encouraging people to either go or continue to go. I think I am more open-minded because of it, and I get pretty excited by what I am learning.

At first Dan may have "used" college for structure as he mourned. But now his new bachelor's degree represents a fresh start in a field to which he feels much more suited.

I hope that by now you are convinced that college is a good idea, no matter what your academic or personal past. The next step, after deciding to return to college, is overcoming any natural worries that may accompany that decision. You may understandably wonder if you're smart enough to succeed. You may have reservations about sitting in classrooms with a bunch of twenty-year-olds, or conquering the algebra that conquered you decades ago.

Well, relax. The back-to-school jitters are part of the process. You'd be unusual if you *didn't* feel some sort of apprehension. In the next chapter, we'll examine the relationship between brains and diplomas, and consider whether or not your innate intelligence has anything at all to do with the number of degrees after your name.

If I Only Had a Brain:
Overcoming the
"Not College Material" Image

If you think diplomas equal intelligence, then you've been watching MGM movie musicals too long. Remember when the Wizard awards a college degree to the Scarecrow in the 1939 big-screen version of *The Wizard of Oz*? Well, those famous words ("But they have one thing that you haven't got: a diploma!") never appeared in the book. Here's what author L. Frank Baum's original Wizard said about intelligence:

> "Can't you give me brains?" asked the Scarecrow.
> "You don't need them. You are learning something every day. A baby has brains, but it doesn't know much. Experience is the only thing that brings knowledge, and the longer you are on earth the more experience you are sure to get."

That's it. No diploma. No long spiel about universities.

Although Baum's family was wealthy, Baum never went to college. Nobody expected him to, for he was successful enough as a journalist and best-selling author. When he published his first *Oz* book, in 1900, only about a tenth of all high school students continued formal studies after high school.

Few people back then would have imagined the Wizard giving a Scarecrow a piece of paper to solve his intellectual problems. But the 1939 myth of the diploma in *The Wizard of Oz* persists to this day. Students quote it on their World Wide Web pages. It appears on T-shirts in college towns.

I remember one beautiful afternoon in a psychologist's office in Washington, D.C., back when I was in my early twenties. The walls were persimmon-colored, and the room was filled with exotic plants. A yellow, green, and peach-colored bird chirped in its brass cage. The psychologist sat in a velvety cinnamon chair and looked at me with intensity and understanding. Gently she nudged a box of tissues my way as she said, softly: "If you could imagine yourself as any of the characters from *The Wizard of Oz*, which one would you be?"

I didn't know. Dorothy the Lost? Lion the Frightened? Tin Woodman the Cold and Unresponsive? Scarecrow the Dolt? I couldn't answer. She urged me to take my time and think it over. I still had no response.

It was only years later that I recalled that scene and filled in one more important detail. One of her walls was covered with diplomas from various universities. Papers bearing variations on her name, both maiden and married, written in calligraphy, obscured that wall. She had a bachelor's degree, a master's degree, a doctorate, and a certificate from some institute in London. Latin terms graced the documents, which she had framed in expensive acid-free glass mounts, not those cheaper do-it-yourself jobs.

To her, since I was twenty-four years old and didn't have a college degree, "Scarecrow" would have been the best possible answer. I had plenty of courage to survive in the working world without a bachelor's degree, and there didn't seem to be any question about my sensitivity or heart. But what about higher education? She tried to help me see how much I needed a diploma for something abstract called *self-esteem*.

Although I believe the psychologist meant well, in retrospect I have to call her error the Oz Diploma Fallacy. That falsehood, simply put, says that the attainment of the paper itself improves you, and represents actual knowledge. Finishing college becomes more important than understanding a philosophic argument or mastering calculus. Instead of standing humbled before history, adults who accept the Diploma Fallacy think they're through with learning when they get that all-important piece of paper. Once they shake hands with the Chancellor and flip their tassels, they're done.

Students aren't the only ones who mistake finishing college for getting an education. University administrators and professional educators today repeatedly fall into this "diploma trap," presuming that no meaningful learning takes place anywhere else besides school. They worry about college dropouts, as if education started and stopped at the classroom door. They wring their hands and fret over how many people are or aren't earning diplomas, and they create Internet-based alternative programs to speed students through the degree process like sheep through a dip tank.

Some of these troubled souls argue on behalf of such ridiculous concepts as adults earning "fast" college degrees at "just as good" lower-tier-but-still-accredited schools, instead of their spending time actually studying something in a rigorous, historically rich way. Authors churn out books about distance learning. They promise readers degrees without going to college at all, "nontraditional" degrees, and shortened curricula offering "life experience credit."

Self-styled experts muse about adult students' special needs as though we're a slow but honest lot who won't amount to much, but who deserve some sort of chance at a meaningful life. These same people express shock that Bill Gates can run Microsoft without his diploma from Harvard (he dropped out) and that former president George Bush, having accomplished the magnificent feat of completing his studies at Yale, could possibly have not known what a supermarket price scanner does.

Despite misguided academics' almost religious faith in its

power, a college diploma by itself won't give you anything. You won't be smarter when you have one. A diploma is a symbol of a particular intellectual process, but it is no guarantee. When I think about the relationship between going to college and intelligence, I remember the minister who said, "Sitting in church won't make you a good person, any more than sitting in a garage will make you a car."

Education, however. Now, *that* will give you something. And you are receiving your education every day. Education is what you received when you faced the death of a loved one, or the night your first child was born. Education is the passion you developed for Egyptian art, bluegrass music, historical nonfiction written by first-rate authors, or whatever else fascinates you. When you first learned how much wiser it is to save your money than spend it, *that* was education, as was the time you actually used your high school French in Paris and found out that *s'il vous plaît* really does mean "please." When you longed for someone and suffered alone, *that* taught you more than any abstract book on romance and sorrow. As Sir Richard Steele said in his eighteenth-century English journal *The Tatler*: "[T]o love her was a liberal education."

Please do not think that you missed out on this just because you didn't earn a bachelor's degree when you were twenty-two. When young adults enroll in colleges and universities and proceed to do everything except study, even if they receive a diploma at the end of it all, they do not—they *cannot*—receive an education. They must all do the same things you and I did and discover for themselves what they love. They have to learn where their intellectual hungers lie. When they act on those hungers by satisfying them with travel, books, film, or long afternoons spent *thinking*, and bolstering that thinking by studying the well-considered ideas of others, then they participate in education at its richest and most substantial.

If you are older and wiser today than you were the day you left high school, then you have some education. That education may lead you to want more. If the "wanting more" means you wish to return to college and earn a bachelor's degree, then you're almost exactly where you need to be to get one. You just need one more thing: perspective.

College will put you in the same community as professors and other people who love certain subjects enough to want to spend a lifetime studying them. Although most of your fellow students won't understand the difference between snagging a diploma and being educated, you will.

Still, many people think that only the young can learn. There's a myth out there which suggests that younger students have more resilient minds than older ones. Jan almost believed that one, until she proved otherwise:

> Even though I had earned a 4.00 in high school and a 3.97 for my associate's degree, I was still afraid that I would not be able to handle college after so many years of being away, and in competition with all those "young" brains.
>
> Twice I took courses that were attended mostly by young people, and found that the discussion really lacked depth and purpose. I also found that age and experience gave me, and virtually all of the other adult students, a decided edge. In fact, the theology awards given to my graduating class went to four continuing-education students (I was one of them), even though many traditional-age students graduated with us.

Once you grasp the concept that education is a lifelong growing process and that the older you are, the more suited you are to appreciate it and benefit from it, then you will know what the Scarecrow knew a century ago: We all have brains. And the older we get, the more ready we become to handle the challenges of a spirited college curriculum. Simply put, if you *want* a college degree, then you are ready to get one. Hunger for academic achievement is all that is required for basic success.

BUT WHAT ABOUT INTELLIGENCE?
WHAT IF I'M REALLY TOO DUMB AFTER ALL?

At this point, you'll probably be ready to stop me, perhaps angrily. "What about IQ?" one reader might ask. "It's all fine and good to say that everyone has brains, but surely you're not suggesting that college is for *everyone*?"

Of course not. College *isn't* for everyone, any more than the same job suits everyone. But I strongly advocate a four-year on-campus college education for most adults who like to read; who enjoy puzzles; who consider religion, history, philosophy, math, theater, or other fields interesting; who spend time thinking about how the world works; and who want to know more. If you want to earn your living in the business world, if you want to teach, or if you want to share in the present power structure of this country, a college degree is a very important tool for opening the right doors. Beyond this, it offers the kind of broad exposure to history, literature, languages, math, and the sciences that you can't easily get anywhere else. If you engage with college in a meaningful way, you will come away from it with a better understanding of your culture and the world. College *can* and *does* educate, if you use it the way it was designed to be used.

Still, the feeling may reasonably haunt you that you "aren't quite college material." Many adult students worry about this. One readmissions counselor told me that returning students made the same nervous jokes to him so many times that he was beginning to expect them:

"The admissions office must have made a mistake, ha, ha!"

"I guess I'm part of your new special-ed program for the terminally slow."

"I'm not what you'd call book-smart, but I do know how to work hard."

Adults who never went to college or who didn't finish often imagine that they'll constantly be playing catch-up just to keep pace with the younger students. It usually works the other way around, however. Colleen was in her fifties when she started college:

> I grew up being told that I was not too bright, I was "just a girl" and that I didn't need to have a job, just to find a husband. A teacher I had in eleventh and twelfth grade impressed me that a profession was imperative, and she helped me to get into nursing school. Although I graduated and passed the RN exams, I never thought I had the capacity for university. After I was married, my husband encouraged me to attend the local junior college. It took me three tries before I got in the door, I was so nervous.

Instead of struggling to keep up, which she expected, she did very well indeed. She completed her bachelor's degree with honors at the University of Minnesota and eventually earned a doctorate from Iowa State University.

Dave, too, feared that he was too slow to handle college. His fears were reinforced when he found classwork more difficult than he'd expected. But he persisted and worked on his study skills. Soon, like most adult students, he became a top scholar:

> I was frightened to return to school. I had poor grades in high school and a belief that I was not smart enough to continue. In addition, I had little family support for accomplishing anything academic. I had attempted college four times previously, only to drop out the first day, overwhelmed with fear.
>
> Upon my admission to community college, I took tests which confirmed my own beliefs that I was deficient. In addition, I took my first test in school, and failed.
>
> However, I finished that first semester with all A's. This was a miracle, and I am well aware that I could not have done it without a great deal of help. Since then, I have re-

ceived a B.A. in psychology and a master's degree in gerontology, with about a 3.9 GPA all of the way through.

It wasn't until I applied for my bachelor's degree after
community college that I realized I was worthy of the title
"college student." At that point, college was not just something I was doing, but it became *who I was.*

Not every student experiences a bumpy transition to college like
Dave's, but many do. Even if your first experiences on campus
aren't perfect, you can still make it if you try. Jennifer had problems during her first semester at the University of Wisconsin–Eau
Claire:

I was frightened. I had lost two years working in my factory
job, which I was still at, working nights. I had never been to
this campus before; I didn't know where anything was located; I didn't know where to get help with simple tasks. I
didn't even know the university had a library. Thankfully, I
was enrolled in an introductory physics class: my professor
went far out of his way to make sure I adjusted.

After the first round of exams, I was a complete wreck. I
had forgotten how to study; I was unused to critical thinking. For the first time in my life, I experienced test anxiety.
It was pretty nasty. Since then, it's been an uphill struggle to
rebuild those skills.

Jennifer completed her first semester with a B– average, and she
only got stronger with time. Soon she was enjoying semesters in
the A range. Her success took patience and dedication, but it was
well worth the effort.

Susan, who attended George Washington University in Washington, D.C., in her late thirties, also struggled before hitting her stride:

I was convinced during my boarding school days that I was
stupid and was lucky to get into any college . . . Most of my

professors were my age or a bit younger and were quite supportive. In the library, the students checking out books were always startled I wasn't faculty, or staff, or a grad student. I used to enjoy watching them squirm as they realized I was just an ordinary undergrad like themselves. Incidentally, I graduated magna cum laude—so much for being "dumb"!

FACING DOWN YOUR FIRST ON-CAMPUS FEARS

Penny, an adult student at Aquinas College, almost let fear stop her. She persisted, however, and now can't imagine life without a college education:

> Once I made the decision . . . fear settled in. The what-ifs were pouring into my mind. I remember just taking a deep breath and thinking to myself that I would be fine. I would just take one class at a time, and slowly the studying and paper writing would become easier. This helped, but the first time I walked into a classroom, I was still terrified.
>
> Because I was taking evening courses, a good portion of my fellow students were not traditional age, but rather older continuing-education students who also worked during the day. I was still feeling terrified, but at least I had lots of company.
>
> By the time I completed my first class, I was hooked! I loved being back in school. I met a lot of interesting people and looked forward to going. Pretty soon, the studying and paper writing did get easier. I started taking two classes at a time. Before I knew it, I was completing my associate's degree.
>
> I managed to hold on to a 4.0 for the better part of the first two years. I will be graduating this May with a GPA of

3.7 (magna cum laude). I also received a letter inviting me to be inducted into the Alpha Sigma Lambda Honor Society. As much as I feel that I really missed out on the true college experience as a young person, I know I am getting more out of my education as an adult than I would have at age eighteen.

Ken, now an adult re-entry administrator at UC Berkeley, made the transition from truck driver and high school basketball coach to college student. Although he didn't start out feeling like he belonged on campus, gradually he fit in. Soon his education altered the way he viewed himself:

It was very intimidating here during my initial semester. After I made necessary adjustments, I believed that I actually belonged here. I most definitely changed identities. Fellow students began asking me to join in their study groups, and professors enjoyed my in-class and office-hour discussions. I began to gradually notice the change, and realized that I was "Cal material" during the middle of my first semester, when a prof responded to one of my comments with "That's a good question."

Ken still takes pride in having made it in life without a bachelor's degree. He enjoyed his pre-college identity. In fact, some of the most successful college students are those who have proven that they have enough good sense to get by without a degree. Once you understand that you can have a personal identity apart from where you went to school or how many diplomas you have, you'll be much more confident when you face academia.

Angie remembers dropping out of college to get married years earlier. She worried that she really didn't have what it took to be on a campus after all:

I was so scared to start college again. I remember the butterflies whirling in my belly. It wasn't so much the unfamiliarity, but the fears of failure again. Was I cut out for four years of college now?

I decided I was college material after receiving my first round of A grades. I realized then that "I can do this" . . . Something changed in me . . . I have so much self-confidence now. I feel like I have purpose outside of my family and that I have more self-worth. I am investing in myself not only for my future, but for the future of my family.

Other students report that they had to overcome "imposter syndrome," the nagging belief that they really belonged at a lower station in life and that they were faking it where they were. Here's how Karen remembered her own transition to college life:

> Quite often I think about what a senior student said during my orientation. For the first year she thought someone was going to walk up to her, tap her on the shoulder, and say, "There's been some mistake, you don't belong here." That's exactly how I felt, and several women in the room smiled and nodded when she said this. This feeling went away after a while . . .

As Judy Garland once said to director George Cukor about her own feelings of being a fake: "I'm always afraid that this is the time they're gonna catch me." If you build up a history of strong grades and an active life on campus, however, your fears will gradually diminish.

Julie discovered this when she decided to return to college at the University of Miami when her daughter began classes there. She was in her early fifties, she had grown up in Chile and Peru, and she hadn't been on a campus since she dropped out of a pre-med program many years before. First she got a job on campus to pay for her daughter's education, and then she began her own academic journey:

My children kept on encouraging me to go back. I hesitated, registered several times and dropped the course. I was afraid I could not make it, or that I could not meet the high expectations I set up for me. I felt very old and that my time had passed. Once I did finish a course, but I did not continue for several semesters. I hated walking across the campus to go to class.

Julie decided to persevere after talking over her problems with a colleague who had once faced similar issues. She found that by asking for support from another adult, she didn't feel so alone anymore:

One day I met a friend from church, Louise, who had a management position in the Continuing Education section of the university, and I told her, "I would like to study, but . . ." She replied, "You'll be here anyway. Time passes, and you will have that many more courses."

I went to see her at her office to start again. She became my counselor and encouraged me to take the courses that sounded interesting to me. I did. All of a sudden I realized I was learning, and that I enjoyed learning. It was work—tough work—but I was having fun, and today I knew a little more than yesterday, and that made me feel real good. All of a sudden I realized: I am getting an education.

Julie completed her bachelor's degree in May of 1998 with a 3.63 grade-point average. She was fifty-seven years old. "I was so happy and excited," she remembers. "My children and three-month-old grandchild could come to my graduation."

When Sharon began a career-exploration class at American River College in Sacramento, she was quite nervous. She had no academic history and had worked for years as a legal secretary while struggling with the responsibilities of being a wife and mother. Her life had been complicated by years of alcohol and drug abuse, and an eventual divorce. College was her first major goal after becoming clean and sober:

> The day I went back to college, I was full of fear. I made sure exactly what time the class was and where I was going to park, and actually which way I was going to walk to class. The class was going to involve looking into who you are and what you want to be. We had group sessions, which were scary. But I survived and got an A in the class and really felt good about myself.

Most returning students report that they started college feeling a little silly. It's part of the process, just like finding the campus bookstore or getting your photo ID. When Ann walked onto the campus of Bryn Mawr College in Pennsylvania, she remembers thinking, "There must be a mistake. How did I get *into* this place?" Many of us once wandered around gaping at buildings that surely weren't erected just for little old us.

But they were. The campus belongs to no one so much as the student who hungers to learn, and is ready to do so.

COLLEGE IS AIMED AT THE AVERAGE STUDENT, NOT THE SO-CALLED GENIUS

To survive economically, most colleges aim toward the average applicant, who isn't as brilliant as you might think. The middle and bottom students—who by definition make up two-thirds of all students—drift through their studies with a casual sense of needing to finish, but not in any distinguishing sort of way. If you yearn to learn, you'll step right over their sleepy heads to the front of the class. These young, partying, unfocused students are present on all campuses, even the best in the country.

Why do great campuses have mediocre and even poor students?

Perhaps it is because the students at the bottom aren't ready for college yet. Many—if not most—eighteen-to-twenty-two-year olds aren't. There are other factors that explain their presence, however.

Some of them went to the top private high schools, where teachers held their hands and gently nursed them through science, math, and the humanities, one carefully cut bite of information at a time. Now they're in the Big Kids' Pool at college, and they're drowning. Others have parents who donated astonishing sums to the university and quite literally bought their way in.

This isn't as unfair as it may sound, and even if it is, it is unlikely to change. After all, it is the parents' money that created the rich endowments and beautiful facilities at America's best campuses. If Higby Detweiler III's parents built the Detweiler burn unit of the new hospital, which serves thousands of critically ill patients every year, then I have no problem trying to teach their son, even if he *is* a little slow and hopelessly unmotivated. Because I respect the larger need of the community to have a burn unit at the hospital, and because I'm appreciative of his parents for spending their wealth that way instead of, say, blowing it at the gaming tables in Monaco, then I'll happily work with a kid who may not have the intellectual capacity of his peers. But that doesn't change the fact that America's top universities are dotted with little Detweilers, taking up space and making it easy for a bright, hardworking adult student like you to shine.

MANY PROFESSORS WELCOME ADULT STUDENTS—WITH GOOD REASON

Over the years, colleges have tailored their curricula for a group of students who are often too young to appreciate them. When you step onto a campus and participate in classes with these promising but unformed youngsters, you will shine simply because you have learned how to listen, how to focus, and how to finish something you have begun. While traditional undergraduates recite their excuses and requests for extensions, you will quietly finish your work on time and do very, very well.

College campuses wouldn't exist today were it not for the one thing they sell best: the bachelor's degree. This means that every member of the university community, including the graduate students, must serve the undergraduates, no matter how unmotivated those undergraduates are. You and your focused attitude will represent a refreshing switch for most professors. As Alice Olson, Director of the Center for Continuing Education at Sarah Lawrence College, puts it:

> Our faculty love to teach adult students. They frequently express surprise at the level of insecurity they see with adult students who are in the early stages of their return to school—an insecurity not at all reflective of the students' actual capacity for work and learning.

Michael Gillan, Dean of the Fordham College of Liberal Studies, agrees:

> Almost all of us who went to college at the traditional age can remember a point at which we realized that we would have gotten much more out of this if we were a few years older, with a little more experience. There ought to be a law that you can't go right through college immediately after high school. Our adult students . . . are doing exactly what many of us wish we had done. They *are* getting more out of it, precisely because they're putting so much more into it.

Does that mean you can expect an open-arms reception when you step on campus? Not quite. There is also no one more lowly than the humble undergraduate. In one of life's great social mysteries, you will be both prized and reviled, necessary and expendable.

Some professors will treat you like a budding scholar and respect your intellectual growth. Others will try to brush your offending dust from the lapels of their tweed jackets. Some administrators will help you, giving you directions, assistance, and advice. Others will seem to be doing everything in their red-tape power to remind you of just how insignificant you and all of your colleagues are. And then you'll meet the mushy middle, those professors who pretend to care but don't, or those administrators who are more worried about five o'clock or their coffee breaks than taking action on your student file.

But hey, that's *another* good part about being an adult returning student. You have lived in the outside world, and you know that college didn't invent these minor insults and petty inconveniences. They are part of that arcane and convoluted mess known as bureaucratic life. You'll never be rid of them, whether you go to the Department of Motor Vehicles, small-claims court, or your local university. As an adult, at least you'll know that the mistreatment, if it comes, is nothing personal. You'll be able to move on and keep looking until you find administrators who will help you and professors who will support you. If you're smart enough to navigate a bureaucratic job, then you'll be plenty smart enough to do well in college.

Here's what Ina, now the Director of Adult Student Recruitment at Aquinas College, says about her first approach to campus, when she was forty:

> The fears I faced were of being humiliated. That has never been the case. I have always felt welcome in the classroom and respected by my peers, faculty, and the traditional-age students at the college.

Jay had the same fear at the University of Wisconsin. He had dropped out of college in 1970 with a 1.42 grade-point average. Somehow, he believed that everyone would know about his past record when he returned to college in 1998:

I was apprehensive about returning, and whether or not I could cut it alongside people who are twenty-seven years younger than me. [But] many students like the nontraditional folks. We usually have interesting stories, and are serious about learning. Some do think of us as real pain-in-the-asses because we sit up front, participate in class discussions, and generally try hard. But I have also found that my professors are understanding, and enjoy having us in class.

What Ina and Jay both discovered is that nobody knew about their academic pasts, and nobody cared about their ages. Professors became their friends as well as their teachers, and these older students made a much stronger connection to the university's superstructure than their younger fellow students. As Sally says:

College . . . is such an invigorating atmosphere. It has made me want to learn more, to be more, and to do more with my life . . . Going back to school at my age has been one of the most positive experiences of my life.

From this chapter forward, we will assume that you have agreed to conquer any early fears and that you have made the decision to return to college. However, such a decision rarely occurs in a vacuum. Most adults have work and family obligations of one sort or another, and we all need to support ourselves. In the next chapter, we'll talk about breaking the news to your loved ones and to your bosses and co-workers.

WHAT'S SCARIER:
TELLING YOUR BOSS,
OR TELLING YOUR FAMILY?

The lie haunted Gordon for years. Every time he walked into his boss Alan's office and saw that framed bachelor's degree from the University of Mississippi, he felt a little pull and heard a soft internal whisper:

"Liar, liar . . ."

It was a quiet voice, which didn't taunt him exactly. It just prodded him. Gordon had never actually told his employer that he had *graduated* from Ole Miss, he just mentioned that he had been a student there, and Alan had filled in the rest. He believed that Gordon had graduated from his beloved alma mater. But Gordon had dropped out in the first semester of his senior year because of low grades and financial problems at home. He had started work right away, fudging the fact that he hadn't graduated by not mentioning it on his job application, but instead simply listing the university that he had attended and the year he had left. Gradually, he built a career. Nobody ever checked his record.

Now, here he was, thirty-one years old, working in Seattle for a man who could expose him at any moment. Would Alan ever notice that Gordon's name didn't appear in the alumni magazine? Did he even care about such things? Would he get a phone call late one night from a gravel-voiced administrator: *"About that so-called marketing manager of yours. Gordon Hollins. Did you know that he's a big fake?"*

When Gordon met his fiancée, Karen, he told her everything, and it felt good to just admit that his whole job was founded on a lie. He was relieved that she didn't become overly upset. Instead of chastising him, Karen surprised him by calling the registrar's office at the University of Mississippi and asking them what he would need to do to graduate more than a decade after dropping out.

"Honey, don't do it," he said as she dialed the phone. "It won't count. After seven years they erase your record! College credits don't keep that long. I'd have to start over!"

"Maybe so," she said, smiling. "Let's find out."

After one or two phone transfers, she talked to a readmissions officer who pulled Gordon's record and confirmed that he had left in reasonably good standing. His grades weren't stellar, and in fact hovered in the lower range. But the officer knew that adult returning students can be highly motivated to improve. She also knew that they represent necessary income to a university. Furthermore, a university's success is partly measured on the number of students it accepts who make it all the way to graduation. It was in the university's best interest to work with Gordon and help him finish. Even though Gordon's former GPA had been just barely above failing, and even though it had been eleven years since he had walked away, she agreed to reactivate his student status once he submitted the required readmission application. Just like that.

Gordon owed the university 18 credits—six classes—in order to graduate. The counselor agreed that he could take four of those classes at the nearby University of Washington in Seattle and transfer the credits to Ole Miss. She faxed him a list of course equivalents and instructions for applying for transfer credit. This meant that he could start in night classes right away and earn those 12 credits in two semesters of two classes each. For the two classes that required residency at the main campus in Oxford, Mississippi, he would have to attend summer school. And that meant talking to his boss, Alan. Summer sessions were five weeks long, and Gordon earned only two weeks of paid vacation each year. Although he could easily arrange to take his vacation during the first two weeks of summer session, what about the remaining three? What would he say?

"I broke my leg on the trip and have to remain in traction"?

"The hijackers took me hostage. You didn't read about it in the papers because the CIA kept it very hush-hush"?

Then he looked at Karen and said, "Honey, maybe I should just tell Alan the truth. Admit that I lied to him and that I've been working at the company for nine years without a bachelor's degree. Be honest. Be a man."

"Don't talk nonsense!" Karen replied. "Of *course* you're not going to admit everything. You're simply going to march in there and ask him for three weeks of leave next summer without pay, tacked onto your vacation."

In this case, I believe that Karen was right. While it may be commendable to own up to most falsehoods in your private life, at work such honesty might get you into more trouble than it solves. Bosses do appreciate and deserve the truth, but if you have been evasive about having a bachelor's degree for years, they won't *want* to know about it, especially if you are an excellent employee. You might inadvertently make your boss feel foolish for not having checked more thoroughly, and you could find yourself in an uncomfortable—and largely unnecessary—predicament. Focus your energies on cleaning up your record and turning what was once a lie into the complete truth.

Gordon thought Karen was too optimistic to insist that he

could finish college now. On the other hand, he knew that she might not want to marry him if he couldn't correct his professional mistakes. So he gambled and asked Alan for the extra leave. He said that he needed it for personal reasons, for self-improvement and for a chance to reorder his priorities. He assured Alan that with a five-week break he would return to the office refreshed and ready to focus on his job, all of which was perfectly true. He promised to take this leave during the last three weeks of July and the first two weeks of August, when business was traditionally slow. In essence, he'd be saving his company money by not demanding three weeks' worth of salary in the off-season.

To Gordon's astonishment, Alan agreed to the plan. By September 1 of the following year. Gordon had a real bachelor's degree from the University of Mississippi. Better yet, he had earned mostly A's in the courses he took. When his grades arrived in the mail, he stared at his final report card for the longest time. He'd made the dean's list for summer school.

Like Gordon, many people who drop out in their youth return to the same university to finish up later. Melinda, a student at the University of California at Berkeley, found it similarly easy to hide her lack of a bachelor's degree. For twenty-five years she worked without one, until she grew tired of the feeling of having left something undone:

> I felt unfulfilled about not having my B.A. When people asked where I went to college. I always replied "Cal," and never volunteered that I didn't graduate. It was a little dark secret of mine. I never lied on my résumé, but I don't think they looked too carefully at the dates.
>
> One day I decided to go to Cal and just inquire about what it would take to get back into school. They had me fill out a one page readmit form, which I thought would be reviewed or something, but that was not the case. I was back in, since I left in good standing, just like that, twenty-five years later!

Melinda's return wasn't without its psychological challenges, however. She had to make the transition from working adult to college student and overcome a quarter-century of inadequate feelings about her academic abilities:

> Going back to campus was like walking back in time for me. I remembered events from when I was eighteen. It was a very emotional experience the first few days. I was nervous, I had forgotten how to take notes and was not used to the academic lingo. I was afraid that the younger students would stare at me, wonder what I was doing there, and would never accept me in their classes.
>
> Well, I got over that quickly. Cal is so diverse that nobody stared at me. There are a lot of older students walking around, and an entire re-entry program for us. My reading and writing skills were weak at first, but I utilized tutors to rub the dust and rust from my pencil, and everything clicked into place after that.
>
> By returning to Cal, I gained a sense of confidence, and I was no longer afraid. My intellectual identity was finally coming. I'd left with a 2.8, but now I have gotten all A's (except one B), and I am up to a 3.4. This experience has totally changed how I feel about myself: that you can accomplish new goals, you can change your lifestyle, you can do whatever you set out to do! My advice would be to pick up the phone, get an application filled out, and just see what happens. It could be the most exhilarating experience of your life.

You may hear a myth about a "seven-year grace period" during which you must complete an undergraduate degree or lose your earned credits forever. None of the universities I researched enforced any sort of seven-year rule. Each individual admissions office sets its own policies, and their deans can always grant exceptions if they wish. Today, with colleges seeking as many sources of revenue as possible, most of them strongly encourage former students to return and earn a degree.

Telling the Boss When You Have to Start College from Scratch

While Gordon worried about his duplicity, another employee in his office had different college woes. Gayle, Alan's personal assistant, quietly resented the education gap that made her everybody else's servant. Alan knew that Gayle didn't have a bachelor's degree because, in Gayle's words, "I was too stupid to know that most people without one lie about it." She had answered the question truthfully on her job application, and now she was stuck in her *third* administrative assistant position. Just like her two previous jobs, it was supposed to give her more responsibility and a shot at promotion.

Gayle felt honest, but she took a hit in her paycheck every two weeks because of it. She made less than half of Gordon's salary, despite the fact that she had trained him and most of the other managers.

Besides living with the professional setback, Gayle also suffered from the stigma that most non–college graduates face. Her boss and colleagues all believed that they were smarter than she was. Their bias was so subtle that even Gayle didn't always notice it, but she received a different standard of treatment based on her social class, which was partly determined by her perceived lack of education. Since most of the people in that office valued college, they never really did respect Gayle enough.

Interestingly, Gayle herself shared some of those same biases. Secretly, she didn't respect herself enough, and her lack of a college degree was part of the reason why. Here's how another assistant described her transition back to college:

I became an administrative assistant because it seemed like a safe, secure job and I didn't feel a pull to any other area. But after about eight years in this position, I realized I would never be challenged, I was likely to always be living just above poverty level, and it would be difficult if not impossible to advance without a degree. It seemed such a silly thing, really. My bosses weren't any more intelligent than I. Nevertheless, my lack of a degree made me feel inferior to them.

That can make it harder to return to college. You begin to build up an idea that having a college degree somehow defines you, and maybe the others who have degrees really *are* brighter.

Gayle struggled with her feelings of inadequacy. She also feared that Alan might fire her if he found out that she wanted to give college a try. She worried about the demands of an academic schedule. How could she juggle school and a 40-hour-plus workweek as an administrative assistant? Would Alan mock her efforts to get a degree?

Gayle saw an ad in the paper for a university program for working adults that allowed them to take regular classes on campus but fit them around a nine-to-five office schedule. Although it meant cutting back on her overtime and adjusting her hours somewhat to accommodate early-morning or evening classes, Gayle felt confident that she could start the program on a modified schedule of two classes per semester. If she went in the summers as well, she could finish a bachelor's degree in five years instead of the traditional four. The program would be affordable if she took out student loans, but she also hoped to earn scholarships.

Although Gayle had feared Alan's laughter over the prospect of her going back to college, he surprised her. Alan didn't say much of anything at first, because he was too surprised. Gayle had seemed like a passive person to him, someone who tended to let life happen instead of taking control of it. From the day Gayle first announced her plans to return to college, Alan began treating her differently. Although he had always been a demanding boss time-wise, he didn't mind letting her adjust her lunch hours and breaks so that she could attend the occasional midday class. Alan let Gayle leave early on afternoons before big tests if she promised to make up the hours later.

For the first time, Alan began to respect Gayle. He considered her ideas worthwhile and her time more valuable. Gayle worked for Alan the whole five years she was getting her bachelor's de-gree, which is the longest Alan had ever been able to keep an ad-ministrative assistant. Although he told himself it was because Gayle needed the job while she was in school, it was more than that. Because Alan treated Gayle differently than the other assis-tants, they developed a level of mutual respect that most bosses and assistants never share. Alan went to Gayle's graduation cere-mony and felt quite a bit of personal pride.

Of course, not all bosses are this cooperative, and a rare few may even try to stop you. One attorney told his secretary that she was giving up a prize opportunity as his assistant for the "risks" of higher education. A businesswoman said that she refused to hire students because they think they're too good for the menial tasks that everyone in the office sometimes has to share. Although these bosses' concerns were largely imaginary, they still prevented their employees from trying to get ahead.

No boss who will try to stop you is worth staying for, however. If you work for a boss who doesn't understand, then why not look for an education-friendly employer *before* you go back to college? You can take occasional night classes now to help yourself adjust to the university environment. Meanwhile, you can search for a job where you will find support during school.

Attorneys have a difficult reputation, and many of them can be quite arrogant about their own educations. But surprisingly, they can also be among the most supportive bosses when it comes to academia. They respect college, and many of them will offer you flexible hours while you are finishing school.

Most employers understand that good employees have ambition, and they will do what they can to accommodate you. In Chapter 7, we'll discuss ways to adjust your job so that it accommodates your academic schedule without driving you crazy. Many employees without families will find that it is better to go ahead and quit their full-time jobs to work on campus or obtain a more flexible part-time position. In Chapter 11, I'll give you many excellent reasons for moving on or near campus and embracing college life without trying to hold on to the past. You may find that the best way out of your present situation is to leave it altogether. As one Smith College student said, "Don't wait for your ship to come in; swim out to meet it."

THE BOSS WAS EASY: NOW HOW DO YOU TELL YOUR SPOUSE?

Since most bosses consider a bachelor's degree a basic requirement for life, they shouldn't give you too much trouble when you try to earn one. Your loved ones, however, can have more complicated responses to your decision to finish your education.

Most spouses are at least reasonably supportive, since they know that a happy partner makes for a happy household. Some of them become quite enthusiastic. You may anticipate a big fight and then find out that your partner just wants the best for you and respects college quite a bit. Here's how Susan put it:

> I have a supportive husband, a really good guy, who never said one word about my not having a tasty dinner waiting for him because I was knee-deep in studying for an exam. Maybe he remembered how hard and time-consuming it was to get his degrees.

Although many spouses, particularly women, fear the conflict that will arise if they decide to go back to college, it usually doesn't happen. In fact, sometimes it works the other way around, with the spouse being the biggest impetus to get ahead. Anne complained to her husband that she was too old to go back to school and that she'd be forty-seven when she graduated.

His response? "You will be forty-seven even if you don't graduate." He encouraged her to do it without worrying about her age. She did, and she enjoyed his full support all the way through.

BE SENSITIVE TO "TRAILING SPOUSE SYNDROME"

Although most couples manage the back-to-college transition very well and benefit from it, the few who do complain usually mention "trailing spouse syndrome." The classic trailing spouse is someone who follows his or her partner around the country or the world while the "star" partner advances a career. In going-back-to-college terms, one partner may sacrifice to help the other succeed, and then may feel left behind emotionally, intellectually, or professionally. Women often report feeling used when they work full-time and put their husbands through one or several degrees. Men sometimes suffer a loss of self-esteem if their wives earn more advanced or more prestigious degrees than they do. Whether it manifests itself as resentment, jealousy, or simple crankiness, frustration on the part of the trailing partner can mean problems for your relationship, and for your academic career.

This is especially true when wives return to college. In a 1997 study, Jan Hansen and Eleanor Hall examined the marriages and achievements of 167 married female graduates of the University of Michigan between the ages of forty-five and sixty-five. The women with the highest level of achievement were the ones who perceived their husbands as supportive. Women with occasionally supportive husbands had greater difficulty unless both believed that their achievements directly contributed to the family's income and well-being. Women with unsupportive husbands had the fewest achievements overall. Even though it is the turn of the twenty-first century, women and men still find themselves stuck in the attitudes of the past more often than any of us would like to admit.

The men who do join the cheering section can find that they're in a somewhat lonely minority. Dana Milbank, the husband of a female student at the Harvard Business School, writes about how his status affected him:

> I'm pledging a sorority at Harvard this term. This would be unremarkable except that I am not a student and I am not a woman. My sorority is the Partners Club, a group of students' spouses at Harvard Business School, where my wife is in her first year . . . Partners Club events—afternoon teas, potluck suppers, self-defense seminars, play groups—are designed to keep us spouses busy while our husbands—er, partners—train to become masters of the universe. But the other men seem to find it awkward enough playing the trailing spouse without joining something that sounds, at first, like the Junior League.
>
> To counter this threat to manly dignity, I've joined with some similarly disgruntled husbands to form a Partners Club splinter group. We don't actually meet—we can't be bothered with such details—but we have a name: the Harvard University Male Partners Club. The idea came at a dinner in Boston's North End with five husbands and our business-school wives. We had slipped into our role-reversal easily, the women talking about their career plans and the men exchanging kitchen tips and lamenting our deteriorating figures. ["My Wives Club," *The New Republic*, May 5, 1997]

Milbank's humorous nervousness isn't as unusual as it might seem. Despite the gains of feminism and a generally more enlightened male population, some men can still feel threatened when their wives move ahead of them on the academic achievement scale. You can rail at this as sexist, outdated, and frustrating, but it is still a real phenomenon, and it can rock an otherwise steady relationship.

So what should the female partner of a man without a college degree do? Should she hold herself back to keep her husband's dignity intact? Or what about a man who feels that his wife is sacrificing her education to put him through school? Should he just stop going? Absolutely not. I never advocate dropping back, not even for a beloved and respected spouse. Instead, why not invite your husband or wife to join you in your academic quest? Instead of asking him or her to sit on the sidelines, bemoaning the unfairness of a relationship that gives one partner opportunities and the other one responsibilities, you could both go to college and learn together.

As we will see in Chapter 7, campuses are remarkably accommodating to dual academic couples. There are many creative ways that the whole family can benefit from an on-campus experience, including alternatives for child care. In the twenty-first century, there is no reason why any partner should have to feel like the academically trailing spouse.

But you also owe it to your partner and your family to schedule "down time" when you don't have to hit the books or beat a deadline. The people who love you will have an easier time supporting you emotionally if you remember to give back to them. Academic work can be a remarkably selfish undertaking, all about ego, hunger, drive, ambition, and other things that have a way of obstructing healthy two-way relationships. But that doesn't have to make you self-centered. If you embark on your academic journey with a determination not to let your personal life suffer, and if you take the responsibility for carving out time with your partner and your children, they will usually do their best to keep you going when you can't be everything to everyone and have to work for yourself.

If you're undecided about school and you don't want to feel as though you're risking your comfortable job or rocking your steady relationship, why not try one night class first in order to orient everyone—including yourself—to your new identity? You will probably need the time to adjust to an academic environment again. What's more, the people around you will have a chance to start thinking of you as a student.

Many of the adult students I talked to while researching this book said that a breaking-in period helped them become comfortable on campus, and also gave their families an opportunity to ease into a new schedule. Once you are relaxed in the classroom and you have a record of strong grades, you can either transfer into another, more prestigious program or continue your present program on a full-time or heavier part-time basis. By the time you're ready to take this step, your family and your co-workers will already think of you as a student.

When you decide to go back full-time or make a larger commitment, then I recommend that you simply tell people and not worry too much about the consequences. Decide and plunge in, trusting that the details—including money and time—will take care of themselves as you go along.

BUT WHAT IF SOMEBODY SAYS NO?

Many people will gratify you by being supportive and helpful when you return to college. But by a quirk of human nature known only to the Creator and certain psychologists, other people simply *must* say something negative. You'll have devil's advocates warning you about imaginary risks. In offices, among friends, and even in families, a crab-bucket syndrome can sometimes take over as the group tries to pull down a renegade achiever to the more comfortable norm.

Most adult returning students ask their families and friends for reassurance and support before they go back to school. About 80 percent of the people around you will be happy to provide it. But it can be upsetting to telephone your parents, E-mail your sister, or chat with your otherwise helpful spouse when you're so excited and then hear something negative. Parents are particularly famous for instinctively nay-saying when an adult child announces a plan to return to school. Many parents will interpret the news as a plea for money, even if you have no intention of asking for financial assistance. "You flunked out once, Stan, so don't expect me to pick up the tab!" was the first thing one man's father told him when he called to share the news.

For some, a decision to return to school can mean confronting drug or alcohol dependencies that may have contributed to their problems. When Clark faced his parents, he began the conversation with "I wouldn't blame you if you didn't trust me, but I want to go back to school." As he predicted, they were skeptical at first. But they also wanted him to succeed, so they bet on him, and won. He is now earning top grades at Georgetown University, at age twenty-seven.

Maggie had physical disabilities that made it impossible for her to continue her job as a garment worker. But when she attempted to return to college, she encountered resistance from both her parents and her in-laws. Both sets of relatives believed that her disability shouldn't keep her from a job that supported her children. Her husband didn't quite understand either, although he didn't complain as much:

> I had decided that I should go [back to college], whether my spouse "approved" or not. He'd been having his own issues to deal with since my life had changed dramatically with my disability. After fifteen years, I was no longer the same wife or mother.

My family was distraught and in disbelief over my situation, while his family was in denial. Some of his family members just couldn't believe this condition was that disabling and wondered why I didn't just go back to work. This was a particularly disturbing time in our personal lives and was difficult on our relationship.

In Maggie's case, it was her children's acceptance that changed things. As she and her family saw how much the children benefited from having a mother who enjoyed life by finishing college, they came around:

My children were a world of support. They didn't quite understand, either, but they willingly helped with chores and offered comfort when I was having extremely painful episodes. My bottom line became, Yes, these changes in my life had an effect on my entire family, but I was the one who "really" had to deal with it, and I was the only one that could change my situation.

Remember that you aren't asking anyone's permission to return to college. Since you're an adult, the choice is all yours. You are simply making a friendly announcement and hoping—hoping!— that the people you love will back you up. If they do—and most will—then that's wonderful. But if they don't, try to rise above any feelings of rejection or disappointment, as Maggie did, and see their reluctance as a challenge. Here are some typical negative responses to your academic announcement, and some ideas for how you might prepare for them and react:

- *"How are we going to pay for this?"*

Sometimes a partner who says "We can't afford it" is really expressing a fear that your college education will ultimately be his or her responsibility. You can allay these fears by researching financial aid ahead of time. Be sure to say the magic words "Don't worry, I'll be responsible for college, and I've got it all under control." That alone should relax those who have been enculturated to feel that everything that happens concerning family finances is up to them, fair or not. If you can present a workable plan for shared child care and household chores, most partners will cooperate. They'll also breathe a sigh of relief that you understand how scary new responsibilities can seem.

Parents usually launch into a predictable, and easily diffused, litany starting with one of these objections:

- *"Aren't you afraid you'll just flunk again?"*
- *"You never were bright in school."*
- *"Your brother could probably handle it. He could have been a doctor. But you?"*

If your folks give you any of these classic responses or variations thereof, just remember the Petulant Parents' Rule: All parents love A's. If you show them even one A-laden report card, they will usually change their tune. Remember that when a child succeeds, to Mom and Dad it isn't the child's accomplishment, it's the parents'. They'll have a wonderful time hogging all the credit if you start showing them report cards that put you on the dean's list. Whether you are twenty-five or fifty-five, if your parents are a part of your life, they will undoubtedly soften when your grades come in.

David had trouble convincing his father that interrupting a financially successful career to go to college could be a responsible decision:

> When I decided to sell my home, quit my job, and return to college, my father asked why. I told him I was not happy with my job and felt like there were few opportunities. His response was, "David, no one likes their jobs."

David's dad came around, however, when he realized just what kind of bragging rights David's success would earn him:

> As he was dying, he expressed his pride in my educational efforts and the changes that I had endured . . . Many times he would sort of chant over and over, "Ph.D., Ph.D. . . . Dr. Baker," and smile.

If your family and friends don't embrace your decision immediately, take heart. Most people calm down after a short time. Like David's father, they may just be waiting for proof that you can do it. If they never support your efforts, then you can probably bet that your earlier difficulties with school had something to do with your parents' poor attitudes about academic achievement.

If your boyfriend or girlfriend is the problem, you might want to question the basis for the whole relationship. For example, Kristen noticed that her boyfriend, Derek, began urging her out for beer nights during the week, and pouting when she said she had to study. He had never been a midweek drinker before. She soon realized that he was subtly trying to undermine her academic achievement because he felt belittled by her potential success. He was also terrified that she would fall for a new man at college. When she suggested that he stop whining and go back for that master's degree he'd talked so much about, he became angry. Then he asked her to marry him and give up college for good.

When Kristen assessed her relationship honestly, she realized that it was built upon the power structure of her being a shipping clerk without a college degree, and Derek being the "educated" one. He was insecure about his own intellect because of his unfulfilled ambitions, and he liked having a girlfriend who always stayed a step behind him. If he and Kristen had been married, I might have suggested that she try harder to convince him to enroll in a master's degree program. Since they were only dating, however, my advice was simple: Dump him. If he's just being childish, he can repent and try to win her back. But if he insists on these Stone Age attitudes, then she is better off without him, since their relationship could never survive her success in the long run.

Remember, however, that most of these scenarios represent the exceptions, not the rule. More than three-quarters of the students I talked to said that their best support came from family and friends. Jay was forty-six when he started classes at the University of Wisconsin–Eau Claire. He had little trouble enlisting his family's support:

> My wife and my parents were very supportive. Both my parents are college graduates and retired teachers. My father retired from the Army prior to going back to school (while I was in elementary school) to get his degree to teach. I am following in my father's footsteps, which is making him happy. He was afraid that I was going to be a bum back in the early seventies.

Instead of criticizing him, Jay's father supported his later-life decision, and even helped him pay out-of-state tuition until he established in-state residency.

Heather's husband complained for a brief while when she first returned to college, but he calmed down after he realized that she was serious about her education:

> My husband was a little [irritated] about being forced to "baby-sit" while I went to class. I responded by reminding him that while he was on a submarine I was left alone with the kids every few days while he had twenty-four-hour duty. I took them for months at a time while he was on deployment.
>
> After he saw how committed I was to going back to school, he became very supportive.

Some men will default to an outdated attitude about child care or family responsibilities, but most will come around once they realize that a good education for both partners is vital to the economic and emotional security of the family. Remember that asking a man to care for his own children is perfectly fair. Despite what he may say, looking after his own offspring is not baby-sitting. We are many decades away from an economy that supports or encourages only one educated "breadwinner" per couple. If your husband is not yet aware of this, then your return to college will be a fine opportunity for him to catch up.

Some men will surprise you by embracing your decision right away. Beth, a student at Aquinas College, remembers how gratified she was by her husband's response when she finally broke the news:

> I called my husband (who, by the way, is wonderful) and told him I'd quit my job to go back to school. His response: "Fantastic!" You should also know that at this time he did not have his degree, and in fact didn't receive it until 1990.

Other husbands, wives, parents, partners, and children will be immediately supportive from the start, and all the way through the process.

When Ann completed college, she brought her diploma home and presented it to her father. She had plans to go to graduate school, and she wanted to give him a symbol of her first major success after a troubled adolescence and young adulthood. She put the diploma in his hands:

"This is yours."

"No," he replied, smiling and handing it back to her. "This is *yours.*"

She pushed it back at him, insistent. "No, this is yours. But the next one is *mine!*"

Choosing a College
or University:
Prestige Does Matter

There is no such thing as intellectual "old money." Wealthy people can inherit money, businesses, land, and pedigrees going back to the *Mayflower*, but they can't inherit their educations. You have the same opportunity that any other student has to achieve academically.

Earning a degree from a reputable college or university is one of the few ways to change social classes in America. If you graduate, you will gain social standing that will make you the perceived equal of any other alumnus of your college, no matter how wealthy or how humble. If you also earn honors or otherwise distinguish yourself, you will match and even surpass your peers no matter how much of a head start they may have gotten in life.

But why would you want to earn a prestigious degree? There are many good, practical reasons why.

CAMPUS LIFE AND TOP DEGREES
MAKE YOU VISIBLE TO THE POWER ELITE

Since World War II, campus life has been an important aspect of how Americans identify themselves as participants in our power structures. America's power elite distinguish among people by social cues that have little to do with how inherently capable you are. You may have more raw talent than your bosses, but it won't matter unless you possess the same credentials that they have earned.

You can't entirely fake your way into this world. America's great businesses may have been founded by scrappy entrepreneurs with eighth-grade educations and lots of street smarts, but now they are largely run by people who were successful in school. These bosses participated in a traditional campus culture defined by interaction with professors and peers and by a social system that taught them certain shared values. If you didn't go to college, then you missed out on many of their experiences, and nothing you can do outside the university gates will make up for that. There isn't an Internet program or correspondence course in the world that can teach you how to talk to these people, and how to understand what's important to them. In college, you will learn to speak and act so that they can "see" you in the professional world.

Most of what really matters about higher education is the intellectual and social changes that college students undergo. By discussing subjects firsthand with professors and listening to the ways in which academic material is traditionally conveyed, you will develop different ways of thinking, and even adopt new patterns of speech.

"Experts" selling quick-degree programs say that certain college courses of study such as philosophy or classics are unnecessary in adults' daily lives. But they're wrong. It is precisely these subjects, along with history, languages, and other disciplines, that shape the intellect in a rigorous manner. Your conversations within the classroom, and your casual interactions with fellow students outside of it, will expand your ability to think critically and to socialize with others who value that ability.

The same leaders who were trained in our university system are the ones who will hire and promote you. When you attend a great university, you become recognizable to them as the product of a system they respect and trust. They may initially be attracted to the name of your alma mater. But in daily life, they will be attracted to the way that you handle yourself in their well-established world.

Attend the Top Schools and Great Jobs Will Find *You*!

America's best companies do much of their recruiting exclusively on campuses they know well. Many available jobs will never appear in the want ads because corporations already know where to find the largest number of what they consider the best candidates.

You might logically ask why these companies aren't more egalitarian and why they don't consider you as an individual rather than just focusing on where you went to school. But if you think about it, corporate recruiting at colleges makes a lot of sense in their world. Companies don't have the time or the interest to weed through scattershot applications from newspaper ads in order to find a few hidden greats who happened to notice them that week. Recruiters would rather go to the top schools and simply ask for their most promising candidates.

If you don't think this selectivity is justified, then consider it from the other side of the desk. A company's personnel department is often rated by how many excellent employees it can attract. You may think of the hiring process as nerve-racking for job seekers, but it is also tense for recruiters. They circulate memos dotted with statistics showing how many hires came from which academic and employment sectors. The more recognizable and reputable your degree, the better these people will feel about hiring you. It will be simpler for them to say yes instead of no to you if you can drop a known university name and demonstrate success in a program they trust.

Elliot, a manager for a Big Six accounting and consulting firm, develops ongoing relationships exclusively with particular tier-one universities because their graduates are candidates that he can confidently hire. Instead of looking at every résumé that comes across his desk, Elliot goes straight to the campuses that he already knows he likes and asks for their top picks. For example, he gets especially good technology-based candidates from Georgia Tech. It has a large engineering school, with strong computer science and information systems programs. Why should he search through the dozens of unsolicited résumés he receives each week when he can fly to Atlanta for a prearranged series of recruitment interviews? Since Elliot already knows what kind of employee he's looking for, this allows him to "one-stop shop" and get the best results for the time he expends. Here's how he puts it:

> We keep going back to the same places because it's like mining for gold. You get a broad base of exceptionally qualified talent. Can you imagine going to a no-name college or trying to find onesies and twosies to interview? How much time would *that* take? Going to the tier-one schools is an economy of scale and an efficient way of doing business. You get a known commodity, and a lot of it. Students who attend these schools make it easy for me to find them, and hire them.

While Georgia Tech isn't the only school Elliot favors, it is one of a small number in his region that offer programs in line with his standards. He also knows that it will do a lot of his selection work for him. A student can't graduate until he or she reaches a predefined standard of excellence. Nonselective schools such as Internet universities and "just as good" diploma programs simply can't offer an employer this kind of assurance.

If you want an academic job after graduation, the necessity of enrolling in a respected program is even greater. Sociologist Stéphane Baldi has established a correlation between the ranking of departments where social scientists received their degrees and the quality of the departments that hired them after graduate school.* Even if these social scientists did top-notch original research, if they studied at a second-rate school, then they didn't get as good a job after graduation. Similarly, Jeffrey H. Blair and Myron Boor showed that the nine top-ranked law schools tended to hire one another's graduates, thereby reinforcing their own sense of prestige and power.† Whether or not you perceive this as fair, it is what happens, and it will only continue to happen more as adults earn bachelor's degrees in greater numbers.

COLLEGE ENDOWMENTS MAKE
GREAT SCHOOLS A BARGAIN

But what makes the *great* schools such a big deal? Can't you do just as well at an okay school that's closer to home? Wouldn't it be smarter to save time and money by attending an inexpensive technical institute, or seeking a campus specially designed for commuters? Why spend what seems like a fortune at a traditional, respected campus?

In addition to recommending the intellectual identity and shared culture a good school can provide, I insist on a traditional campus experience for adults because a great school offers an

---

*"Prestige Determinants of First Academic Jobs for New Sociology Ph.Ds," *Sociological Quarterly*, Fall 1995.
†"The Academic Elite in Law: Linkages Among Top-Ranked Law Schools," *Psychological Reports*, June 1991.

array of important extras that you can't find anywhere else. Through endowments, collections, and resources amassed over decades or even centuries, traditional campuses provide students with far more than they ever ask in mere tuition.

Let's start with money, known in college parlance as *endowment*. The term is related to the word "dowry," which in times past was the amount of money a family bestowed upon daughters when they married. The older and richer the family, the more likely that the daughter would have not just money, but land, houses, and even important political connections, all of which were vital to the couple's rank in society.

If your future college has a rich endowment, that will mean much more to you than just pretty buildings or well-manicured lawns. It will also mean that your school can offer you excellent research labs and libraries, computer access to on-line networks and the Web, free E-mail, radio, television, and multimedia facilities, connections with other top colleges around the world, foreign study programs, internship opportunities, and other valuable extras that you will be able to use and enjoy without paying an additional penny. A well-endowed college will pay you back much more than you ever put in through tuition. At its best, a wealthy college represents a shared pool of resources that simply cannot be duplicated without investing enormous amounts of money.

You can find information about a college's endowment in its catalogue or on its website. Endowments run into the hundreds of millions and even *billions* of dollars at many universities. The University of Texas system has an endowment of over $7 billion spread out among its many campuses. Ohio State University's endowment is nearly $1 billion. The Indiana University system boasts well over $.75 billion. Even at more modest institutions, the amount is generally counted in the hundreds of millions. Atlanta's Spelman College has over $200 million, as does the University of Utah. The University of Kentucky and Iowa State University both number their coffers at close to that figure.

When magazines like *U.S. News & World Report* or *Money* or guidebooks like *Peterson's* rank colleges, they use endowment as one indicator of standing. Analysts compare the size of the endowment to the size of the student body and come up with a per capita figure that represents how much a college "spends" on each of its students.

THE BEST COLLEGES HAVE A LONG HISTORY OF INTELLECTUAL RIGOR, COUPLED WITH ACADEMIC FREEDOM

After endowment comes history, and many top schools have a rich one. Many of our great universities began around the time our country was born, when settlers sought religious and academic freedom. Some were the direct efforts of the same visionaries who established this country. Benjamin Franklin founded the University of Pennsylvania—a member of the Ivy League—in 1740 as a charity school for the children of Philadelphia. Thomas Jefferson founded the University of Virginia in 1819 to realize his vision of an "academical village" to educate and civilize the rough-and-tumble planters' sons who he knew would go on to run his beloved fledgling country. Franklin's and Jefferson's experiments paid off over time; now you and I can enjoy over two hundred years of growth and contributions.

No matter what your faith, you can benefit from a school that has its roots in religious freedom. Catholic priests founded such institutions as Notre Dame in Indiana; St. Mary's College in southern Maryland; Fordham University in New York; Loyola University in New Orleans and Chicago; and Georgetown and Catholic Universities in Washington, D.C. Exiled Mormons founded Brigham Young University in Salt Lake City, Utah. In 1876, Protestant immigrants fleeing religious persecution in the Netherlands started Calvin College in Grand Rapids, Michigan. Earlham College, Cornell University, Johns Hopkins University,

Swarthmore College, and Haverford College were all founded by the Religious Society of Friends, commonly known as Quakers. They hoped to establish a peaceful and just society in the New World and saw education as a primary agent of this kind of social change.

Yeshiva University began in 1886 as a day school founded by Jewish immigrants on New York's Lower East Side. Both Yale and Harvard also have religious backgrounds: they began as Puritan institutions. A university built upon religious freedom and moral principles can feed the minds of many scholars, not just its religious adherents.

You may be concerned that some of these universities have another history: one that includes racism and sexism. It is often true that some of our greatest campuses have been the worst offenders here. But now is an excellent time to consider applying to them, simply because they have an official public mandate to right the wrongs of the past. Even with the gradual demise of affirmative action, the continued funding of many public universities depends upon their efforts to make their student bodies more representative of their home states. Women and minorities will find exceptional new opportunities available to them, even on America's most traditional old-boy private campuses.

In fact, some of these schools may be so eager to speak to you that they will let you apply for free. Cordelia, an African-American student, applied to twenty outstanding universities, including several Ivies, and requested application-fee waivers. Every university complied, and she received nineteen offers of admission, including generous financial aid. If you worry that once you get on campus you "won't belong," take heart. Since the early 1970s, women and minorities have made impressive inroads on most campuses, and you will find a support structure. Better yet, your presence on a campus will help change it, and open it further for generations to come.

There are also campuses with big endowments that are specifically geared toward members of minority groups or women.

Howard University in Washington, D.C., is one of the best-endowed of the historically black colleges in the country. Pennsylvania's Bryn Mawr College was founded in 1885, when women could not participate in the same education as men. Among its aims was to give women access to Greek, mathematics, and philosophy, which at the time they were forbidden to study in other universities. By copying the models offered at Princeton and Yale in the United States and Oxford in England, Bryn Mawr mimicked their successes. Today, in addition to its mission to traditional-age students, it offers one of the country's most respected programs tailored just for adult learners.

Time has proven these institutions. They have turned out great leaders, and they will help you shape yourself into a scholar and a more confident adult. When you step onto their campuses, you will feel awash in their rich history, and you will eventually become part of the university culture. As a student and as a future alumnus, your presence will affect the university identity as it affects yours, until you and the school figuratively become one. In the future, when you introduce yourself to others—whether prospective employers or new friends—you won't just be Alicia Feldman, but *Alicia Feldman, University of Michigan, class of 2005.*

THE BEST COLLEGES HAVE EXCELLENT ON-CAMPUS RESOURCES

Besides endowments and rich histories, the best schools have superb facilities and resources. Let's start with libraries. Our top universities, especially the older ones, have amassed wonderful library collections through many decades, even centuries, of careful acquisitions. The archives often house priceless collections, many of which were established back when their oldest acquisitions were new. A library that has diligently acquired books for over two hundred years can offer you a matchless array of historical materials that no recently assembled collection can rival.

Many library treasures began as modest gifts and have attained value over time. From the Louis Armstrong jazz archives at Queens College of the City University of New York, to the English poet William Blake's art and papers at the University of California, Santa Cruz, to Howard University's Moorland-Spingarn Research Center—which houses one of the world's most comprehensive collection related to the history of people of African descent in America and other parts of the world—university libraries contain many items that became treasures over time.

Your university may also have performing arts centers that serve the community, art galleries, a teaching hospital, sports arenas, and other extras that distance-learning proponents love to decry as "unnecessary." Are they really so frivolous? The next time you listen to Garrison Keillor, who got his first on-air training at the University of Minnesota's college station, WMMR, remember that without those campus facilities, *A Prairie Home Companion* might not exist today.

STRONG PROFESSORS MAKE THE DIFFERENCE BETWEEN "BOOK LEARNING" AND AN INTELLECTUALLY RICH EXPERIENCE

Finally, let's consider faculty. Universities today graduate many more Ph.D.'s than the job market can absorb. At the same time, the tenured faculty from the hiring booms in the 1950s and 1960s are retiring. There are still more graduates than jobs, however, so universities can have their pick of a very large and talented crop when professorial jobs open up.

Does the quality of the professors count? Of course it does.

Craftsmanship and excellence show in teaching as much as they do in shipbuilding or furniture making. At top universities, professors are required to write books, give talks, publish articles, and participate in research in their fields. They will have the ability to convey to you much more of the actual profession than just what they glean from books and other professors. They are also required to maintain a high standard of teaching, as measured by student evaluations.

Some people cite the overall high quality of professors as a reason to go to a second-rate school for a convenient and inexpensive degree. But while it's true that many capable professors are stuck on lower rungs simply because there aren't enough top jobs to go around, using this rationale to attend a substandard university may well backfire on you. Yes, you might find a talented professor at a lesser school just trying to stay afloat financially until a better job comes along. But the chances are that your professor won't be happy at the school and that he or she won't be around long enough to mentor you and write letters of recommendation.

If you're just using a lower-level school as a stepping-stone to the school you really want, then fine. Enjoy the relatively high level of professorial quality you'll get for a brief time, and move on. But if you earn a diploma there, you run the risk of working hard for a degree that has less value on the open market. Even if a mediocre school does attract an excellent young professor because of the current job crunch, that person won't stay long, because he or she will be working the job market every year to try to trade up to a better school. A professor with one eye on her watch and another on the door won't give you the kind of personal attention you need.

Some of the professors at the best schools are famous, and their reputations can enhance your résumé. You can take a poetry class with Nikki Giovanni at Virginia Tech. In computer graphics, you can study with Chandrajit Bajaj at the University of Texas at Austin. You can work with novelist Doris Betts at UNC–Chapel

Hill, or novelist Reynolds Price at UNC's archrival, Duke, right down the road. A rich university endowment makes it possible for your school to hire stars and make their expertise available to you.

A GREAT CAMPUS CAN MAKE YOU FALL IN LOVE WITH LEARNING

It's exhilarating to step onto a lovely campus on your first day. I remember walking on the grounds at the University of Virginia back in the 1980s, before I had even gone back to college. Yellow leaves from the gingko trees twirled gently to the ground. Delicate red-brick buildings with white arches and eighteenth-century charm lined the walkways. A student buzzed by on a bicycle, scattering a pile of pumpkin- and squash-colored leaves. Some other students laughed in a distant courtyard. *I could never belong in a place like this,* I thought.

Years later, as a graduate student on the same campus, I remembered my early walks on the grounds and how inadequate I'd felt. But as a Virginian who had worked hard to become a top student, I eventually earned a place there. It took many months before I felt as though I "belonged" at U.Va., but once I did, I never lost that sense of being connected, not just to academia, but to one of the jewels of my home state.

Many of our great universities now have programs for adult returning students that honor the traditional educational path. Smith College in Northampton, Massachusetts, offers the Ada Comstock Scholars Program for women who interrupted their academic careers and want to return later in life. There are similarly excellent programs at NYU, Tufts, Bryn Mawr, George Mason University, Trinity College, Mount Holyoke, and many others. For information on these and other outstanding programs, please consult Appendix A.

BETTER SCHOOLS MAY COST LESS
THAN THE "BARGAIN" PROGRAMS

But what about the cost? How can you afford an education at one of America's top colleges if you didn't come from money?

First you will want to consider the academic offerings of the top state universities in your region. You should also research the financial aid packages that expensive private colleges can afford to offer to their students. We'll consider both of these options, beginning with America's state university system.

If you attend one of our great state universities, such as the University of Texas, Seattle's University of Washington, the University of North Carolina, or the University of Tennessee, you'll be the recipient of a bequest that generations of citizens have worked hard to provide. Your state taxes also help support such institutions. Consequently, state universities have a mandate to serve their citizens.

Some of these schools are highly selective, which means that they turn down many more students than they accept. But if you're a resident of their state, they have a commitment to consider you. When you finish this book, you will know the path for getting into any one of them.

The major factor keeping most adults outside the gates of a great state university is the resistance in their own minds. Once you see yourself as a potential candidate for admission, you'll be halfway to your goal.

Some of the top state universities, such as UC Berkeley and UNC–Chapel Hill, are also quite inexpensive for residents, and their on-campus resources can be even better than those at expensive private schools. Tuition for state residents was so low at the University of Virginia that I paid less to attend U.Va. than I did to attend George Mason University, which began as one of U.Va.'s younger sister campuses near Washington, D.C. Once I started earning fellowships and grants at U.Va., my tuition dropped from a modest $4,000 a year to the point where the university was paying me to attend! Who would have thought that one of the most beautiful, historically rich, academically challenging campuses in the nation would be within my financial reach?

This doesn't mean, however, that you should entirely rule out private colleges. It is a little-known fact that there is much more financial aid available on the most expensive campuses than at the so-called "bargain" institutions. The former can afford generous financial aid packages thanks to their endowments, some of which are enormous. Also, loyal alumni frequently set up scholarships, and many of the expensive private schools have a high percentage of wealthy alumni donors.

Instead of worrying about how you will pay for college, begin by choosing the programs that best match your interests, your ambitions, and your talents. Apply to all of them. You may receive an offer of financial aid right away. Even if you don't, once you're in, you can begin negotiating with the university about how you're going to pay for it all. In Chapter 5, we'll discuss your finances in depth.

THREE PRINCIPLES BEHIND AIMING FOR A GREAT COLLEGE

So how do begin to position yourself as a prospective student at a great college? How can you end up on an excellent campus even if your previous grades were low or you never went to college at all? You can start with changing the way you think about what you want, and deserve.

1. BELIEVE THAT AIMING HIGH IS IMPORTANT. Many adult students have been trained to expect very little, since school wasn't a rewarding proposition in the past. For instance, Edward's high school guidance counselor refused to write a letter of recommendation for him to attend the best university in his state because

she perceived it as being elitist and beyond the reach of her rural students. Instead, she pushed Edward into an adequate but far less distinguished local college. Years later he applied to the great university and read his acceptance letter with amazement. He thrived in its challenging environment and went on to earn graduate degrees there. The moral? If you believe that you would be happier at a great university, then that's where your focus should be, even if it seems like a dream to you now.

2. SEPARATE YOURSELF FROM YOUR RECORD. Forget any low grades from the distant past. After all, everyone else has. Elementary school is ancient history. High school was a long time ago. Even your first run at college, if you had one, is absolutely meaningless now, unless you earned a salvageable credit or two that you would like to transfer.

If your past record bothers you, remember that no one cares whether you got an A or an F in high school biology. *Recent* grades are all that matter to college admissions officers, along with high SAT scores. Any courses that you transfer apply as credit hours, but usually the grades aren't applied to your grade-point average, so you can start all over again at a new school with a new GPA. In Chapter 6, I have listed several options for improving your record, no matter what your academic past.

3. APPLY ONLY TO UNIVERSITIES THAT YOU RESPECT. We'll discuss strategies for choosing an excellent program later in this chapter. When you love your university, you will learn to appreciate your own efforts more, and you will try harder to impress your professors and earn a top degree. Imagine, for example, that you are on a dinner date with the person of your dreams. How will you dress? How will you act? What will you hope to get out of the evening? Now imagine that you are on a date with someone dull you went out with to please your parents. Will you care? Will you try? *Of course not.* You'll do whatever you have to do to get the evening over with as cheaply and quickly as possible.

Colleges are similar. Attending a convenient but nondescript turnpike tech program that happens to be on the way home from the office may eventually sap your spirit. But step onto a great campus and you just may find your life changing along with your attitudes.

WHY YOU SHOULD USE "BEST SCHOOLS" GUIDES WITH CAUTION

After all this emphasis on great schools, however, I will warn you that you can't learn everything you need to know by simply buying a magazine that publishes a guide to the so-called best colleges and universities and believing everything it says. Trying to rank all college and university programs in a popular magazine is like trying to tell everyone in America what the ten best professions are, or the ten best cities, or the ten most convenient lovemaking positions for busy professionals. America's fascination with top tens can even be harmful, especially when it comes to discussing such a personal matter as the college one attends.

U.S. News & World Report publishes the most famous guide. You can purchase a copy and learn that Harvard, Yale, Stanford, Princeton, and other elite schools usually jostle for the number-one position.

Do you care? Will this help you?

Probably not. The magazine uses an opinion poll to determine 25 percent of its ranking criteria. Yet fewer than three-quarters of the college administrators who receive the form even bother to fill it out. Many of those who do fail to complete the entire survey.

The other criteria for ranking are alumni donations, a school's selectivity score, its faculty's star power, and how many students graduate. These are remarkably complex categories, subject to extreme manipulation by the colleges in question. For example, the selectivity score is the subject of a high-stakes game in which universities try to lure as many applicants as possible so that they can reject most of them and appear choosier. There are other elements in a selectivity score, too, such as the class rank of the high school seniors a college accepts, how many of these accepted students actually enroll, and what their SAT scores were. Because of the rankings lists, colleges now go through elaborate processes to compete for the same small pool of top high school seniors, even if lower-ranking students have spectacular talents.

If you think it would be hard to come up with an accurate math formula to fairly express the value of different facets of just the selectivity score, you're correct. Worse, the rankings try to compare apples and oranges by pitting state schools against private schools, small colleges against large ones, and regional stars against national ones. This opens the rankings up to obvious biases: the old, elite private schools usually win. Their alumni give more money; they enjoy more name recognition; and their endowments are already among the richest. How can an excellent small college with mere millions in the bank compete with an Ivy that draws interest on *billions*? Although I have been touting attributes such as wealth, many colleges, even those in the top several hundred rather than the top ten, share them.

PUTTING THE TOP-TEN LISTS IN PERSPECTIVE

All rankings and guides aren't useless, of course, but they *must* be seen in perspective. Here's a way to make more sense of them. Rather than focusing on an arbitrary top ten, consult *Money* magazine's list of best academic buys. Also, check the indexes of magazines that may more accurately reflect some of your personal search criteria, such as *Ebony* or *Hispanic Magazine*, political journals like the conservative *National Review*, or religious journals like the *National Catholic Reporter*. These publications will make the kinds of audience-specific distinctions that no single ranking can address.

You will want to consider many other factors besides rankings when choosing a university. To begin with, you will want to assess your needs and interests, and your academic background. There is an excellent chance that you will be happier at a strong state university, or at a small private college, than at one of the magazines' favorites. It may be more useful for you to focus on rankings for particular programs rather than for schools overall.

For example, Tracy accepted an offer from the top public university in her state but never checked its individual reputation in the fine arts. She was surprised to find an inexplicably third-rate drama program and almost no legitimate instruction in dance or music. And she felt like a social outcast among all those competitive kids who were majoring in pre-med or pre-law. By trusting rankings alone, she found herself on the wrong campus.

This wasn't the only university that had accepted her—just the biggest. She was so flattered to get accepted by an elite public university that she had turned down a small fellowship from another state school which ranked only slightly lower overall, but which had some of the best fine arts programs in the nation. Eventually she transferred and was happy at the hipper, more arts-oriented campus.

The best way to identify programs that interest you is to go ahead and read whatever you can about rankings, but seriously question the results. You can also use the Internet intelligently to identify great programs that the lists might have missed. Most colleges have websites, and nearly all of them are as carefully constructed as their catalogues. Visit Yahoo's home page (*www.yahoo.com*) and click on "College and University" under the "Education" category. Click on "Colleges and Universities" on the next page as well. You'll find an enormous listing, sorted in various useful ways. You can search by region, by category, and by state. Visit as many of these websites as you can, and request catalogues on-line from the ones that interest you. You'll get the best picture of a college from its own website and catalogue.

You can assess a university yourself by examining the credentials of its faculty. How many of its business professors come directly from the corporate world and still work as consultants? How many of its English professors are published scholars? Do its law professors practice law? Are its history professors top historians?

You can request free packets from a college's public relations office, including newspaper articles and magazine profiles. You can also see how guidebooks that aren't so obsessed with "top tens" rate that particular school. Appendix B lists some excellent book and magazine resources for locating top schools.

Of course, I'll stick by my original advice and say "Aim high." Very high. But you may well have to go through more steps to get where you want to be. Right now you are looking for an academic start and a nurturing environment, not a prestigious cold shoulder.

Consider one of these strategies. You can earn a bachelor's degree at a good state university in your region and distinguish yourself with high grades and honors. After you graduate, even some of the most selective campuses will probably welcome you as a graduate student. Or you can earn some credits at a decent, lower-tier school and then apply to one of your dream campuses as a transfer student after you have proven yourself at a more modest, accessible level. In Chapter 6, we'll discuss the application process and examine the various nontraditional routes into the traditional, respected college classroom.

You will soon learn to think about colleges as an interconnected system through which you can maneuver, depending upon your tastes, your goals, and your academic record. You will also learn to see your transcripts as something over which you have complete control. You just have to be practical enough to start where your credentials place you. With determination and patience, you can usually work your way onto the campus of your choice.

Paying for It:
The Simple Math of
Financial Aid

Despite what you may have read about college being unaffordable, undergraduate tuition varies greatly. One 3-credit course can cost anywhere from $75 at a community college to $2,700 at a top-ranked private university. However, the typical college student in America still pays tuition at the lower end of the scale: around $310 per course. When you add in fees, a four-year education at a typical state university, *including books*, costs between $16,000 and $20,000. That's less than the price of a new midsize domestic automobile.

The good news is that if you have a job, you can probably pay resident tuition out-of-pocket. The better news is that you probably won't have to pay every penny by yourself. If you earn a high grade-point average, or if you fall into certain demographic categories, you will qualify for all kinds of financial aid, including grants and fellowships that you don't have to pay back.

Nearly half (44 percent) of the students on today's campuses receive some form of financial assistance, and 25 percent are recipients of grants and scholarships they won't have to repay. Better yet, the more expensive the college, the more of its students receive financial aid. In this chapter, we'll examine reasonable college costs for an adult returning student, and then we'll look at potential sources of money. It is quite possible to finance your college education without having to take out enormous student loans.

Of course, this rosy picture presumes a great deal about your personal financial situation. I'm assuming that you have a job and that you are not trying to put three of your six kids through school at the same time. What if you *do* have children in college at the same time you are planning to go? Or what if you support your elderly parents? Perhaps, like Ellen, you feel as though you were "born unemployed" and will always stay that way because you haven't been able to find adequate work without a degree. Even if your situation is a little trickier than most, don't despair. I have collected examples for you from single moms and dads, parents of college-age kids, and people in all sorts of financial predicaments, including poverty. Even if your life isn't quite perfect, you *can* find a way to put yourself through college.

MOST AMERICANS OVERESTIMATE THE REAL PRICE OF COLLEGE

Why do many people complain that college is so expensive? It's true that many of the top private universities cost a lot of money. In part, this is because parents and students *want* them to. At the elite private colleges, applications might actually drop if they lowered their prices, simply because much of the marketing at these colleges is based on class consciousness. The more selective a university is and the more it costs, the more wealthy families will do whatever it takes to send their children there.

What the journalists who write those scary "college costs too much" articles *don't* tell you, however, is that the most expensive schools use their rich endowments to offer much more financial aid. At some of the priciest campuses, as many as three-quarters of the student body pay much less than the full tuition!

An American Council on Education poll showed that most Americans drastically overestimate college tuition and fees. They read startling headlines about out-of-control prices and assume that those headlines always reflect reality. But the journalists who write these stories will readily admit that they base them on private or out-of-state tuition rates only, even though most students receive financial assistance at private universities or pay in-state rates at public ones. You can get an artificial sense of "sticker shock" when you read these articles, since most skew the statistics to make it seem as though every family that sends a child to college must go into crushing debt.

YOUR TAX DOLLARS HAVE ALREADY HELPED PAY FOR STATE UNIVERSITIES

Every state has one or more great universities to its name: campuses that are specifically funded from public money in order to educate its citizens well, and at a reasonable cost. Not all state university systems are equal, of course, but in most states you can get an excellent education that rivals much of what the private colleges have to offer.

These state universities are the main reason why the largest single category of students (42.2 percent) pay between $2,000 and $3,900 for a whole school year's tuition and fees. That's a good buy, especially when you consider that the average college graduate will earn *at least* $10,000 per year more than her less-educated counterparts for the rest of her professional life. Here are just some of our many great state universities, along with their in-state tuition and fees for two semesters (ten courses) during the 1999–2000 academic year:

Florida State University	$2,240
University of Iowa	$2,666
University of Kentucky	$1,956
UCLA	$3,858[a]
University of Texas at Austin	$2,754
University of Wyoming	$2,144

[a] Three quarters (quarter system)

Even though it usually costs much less to go to a state college than a private one, some of the best, such as UNC–Chapel Hill, actually have *better* facilities, simply because the public coffers keep them so well funded. They may also receive enormous grants from big businesses in their states, allowing them to operate state-of-the-art research centers that these businesses fund. Loyal alumni also account for much of their wealth.

If you are at or near retirement age, you might qualify for free tuition from your state government. Many states offer free tuition for legal residents over a certain age, usually sixty or sixty-five. When Emily was a student at the University of Arkansas, she received a tuition bill every semester, just like any other undergraduate. Instead of paying it, however, she put it away. The business office later waived it automatically because she was in her sixties. If you think you might qualify for this benefit, call the financial aid office at any state university that interests you to find out about tuition remission for older adults.

YOU SHOULD ALWAYS AIM HIGH, BUT CONSIDER *STARTING* SMALL

Many state universities have numerous campuses. If you have never been to college before, or if you need to establish a record of recent strong grades, it can make sense for you to start at a smaller, less competitive campus in the system, especially if it is closer to your home and job.

Let's say you live in Maine and you would like to attend the University of Maine at Orono, near Bangor. But you live much closer to Augusta, and you're a nervous new student with limited resources. You might do well to start at the University of Maine at Augusta and pay the tuition ($2,835 per year) yourself.

Then let's say you make the dean's list both semesters and you're feeling confident. You could try transferring to the flagship campus at Orono. Even though this school is much more selective, and even though it costs about one-third more ($4,139 per year), your chances of getting in and possibly even receiving a scholarship are quite good. Of course, you also may choose to stay at the Augusta campus and continue earning top grades. An honors degree, even from a smaller school in an excellent state system, will stand you in good stead for work or for graduate study. Although it is true that a degree from the more prestigious and selective campus may open even *more* doors, you will be in the enviable position of having options after your first successful year. You will be able to assess your own goals and budget, and make a decision that's right for you.

Top Community and Junior Colleges Can Be Useful Paths to Four-Year Campuses

If your budget is extraordinarily tight, you can start at a well-ranked community college or a respected junior college that has a strong working relationship with a nearby state university. Tuition and fees will be lower there, and you will also be able to establish the necessary academic record. Jo attended St. Louis Community College for two years before transferring to the University of Northern Iowa. She appreciated the higher ratio of adult

students on the smaller, less competitive community college campus:

> I was not the oldest person on campus at all. There were at
> least two women older—one in her seventies and the other
> in her fifties—and many my age. I was in my forties at the
> time. The ratio of nontraditional to traditional [students]
> was considerably higher there than at the University of
> Northern Iowa, where I now attend. I'm sure that helped my
> transition.

Tuition at St. Louis Community College was only $35 a credit
hour. Now Jo pays around $100 per credit hour for classes at UNI.
All of her course credits transferred, and her diploma will say
"University of Northern Iowa," just like any other grad's.

If you can go straight to the state university campus of your
choice, you should. But well-respected community and junior colleges can be a reasonable first step in certain situations, especially
if funds are a serious problem. Here are some examples of how a
top community college can help you step onto a great American
campus. You could study for a year at Northern Wyoming Community College in Sheridan ($646 in-state; $1,616 out-of-state). If
you earn top grades and then do well on the SAT, you might be
accepted by and even win a scholarship to the nationally ranked
University of Wyoming ($1,165 in-state; $3,709 out-of-state).
Students at Macomb Community College in Warren, Michigan, have an excellent record of transferring to the University of
Michigan. Piedmont Virginia Community College in Charlottesville sends many of its top students to the University of Virginia,
William and Mary, Virginia Tech, and other great Virginia campuses.

Don't try this with just any community or junior college, however. Talk to admissions officers at state universities to find out
what kind of a placement record community colleges have and
how well respected they are. You can also ask the community

colleges themselves. Most will try to convince you that you can transfer anywhere, but press harder and ask for actual placement statistics. This is public information, and it should be able to help you decide whether community or junior college is the right step for you.

IN-STATE STATUS IS ONE KEY TO AFFORDABLE TUITION

If you don't already have in-state (resident) status, it can be complicated to establish, especially if you have moved often. Most state universities will ask you to prove your residency by showing one year's worth of documentation if you weren't born or raised in the state. Even then, you will have to be meticulous in your documentation and quite persistent to win your case. Despite recent court rulings that most state universities' resident admissions criteria are too strenuous, these schools will usually do what they can to force you to pay the out-of-state rate.

There are some loopholes, however. If you're a legal resident of Alabama, Arkansas, Delaware, Florida, Georgia, Kentucky, Louisiana, Maryland, Mississippi, North Carolina, Oklahoma, South Carolina, Tennessee, Texas, Virginia, or West Virginia, you can qualify for in-state tuition in any one of these states through the Southern Regional Education Board (SREB). The catch is that the degree program must be one that universities in your home state don't offer. The SREB offers a list of qualifying programs. You can contact them at 404-875-9211 or visit them on the Web at *www.sreb.org*.

You can also try applying to a college in your original home state even if you no longer live there, using records from earlier years as evidence of residency. For example, I had a much easier time proving legal residency in Virginia, my home state, than in North Carolina, the state where I then resided, when I applied to colleges, and later to graduate programs. Other students report being granted immediate in-state status for states in which they were born or grew up, but where they haven't lived for years. Remember that in-state students qualify for many more scholarships and fellowships than their out-of-state colleagues, so it really pays to make the best use of a state university system as an in-state student.

You may also qualify for in-state tuition elsewhere if one of your parents graduated from a state university. Indiana State University offers in-state status to children of alumni as long as they meet its standard entrance requirements. It doesn't matter where those children were born or where their families live now. Other state universities offer the same deal, but they require that the parent be a lifetime member of the alumni association in order to qualify. A lifetime membership usually costs between $500 and $1,000, so it could be in your best interest to ask your mother or father to join an alumni association and to pay their alumni dues for them. You will save much more than that over the course of your university career.

CAMPUS EMPLOYEES OFTEN RECEIVE GENEROUS TUITION WAIVERS

Don't overlook on-campus jobs as a way of establishing residency and earning your way into a state university. It can make a great deal of sense to work in one of the campus offices if you receive tuition remission or even a tuition discount for your trouble. Even if the job pays only a modest salary, the tuition benefits on top of that can add up to an excellent deal.

Diane worked at Smith College in Northampton, Massachusetts, for a year before she decided to finish her own bachelor's degree. She was delighted to learn that she could take classes without paying tuition. This was a remarkable benefit, since Smith courses cost over $2,500 *each*. Remember that most colleges do require a waiting period. You may have to work for a year or more before qualifying for tuition benefits. But nothing can stop you from taking a course or two elsewhere, or through the college's continuing education program, while you wait, and then signing up for more when your benefits kick in. Diane takes two courses per semester while working full-time. She pays for her own books and course materials. By taking advantage of Smith's generous tuition remission program, she effectively earns an additional $10,000 per year in benefits.

Julia moved from her native California to New Jersey when her husband's company transferred him. She wanted to attend highly ranked Rutgers, a state university, but she couldn't afford the out-of-state tuition of over $515 per course. Instead, she accepted a clerical job in the university's pharmacy school. After one year, she was able to begin taking undergraduate classes at the in-state tuition rate of only $253 per course, and eventually she qualified for tuition remission as an employee. She saved more money overall than she lost in the pay cut she took to work at the school, and her new bosses were quite flexible about letting her adjust her working hours around her class schedule. She also saved gas money and parking fees by not commuting, and she ended up further ahead financially than she would have been if she had stayed in a more demanding, higher-paying job.

THE MILITARY CAN HELP YOU PAY FOR COLLEGE, AND ALSO GIVE YOU IN-STATE TUITION STATUS

Many adult students return to college after a stint in the armed forces. If you have not yet received your discharge and are thinking about college, consider your options carefully before you leave the military. Most veterans may choose any one of the fifty states in which to establish legal residency. Many automatically select their home state. However, since typically you won't be able to change your mind later, you will want to choose a state university first and *then* declare residency in that state. This is perfectly legal, and it can help you start your education on a much better financial footing.

Many veterans don't take advantage of all of their educational options. For example, you may have a service-related disability. If you do, did you know that under most circumstances you qualify for vocational rehabilitation? This means that the government will pay you to go to college in order to train for a new career. Not only will you receive money for tuition and books, you'll receive a paycheck on top of that to help offset your lost wages. Cal, a veteran of the Navy, qualified for vocational rehab after receiving a 50 percent disability rating from the Veterans Administration. Now he is studying to be a nurse:

> The Veterans Administration (VA) pays for all my books, fees, tuition, and supplies purchased from the bookstore on campus, as well as the uniforms I need for the nursing program, stethoscope, white shoes (required for hospital clinics), shots, etc. They also provide me with a monthly stipend of $737.19, because I have four kids. All of my VA disability above the monthly stipend while I'm in school is tax-deductible.

Cal is using this generous package, along with a combination of federal Pell Grants and Wisconsin Higher Education Grants not only to pay for school, but also to support his family while he finishes his degree.

Make sure that you research your full education benefits before you leave the military and that you collect on them afterward.

Check with your discharging officer for complete information, and investigate on your own by talking to veterans' groups. Veterans can be your best source of information on completing all of the necessary paperwork and tracking down every penny that you're entitled to for your education. Many of them worked very hard to master all of the intricacies of the military benefits system. They'll be happy to help a fellow vet, and you'll have a much easier time figuring out what choices are best for you.

Start *Now* to Discover Your Many and Varied Financial Aid Options

Adult financial aid recipients who told their stories for this book were unanimous on one point. They all agreed that it is never too early to begin the money hunt. Many reached for their checkbooks in a burst of enthusiasm when they began college. They sought financial aid on an emergency basis only when money got tight. Most of those who have received scholarships, grants, and other academic awards said they wished that they had begun looking for money earlier.

There are several good reasons to start early. First, you may need to file your income taxes differently in order to qualify for some financial aid. For example, if you are twenty-three and plan to request financial aid as an independent adult, you'll want to make certain that your parents aren't still claiming you as an exemption. Plan ahead so that you can file in the state where you will be claiming in-state status, even if that means moving before you are ready to begin school there. If necessary, talk to a tax accountant about filing *amended* returns for past years. Take every legal step you can to assure yourself the proper tax status for in-state, self-supported tuition.

SOME FINANCIAL AID OFFICES
ARE MORE HELPFUL THAN OTHERS

The bureaucracy in the typical financial aid office is another great reason to start hunting for money as early as possible. Financial aid offices can seem like a blackberry bramble of regulations and delays. In most cases, nobody is deliberately trying to make your life miserable. It's just that financial aid officers have to deal with changing federal and state rules, university policies, quirky private lenders, and the myriad legal complications of foundations, grants, and donors. No two sets of rules are alike. Instead of running in terror, visit early, visit often, and learn from former nontraditional-age students about smart ways through the paperwork thicket.

Cynthia, a student at the University of Arizona, has to budget every penny. When she first approached financial aid, she encountered "red tape up the kazoo. I worked hard to get things processed, but sometimes it was a nightmare." She learned a nifty trick for cutting through the glaze of an often-overworked state university staff: "Make copies of *everything*. Write down *everyone's* name you talk to, along with the date and time." By documenting each step with financial aid and pushing those state employees to take personal responsibility for their answers, Cynthia was able to cover all of her tuition through federal grants.

Evelyn, at the University of Wisconsin, said that asking questions even when she felt like a pest made her transition much easier:

> There were so many hoops to go through, and there still are every single semester. It takes a lot of time running around with all the little administrative things a student needs to do. When I first reached campus, I was bewildered. I just didn't know where to start. Thank God for helpful advisors who know just where to direct you. I was never afraid to ask questions, no matter how stupid they seemed to be. I didn't have a lot of time to waste trying to find it all out on my

own, so I was constantly asking questions. That's one piece
of advice I'd give future nontraditional students. Don't hesitate to ask questions.

Stories about financial aid officers varied, even when different
students went to the same office at the same university. Some students lauded the helpful staff who held their hands and taught
them how to use the system to their advantage. Fern can't say
enough nice things about the staff at American River College:

> The financial aid office at this school is great. I had to buy
> my books, since I was not eligible for a book voucher. I
> didn't have the money one semester, so the Dean gave me a
> $200 emergency loan which I paid back before the semester
> was over. If my Pell grant money happens to be late in com-
> ing, the school waives the fees until it comes. No other col-
> lege that I've found is this helpful.

Fern's good experience was by no means universal, however.
Others complained that staff ignored them, argued with them, and
denied legitimate claims. When I asked Maggie if her financial aid
office had been helpful when she tried to claim her low-income
and disability benefits, she was incredulous:

> You're kidding, right? . . . They have given me the biggest
> runaround and have a problem understanding that a person
> like me could have such a low income. I'm not sure if these
> are disability-awareness issues or if they believe they per-
> sonally control this money. A couple of financial aid coun-
> selors have acted as if the money comes from their own
> pockets. A student really has to be assertive to make the
> right things happen!

Financial aid offices in private universities tend to do a better job
than their state counterparts, but again, your mileage *will* vary.

My best advice is to prepare for the worst when it comes to any bureaucratic office. Walk in with a resolve to be cheerful and persistent. At the same time, wear enough emotional armor to keep yourself protected if things get ugly. Above all, *never* take no for an answer. Just keep trying at higher and higher levels until someone takes you and your concerns seriously and does something to help.

THE ART OF CONVINCING SKEPTICAL OFFICERS THAT YOU ARE INDEPENDENT

Need-based assistance looks at how much money you earn, and at how much your parents earn if you are still a dependent. Most adult students are independent, however, and you may need to emphasize this, *firmly,* to administrators who persist in asking you how much your parents plan to contribute to your education. It may be a challenge to remain patient at times. Remind yourself that these officers usually deal with traditional students between the ages of eighteen and twenty-two. You are an exception to all of their carefully typed rules, and you may have to repeat this so often that you begin to feel like an answering machine on an endless playback loop.

Although it usually has a reputation for having a helpful financial aid office, some staff members at the University of Wisconsin refused to believe that Heather was a self-supporting adult:

> Despite the fact [that] I had been living independently of my parents since I was seventeen, they insisted I must be at least partially supported by my parents until I was twenty-four and refused to even attempt to search aid for me until then.

I myself encountered a similar problem at George Mason University. They didn't have an easy-to-place category for me, either in their minds or in their paperwork. Although I was twenty-eight and had lived on my own for seven years, officers kept asking me how much money my parents intended to contribute to my education.

Many students have found the magic words by saying, assertively, "I am an adult and I contribute money to support my parents." By emphasizing the reversal of support, these students won the attention of most of the financial aid officers they encountered. Edna's parents went along with this, agreeing to confirm that she contributed to their household expenses rather than vice versa. Whenever Edna had a meeting with a new financial aid officer, she *began* the conversation by stating: "My situation is different from most students'. My parents have not supported me since 1985. I contribute to *their* support, along with my brothers and sister." By starting off with this assertive statement, and by politely repeating it whenever an officer suggested that Edna's elderly parents should somehow dip into their meager retirement savings to send their adult daughter to college, she prevailed. Her assertiveness silenced those financial aid officers who were more used to talking with nineteen-year-olds driving Mom's Range Rover and using Dad's Platinum MasterCard.

You can use this same strategy if you have children or if you support other family members. Don't wait for someone to ask you. Instead, introduce yourself at the start of every meeting by saying, "My name is Clark, and I am completely independent. Not only do I help support my parents, I have five children, the youngest of whom is in an expensive special school that understands his autism."

Don't expect the officers to remember any of this, either. Be prepared to repeat it at the outset of your financial aid conversation every time you go to that office. If you really want results, you can even hand the officer a typed sheet that clearly shows your financial obligations and your demonstrated need. Squeaky wheels definitely get the extra WD-40 in financial aid offices. By never giving the officers a chance to see you as anything other than needy, you will qualify for more assistance than typical college undergraduates.

IF YOU EARN TOP GRADES, ENTER WITH YOUR REPORT CARDS BLAZING!

Merit-based assistance looks at your grade-point average, overall and in your major. It is awarded on the basis of such variables as your class rank, your standing in your department, and your performance on standardized tests. As an adult returning student, you probably will not qualify for much merit-based assistance until you have completed a full academic year, or thirty regular credits. Even after the first year, merit-based assistance is highly competitive.

Of course you will try to earn great grades. Nearly all adult returning students become grade-conscious. It's a natural side effect of being more mature and more able to handle college-level work. The good habits that you developed on your job or caring for your family will help you shine in a classroom, and high grades will probably be easier to earn than they were in your youth. As your grades improve, you may find yourself eligible for merit-based scholarship money. Top students can reasonably expect to have many of their expenses covered by scholarships by the end of their sophomore year.

Your ongoing relationship with the financial aid office will help you identify and apply for as many awards as possible. Again, as with the need-based assistance, you will have to introduce yourself as a merit student every time you walk in the door. "Hi, I'm Deanna, and I have a 4.0 in my major and 3.6 overall" is a fine way to open a conversation. Bring copies of your grades so that the officer doesn't have to look them up. As Melba says, "Learn to shout 'A student coming through!' whenever you get *that look*

from one of them. They'll help you after that." Help the officers
see you not as just another whiner in the lobby, but as an academic star who deserves their best efforts.

LEARN TO IDENTIFY YOURSELF BY RACE, RELIGION, AND EVEN SHOE SIZE, IF IT HELPS

There are demographically based awards that take into account
your gender, your age, your race, your religion, the alumni in
your family, and many other variables. It may pay you hand-
somely to carefully consider various awards for which you might
qualify. Make a list of all of the religious, ethnic, and fraternal
groups to which your family belongs.

Was your grandmother a Polish immigrant? Is your father a
Mason? Are you Japanese-American? Did your uncle join the
Teamsters? Did your mother go to the University of Iowa? There
are a great number of awards for students who fall into broad
and varied demographic categories. If you start a list and expand
it as you identify new sources of money, you may find yourself
the happy recipient of women's club awards, checks from the
Fraternal Order of Eagles or the Veterans of Foreign Wars, stip-
ends from the National Italian American Foundation, or money
from other specialized groups, including private philanthropists.
Most semesters I was surprised and delighted to receive checks
from organizations interested in helping adult women return to
college. There is nothing quite so academically satisfying as receiving an extra $600 or $1,000 from a group that enthusiastically
supports your performance and that worked hard to raise the
money.

Always remember to write a warm letter of thanks to any individual or organization that gives you money, and keep them in-

formed with a yearly update of your progress. For a special touch, send every donor an announcement when you graduate, and enclose a final note of thanks for their generosity, letting them know that they are partly responsible for your success.

TRY NOT TO LOOK *TOO* GOOD ON PAPER

If what you earn seems like a high salary for assistance purposes, and if you don't fall into any readily identifiable ethnic or demographic categories, then you may have a tough time with crusty financial aid officers. Sherrie became frustrated when the financial aid office turned her down repeatedly. She earned $32,000 a year at her full-time job, which seemed like much more than a "typical" undergraduate salary. All of the standardized tables said that she should be able to pay for college. But she was forty-one years old and supported two children, with no husband in the picture. Once she emphasized her status as a single mother with two children, she found that she qualified for more free financial aid than a member of almost any other demographic group on campus. It went against Sherrie's self-reliant upbringing to "cry poormouth" to a stranger, but when she clearly pointed out her situation, she got the financial help she needed.

Carol said that a reasoned appeal was the secret to her successful request for financial aid. She, too, looked like a big earner, simply because she was a self-sufficient adult:

> When I first got my financial aid packet back, marked that I had made too much the year before to qualify for federal or state grants of any type, I thought I was seeing my college career end before it started. I went to the financial aid office and they walked me through the appeal process, which was successful. Had it not been, I would have had to look seri-

ously at not going to college at all. At forty, I was and am still extremely reticent to take out large loans to pay for this education.

The appeals process will send your application to specialists who will be able to re-evaluate you using nontraditional-student criteria.

Some students experience a kind of backlash where they earn one windfall award and have trouble qualifying for anything else. Margaret earned a big scholarship early on because of her high grades. But her financial situation was still tight, and she had to fight to get the officers to continue seeing her as a need-based student once the scholarship ended:

> They seemed to resent the good package I got. Once I did not think the figuring had been done correctly on my package. But the financial aid office wouldn't budge. I call a 1-800 number on my application and a federal aid official intervened on my behalf. Even then, I had to complain through three levels before the Vice Chancellor made them release the funds. They were never happy when I walked in the office after that.

You can also ask your elected state government officials to step in and assist you. Try calling the office of your state delegate, representative, or senator. Often you will find a staffer who is paid to help constituents resolve problems like yours. Many of these staffers will even make phone calls on your behalf once they understand your situation. Give them the opportunity to earn their taxpayer-supported salaries by helping you with financial aid.

It may feel strange at first to announce your private business in what seems like such a public way. But this is the most reliable strategy for identifying yourself in the demographics-based world of financial aid.

SEVEN STEPS TOWARD EARNING THE MAXIMUM FINANCIAL AID

Here are some basic, easy steps you can take to increase the amount of financial aid for which you qualify. If you are thorough and persistent, you will be able to locate many sources of financial assistance to make your college quest much more affordable.

1. MAKE YOURSELF WELL-KNOWN AT YOUR UNIVERSITY'S FINANCIAL AID OFFICE. Introduce yourself early, even before your first semester begins. Learn who's who among the staff, including everyone in the financial aid hierarchy, from the front-desk clerks on up to the Dean. Then greet each staff member and officer by name. Don't just show up when you want something; stop by for regular visits each semester just to say hello. Heather notes that personal relationships with administrators, especially in financial aid, made her academic life much easier:

> Get to know the people in the financial aid office, registration, and especially your advisor. These people can really save your academic butt if you get into a bind. If they don't know you from Adam, then you may only get assistance within their job description.

Remember that financial aid often works on a slow timetable. There is seldom any money available on an emergency basis: you must apply very early for almost all awards. If you give the staff time to get to know you and your needs, they will be better able to assist you in applying for future years' funding. You may have to pay for your first semester or two out of pocket or with loans, but in time you will be in the system. The staff will be able to help you make financial plans months, and even years, ahead of time.

Psychologically, you want to get the officers on your side. If they know you and like you, then they will be more likely to keep you in mind when bequests come available. They may even start cheering you on! They can be especially helpful in assigning you smaller amounts that often don't get posted in the usual lists of funds. An award of $250 may not seem like a lot of money, but when you're at the campus bookstore, offering the cashier your lonely little debit card and hoping the charge will go through, it can feel like a fortune.

2. DO YOUR OWN RESEARCH, AND DON'T EXPECT ANY FINANCIAL AID OFFICER TO HAVE THE LAST WORD ON AVAILABLE AWARDS. Financial aid is a complex process involving many more hours per student than most universities can afford. Fortunately, the Internet has made scholarship research much easier. The Web offers well-indexed financial aid databases. Some of these will even notify you by E-mail when an award for which you qualify becomes available! All you have to do is fill out a few screens of personal information and these sites will do the research for you. Appendix B contains some of my favorite on-line financial aid resources.

Some institutions, such as MIT and Drew University, now have Web-based financial aid programs, and many more will in the future. Just make certain you don't let your university's financial aid web page substitute for regular visits to your friendly financial aid officer.

3. FORMALLY THANK EVERYONE WHO HELPS YOU FIND MONEY. I sent cards with handwritten thank-you notes to every person who assisted me with financial aid. When one officer awarded me a discretionary fellowship that paid for a full semester's tuition—an award over which she had complete control—I even sent her a small bouquet of flowers. They weren't too splashy, since I didn't want it to appear that a supposedly broke student was wasting money, but they were pretty and seasonal. When I called her for help with another problem the following year, before I even finished saying my name, she jumped in with, "Oh, I remember, *you're* the student who sent the flowers!" In an office where she frequently had to deal with tears and accusations, the flowers

made me permanently memorable. I was only mildly surprised when she awarded me another discretionary fellowship the following semester.

4. LET YOUR ACADEMIC DEPARTMENTS KNOW THAT YOU HOPE TO RECEIVE FINANCIAL ASSISTANCE. Be sure to notify the chair, the assistant chairs, and all of your professors that you are a self-supporting student who is eager for opportunities to earn scholarship and fellowship money. Departments often receive notification of awards and prizes that are specific to a certain field. Individual professors may be on specialized mailing lists for their disciplines. If you are a top student, and if you make it known that you are struggling financially, your department will be able to nominate you for discretionary money much more easily. Remind members of your department at the beginning of each semester that you are still seeking financial aid.

If your grades are excellent, be sure to prepare a brief memo including your overall GPA and a copy of your recent grades. Don't just hand it shyly to a department secretary and slink off, either. Distribute it by hand to faculty members with a warm greeting and plenty of questions about their kids, their careers, and their lives. If you are doing your best to earn top grades, then your department will consider you one of its own, and these professors should look forward to hearing from you now and then and helping you when they can.

5. CONTACT FEDERAL AND STATE DEPARTMENTS OF EDUCATION. You can search the federal Department of Education website (*www.ed.gov/offices/OPE/Students*) to get the latest information by mail and on-line. Also, contact the department of education in your home state, and—if it is different—the state in which you live now. Most states have a commitment to educating their citizens, and you may find sources of locally based financial aid or hear about state programs that may not have received national attention. Most state departments of education have important links to state

universities, adult learning programs, and state offices concerned with education issues. Many of these departments are on the Web. Visit this Yahoo! page for a list of state education departments: *www.yahoo.com/Education/Government_Agencies/United_States.*

6. CALL THE OFFICES OF YOUR FEDERAL AND STATE OFFICIALS. This includes your local representatives, state senators, and members of Congress. Talk to the staffer responsible for higher education. You may learn of special programs for adult learners in your state, or discretionary money available for working parents or members of demographic groups important to the state, such as Native Americans and other ethnic minorities. Remember that your success may end up making your elected representatives look good, so be sure to give their offices the full opportunity to help you in your search for financial aid.

7. USE A FOUNDATION CENTER LIBRARY TO FIND OUT ABOUT PRIVATE PHILANTHROPISTS WHO MIGHT WANT TO ASSIST YOU. The Foundation Center, a clearinghouse for information on foundations and corporate giving, has libraries in Washington, D.C., Atlanta, San Francisco, Cleveland, and Manhattan. You can also visit the Foundation Center on the Web, at *fdncenter.org.* Using their resources, you can learn how to assess yourself demographically and how to apply for money to complete your education. I found whole award reports dedicated to resources for women or for members of various ethnic groups. Each Foundation Center has a well-stocked library pertaining to higher education and financial aid.

THE COSTS AND BENEFITS OF CORPORATE TUITION REIMBURSEMENT

Many adult students rely on their companies for tuition benefits. While some of these programs can be quite generous, in my experience they are a mixed blessing. Before you embrace your company's tuition reimbursement plan, and especially before you change jobs in order to get tuition benefits, you will want to consider the necessary restrictions that companies place on these programs.

Some companies offer tuition reimbursement as part of their employee benefits package. They receive a federal exemption from payroll and income tax on any money they funnel into the program. Employees who enroll in approved courses can actually get their tuition and books paid for by the corporation. Tuition reimbursement benefits are increasingly popular with professional recruiters, many of whom try to lure top students as early as high school.

The catch (and there's always at least one, isn't there?) is that tuition reimbursement often only covers core courses, and then only in narrowly specified majors. For example, I worked for NASDAQ, a stock exchange that offered tuition reimbursement benefits. But I had to major in accounting or finance, neither of which taps into my particular skills. After some wheedling, I convinced my employer to pay for a communications class before I declared my major, but I had to carefully document that the class was a requirement for finance majors. An executive became angry when I dropped the class and did not immediately pay back the money because I was waiting for the university to refund it to me. He wrote a memo to my boss accusing me of all sorts of nefarious conduct. In the end, the benefits weren't worth the trouble. I switched my major to English, which I loved but which my company would not subsidize, and I simply paid for school myself.

Company reimbursement plans are most useful when you want to take just one or two courses to sharpen your skills. For example, many companies will pay you to take courses in information systems, Web development, or other computer-based disciplines. Your boss will probably give you the time off, since the company supports such education enhancements, and you'll get an easy reintroduction to the realm of higher education. If you like computers, or if you picture yourself in a technology-based major, then these one-shot reimbursement offers can be a wonderful bonus for you.

But what if you're a historian at heart? Should you take your company's money and major in accounting or finance just because that's what they'll pay for? Remember that academic satisfaction and high grades are much more important than the name of your major. Although tuition reimbursement programs are a great benefit for workers who want the majors they support, for more artistic, literary, or right-brained people, left-brained disciplines can feel like a lifetime prison sentence. If you don't enjoy business or technology but major in it, even if you earn a bachelor's degree at the end of it all, you'll be bored and frustrated throughout much of your college career, and your grades will probably reflect your fundamental malaise. Worse yet, your new degree will only help you in a field that you have now proven you don't enjoy.

Besides restricting majors, many companies offer tuition reimbursement only for graduate-level study. And most companies offer tuition reimbursement on a stepped scale, according to grades. They'll reimburse you 100 percent only if you earn an A in the class. For a B, they'll reimburse you 75 percent, and for a C or lower they won't pay at all. Although the percentages vary and a few companies will offer half reimbursement for a C, this grade-based remittance scale is part of almost every tuition benefit package. Unless you are certain that you can do very well in a class, you may find yourself unable to cash in on any benefits.

Other companies actually play bait-and-switch. They'll convince you to sign on by promising you tuition benefits and then inform you later that they'll only pay for a core of five or six classes leading to a certificate. Certificates have become quite popular in business as a lower-level "substitute" for primary or additional college degrees. While certification may help you within your own company, it is meaningless in academia and may not have any value to other employers. If you plan to go to graduate school or to use your education to get a better job someday, you may waste valuable time in pursuit of a certificate. Furthermore, many universities will not accept certificate courses for transfer credit, since classes leading to certification are often narrowly specialized and skills-based and do not meet broader academic criteria.

Dan, a biology major earning his second bachelor's degree, offers another reason for paying for college out-of-pocket instead of accepting corporate tuition reimbursement: motivation. He pays tuition himself,

> even though the company would cover it, because I believe it keeps me focused on what I want . . . One of the things I really like about paying for my own classes is that I feel very committed to what I'm doing. My class selections are things I really want, versus knowing that I could take anything because the employer would pick up the costs anyway.

Dan is a top student now, and he has the luxury of not having to justify any of his academic decisions to a boss or a committee.

Before you sign on with a company because of its tuition reimbursement program, here are six basic questions to ask:

1. Will you cover *all* of the courses, including electives, leading to a traditional, four-year bachelor's degree, or do you focus only on core courses leading to certificates?
2. Is the program just for executives, or may any employee participate?
3. Will you support my chosen major? If not, will you pay for individual requirements or electives within my major that pertain to our company's business, such as statistics, marketing, advertising, finance, or communications?
4. Is there a grade-based reimbursement scale? If I earn one or two C's but maintain a high GPA overall, can I still receive full reimbursement for those courses?

5. Do you pay in full for additional fees and books?
6. Is tuition reimbursement a guaranteed benefit, or can my boss terminate my schooling if she doesn't see the need for my degree?

Although no company's answers will please you 100 percent of the time, some companies are much better than others about meeting *most* of your reasonable academic requests. You can avoid making a serious professional misstep if you clarify these basic points before you change jobs or sign an employment agreement.

ASK YOUR COLLEGE ABOUT THE FUNDING FOR VARIOUS MAJORS

On many college campuses, certain majors are better funded than others. Although I strongly advise you to major in something you love (see Chapter 9), there may be variations on your chosen profession or major that will pay you more to be in school.

Jan thought that the tuition at Aquinas College, at slightly over $800 per course, was too high for her budget. She investigated, however, and found out that generous funding was available for one major that intrigued her:

> I had no help from my employer, even though the Diocese of Grand Rapids encourages parishes to reimburse its employees for theology courses taken. Aquinas, like all private colleges, is quite expensive: about twice the cost of local state colleges or universities.
>
> One nice break was that Aquinas offers a 50 percent rebate on theology courses for those employed by the church. This brought the cost for all but five of the courses I needed down to the same rate that a public institution would have

charged. By the time I finished last spring, 3-credit courses
ran $805. My part was $402.50, plus about $50 per course
for textbooks.

By majoring in theology—which she loved anyway—and by
working in a parish as a complement to her chosen major, Jan
managed to cut the cost of college in half while earning money toward the remainder of the tuition and giving herself a top professional credential.

You might be able to find work-study programs at your university that combine funded majors with field experience. Many of
these are available in the sciences, in conjunction with local tech-
nological or research firms that may fund specific programs. You
will have to hunt around from department to department and
make lots of phone calls, but it will be worth it if you can find
deals like Jan's.

I don't recommend majoring in something you don't like just
to save money. However, if the difference between paying full
price and getting funded is a simple change to another version of
something you are already interested in, you may find useful
partnerships between your university and the professional community. You can also gain work experience and increase your
chances of being hired in that field.

STUDENT LOANS SHOULD BE YOUR LAST RESORT

After all this discussion of free funding as opposed to out-of-
pocket expenses, it is only fair to stop and consider the most common form of tuition financing: the student loan. I don't generally
recommend loans at the undergraduate level. If you don't qualify
for financial aid or tuition reimbursement, then you should attend
a college you can afford and try to pay your tuition out-of-pocket

as you go. After all, you may want to consider graduate or law school someday, and you'll find yourself with more options if you don't assume too much student loan debt in undergraduate school.

My only exception to this rule is if you get into a *very* highly ranked university, but without an offer of financial aid. Your education at that elite school may be worth so much to you in terms of future earnings that the student loan option immediately becomes "worth it." I do believe, however, that you should exhaust every other option for academic financing before filling out those tempting forms and accepting a tuition check.

If you must take out a student loan, the federal government has recently made it easier and cheaper to do so. By early 1999, student loan interest rates had dropped to 7.5 percent, their lowest level in almost twenty years. The loans are easy to obtain even if you have a limited credit history. You can always accept a loan that you don't need, bank it to earn interest, and then use it to pay off future loans in order to buy yourself a little time between your bachelor's degree and your first good job.

However, I don't recommend student loans, primarily because they *are* so easy to get. If you meet certain financial aid criteria, the lenders will waive charging interest until you graduate. Some students gradually slip into staggering debt loads. Alison graduated owing $35,000 to the Student Loan Marketing Association (Sallie Mae). Jason, an attorney, had racked up a debt close to $90,000 by the time he finished law school. Even though they both earned fine salaries after graduation and eventually paid their debts, they could have avoided this trap through more careful financing. As one student said, "Student loans made it easy for me to just not look for other sources of money. They let me be lazy about my finances, and now I'm paying for it." Another writes, "If I could do anything differently, I would not have borrowed any, or at least not as much."

Ina, however, thinks the sacrifice is worth it. She makes the important point that even big student loans are better for you financially than not finishing college at all:

Take out loans if you must. The return on investment for the degree is often greater than the returns on investments in the stock market, and much more of a sure thing. The degree costs less than a new car, doesn't depreciate, and does wonders for your self-esteem.

Margaret, who began her studies at the University of Arkansas in her late forties, agrees. She has mixed feelings about her student loans, and wishes she hadn't taken so many. But she'd rather have them than not have a degree:

> The loans were to insulate my husband and daughter from feeling deprived while I was in school. We were used to my income, but we probably could have done without the loans. I wound up borrowing $14,000 after the four years of my bachelor's degree . . .
>
> Anyone who gets a loan had better be sure that he is getting the skills and degree to get a good job, which may only mean a different minor.

If you do take out student loans, try to repay them before you leave college and the interest clock starts ticking. Even if you only send a hundred dollars now and again to pay down your principal, you will save a great deal in interest over the life of the loan.

How to Pay for Your Education When Your Kids Are Students, Too

Sometimes, sending your own children to college will convince you that you ought to give it a try yourself. A surprising number of parents reported being back in college at the same time as their traditional-age children. Some parents, like forty-four-year-old

Dave at the University of Massachusetts at Dartmouth, are actually on the same campus with their kids. When Anne was in college at the University of North Carolina at Greensboro, she and her daughter shared a classic undergraduate experience:

> My daughter, by that time a senior, and I decided to take a class together—Russian Literature in Translation—and we stayed up all night in her dorm room before the exam, drinking gallons of tea and coffee to stay awake. I fell asleep at 5 a.m. at her desk, with my head resting atop my notebook. I had finally made it as a student.

How do families with children *and* parents in college pay for it all? Whose education is more important?

You can resolve this seeming conflict by restructuring the way the family thinks about college costs. Many parents assume that they *owe* their children a fully paid college education. They smile and say that they don't want their kids to have to work or struggle during college because the responsibilities of adult life will come soon enough after graduation.

The reality is different, however. College students, including your traditional-age kids, appreciate their courses more if they have to help figure out how to pay for them. When I went to college in my late teens and early twenties on a full ride from Dad and Mom, I partied around, did as little homework as possible, and constantly calculated the least amount of effort necessary to pass a course. Years later, when I paid for college myself out of money earned at a challenging job, I strove for excellence and proudly earned top grades. What changed? One fundamental difference was paying for school myself. Students who earn their tuition work harder, and demand more for *their* money.

Most students are like this. I can tell the difference today between my Georgetown students who have jobs, or who have to maintain high GPAs to keep their scholarship money, and those who know that their parents will pay the hefty tab semester after semester. As one student who worked at the food counters at Dean & DeLuca put it, "I paid dearly for this semester. I'm not going to sleep through it."

This advice goes for rich kids, gifted kids, average kids, *any* kids. The American concept that parents "owe" their children four years of paid tuition runs exactly counter to the basic principles of self-motivation and achievement. No matter where your children are—whether presently in college or planning to go in the future—now is the time for you to make them partners in their own educations. It is perfectly fair to ask them what kinds of jobs they plan to get and how they plan to improve their grade-point averages in order to qualify for scholarships and fellowships.

If you're laughing right now and saying "*My* Brian? The one who thinks that the grading scale only goes as high as C plus?" then it might be time to ask yourself why the family is sending him to college at all. Four-year degrees are important, but they mean something only if they represent an actual education. Many lackluster students become remarkably motivated when they know that their funding is about to be cut off because of nonperformance. I have counseled tearful students in my office who begged for higher grades "because Dad says if I don't get at least a B in here, he's going to pull my money. *All* of it!" I just smile and say, "Well, then, it's time to figure out how to make that happen, isn't it?"

If every college student in the family becomes responsible for her or his own tuition, then it makes sense for the family to take out loans to cover whatever on-campus jobs and fellowships don't cover. Nonperforming students, whether parents or children, should have to make the decision to shape up or drop out. After college, children and parents together can decide how to repay the loan debt that the family has accumulated.

You may worry that your children will resent you for pulling the plug on free college funding. Most don't, however. My students consistently report that they enjoy being responsible for their own success. As one student who waits tables at a nearby restaurant put it, "My parents could pay for college, but I *wanted* to earn some of the money myself." Students also feel more comfortable choosing majors that reflect their interests when they pay for college themselves. The academic process shifts from being a grind to being an exciting challenge. And when that happens, their grades automatically improve, along with self-esteem and natural confidence.

Here are some closing comments and advice that nontraditional-age students offer about financing a college education:

- *Angie (University of Wisconsin):* "As far as paying for school, you'll figure out where the money will come from and you'll be amazed at what you can do to afford it, like giving up something. It's worth every dime, and no one can take your education away from you."
- *Ken (UC Berkeley):* "I wish that I had done more investigation regarding scholarships. Since my involvement at Cal and with the re-entry program, I have discovered that there are considerable scholarship opportunities available for students."
- *Jorgiana (University of Arizona):* "Fill out those forms and mail them off. The sooner you mail, the more you get."
- *Sue (University of Wisconsin):* "Don't let not having money be an excuse for you to not go to college. There is no shame in accepting these grants, or scholarships, or student loans. The majority of Americans do not have adequate resources to pay for college tuition. That's why our tax dollars help to supply these grants for anyone who wants to go to college."
- *Susan (George Washington University):* "I still worry a bit about my finances in my old age, since I have no children who would gladly or begrudgingly help me. But I

would cash in those stocks again and head back to school in a heartbeat."

- *Heather (University of Wisconsin):* "Take the time to apply for every scholarship you may remotely be qualified for if you are not able to meet your needs with loans and grants. There are so many scholarships available that no one even applies for year after year. Oftentimes you can write one general essay and then just massage it to meet the needs of each scholarship. Think of it as earning $500 for two hours' worth of work."

- *Lynn (Bryn Mawr):* "If it really is the right time for you to go to college and you have found the right school, I'd say you should pay for it any way you can. I have one friend who went on welfare to support her son while she did it, and one who used all her rehabilitative alimony. There are no regrets on anyone's part."

- *Dan (Aquinas College):* "It is important to make the school expenses a priority, just as you have to do with the time you invest. Try to pay as much as you can so the costs don't trail along after you finish classes."

- *Evelyn (University of Wisconsin):* "Don't hesitate to fill out financial aid forms. Initially I didn't think I would receive anything because I wasn't a single mother or living in poverty. But I did receive several hundred dollars, which has made it much less of a burden financially. I am sure it helps that I have four children at home, one a preschooler."

- *Emily (University of Arkansas):* "If nothing else, borrow the money for one year's tuition, work hard, excel, and scholarship money will become available. A thirty-five-year-old friend of mine did just that, and has obtained scholarship money for the remainder of her education. She will graduate in May and has scholarships that will carry her through her entire postgraduate work."

- *Melinda (UC Berkeley):* "Just do it . . . credit, loans, cocktail waitressing, whatever it takes!"
- *Anne (UNC–Greensboro):* "After studying all of your options, pick the best one for you, take a deep breath, and plunge in. When you think you're drowning, swim like hell. You'll be glad you did."

The Inevitable
Application Process

Applying to a college or university is about as time-consuming as doing your taxes. Fortunately, however, the first application is also the hardest. If you apply to several schools, each successive application package will be easier, since you will use many of the same materials again and again.

You will want to start as early as possible. Although the process can seem rather cumbersome and bureaucratic, it can also be exciting.

Every university has a different "best way in" for the adult returning student. Some, like the University of California at Berkeley, have a special office for adult and re-entry students. There you will find trained experts to guide you through the application process. This is the exception, though. More typically, you'll have to apply through the general admissions office, just like any other student. There are ways to get into college, however, and then there are *ways* (she said with a wink). In this chapter we'll examine time-tested methods for proving your worthiness for college work, even if you don't have much of an academic record yet.

DECLARING THE PAST OVER:
HOW TO EARN A BETTER RECORD

The biggest fear for many adult students is that a past record of poor scholarship will come back to haunt them at application time. However, old grades are almost meaningless to admissions officers. They want to know what you have done with your academic life *lately*.

Joe Carver, a former admissions officer at the University of Massachusetts at Dartmouth, has seen many nontraditional applications over the years. He says that past history is less important than present-day determination. Instead of worrying about high school grades, he examines other, more relevant criteria:

> One of my favorite stories is about a woman, age forty-seven, who was serving as the treasurer of her husband's manufacturing company. When I asked why she wanted to complete her education after twenty-eight years away from the books, she responded that she wanted to be president. We waived most of the standard requirements (SAT, high school transcript) and based our decision on her personal statement and her junior college record, which was decent, but not outstanding.
>
> After her first year, I looked up her record in the registrar's office. Surprisingly, she had submitted the SAT (taken that year), which I had not seen. She had scored over 700 on the verbal and 550 in math. Better than that, she had earned a 3.75 GPA! She continued at that pace for two more years, accelerating her program and graduating in three years.

By having the bravery to approach a top school like the University of Massachusetts with a goal and determination, this student bypassed many of the typical hurdles. You can "brave your way" through the system, too. Here are six tips that worked for me and many other returning students:

1. EARN SOME GOOD RECENT COLLEGE GRADES BEFORE SUBMITTING
YOUR APPLICATION. Take a few classes, either at the school you are
applying to or at a reputable community or junior college, before
you approach a university for formal admission. Two or three A's
and B's will convince even the crustiest admissions officer that
you are now ready to handle college. Even if you never went to
college, successfully completing these classes will give you a pre-
sentable and impressive record.

The best way to earn solid recent credentials is to take some
regular undergraduate courses on your own in summer school,
or as a continuing education student. Just make certain you
take traditional undergraduate courses taught by the school's
regular professors, not shorter classes taught by nonfaculty.
Many non-degree-seeking adults enroll in regular classes for
the fun of it, or to enhance their résumés. You can usually sign
up with no formal admissions requirements. You'll get a transcript just like any other student; the only difference is that yours
won't count toward a degree unless you are formally admitted
later.

Be sure to take these courses at the highest-ranking university
you can find. Admissions expert Bill Mayher notes that many
adults in Boston attend night classes at Harvard Extension School,
paying a reasonable price per course and earning impressive credentials at the same time. These are real Harvard classes, and they
represent a legitimate "back door" into a top university's good
graces, including Harvard itself. Harvard Extension's website
notes that graduates of its ALB (Bachelor of Liberal Arts) program
have also gone on to MIT, Stanford, Yale, and many others. Please
see Appendix A for more information about the Harvard Extension School programs.

Joe Carver also stresses the importance of continuing education
when he considers whether to admit applicants to the University
of Massachusetts. He tells of a fifty-year-old applicant who lacked
even a high school diploma:

> He took the GED [General Educational Development test]
> with some trepidation, enrolled in a couple of continuing ed-
> ucation courses just to try his hand at going to school, did
> well, and came in to talk about what he needed to do to apply
> for a degree program in fine arts. In less than two years, he is
> more than halfway toward the degree, and doing famously.

Universities try to downplay the usefulness of continuing education or extension courses for college admissions, but they really
can get you in at a top university. You'll learn study skills in a
less-pressured environment, and you'll find out if you and the
school are a good match. If you like the university, and if you earn
top grades and get the professors to write letters of recommendation, your chances of being welcomed by the university's administrators will sharply improve. Best of all, most universities will
allow courses taken under continuing education to transfer into
the degree program. As Carver notes:

> I encourage most returning students to begin with two
> courses as special students before applying for degree pro-
> grams. That does two things: first, it enables the student to
> discover whether this is a good fit and helps to develop some
> self-confidence; second, it produces evidence for us that the
> student can cut it and provides a standard on which to make
> a more sound admissions decision.

Don't try to call ahead and get a college to admit this, though. It is
a well-kept secret that you can quietly use to your advantage. The
university does not have to transfer the credits, and some won't.
But many will, and you'll be ahead no matter what.

Please don't confuse continuing education with adult education.
Adult education is the general term for informal night classes designed for non–degree candidates. Often these classes are less rigorous than standard university courses, and many of them are

shorter than a full semester. You will want to take regular, for-credit courses through the formal summer school, continuing education, or university extension program. The terminology used by different colleges can be confusing, so be sure to request all of the relevant catalogues and brochures ahead of time, and find out if the hours can later transfer to a degree program.

2. NEVER SUBMIT A POOR TRANSCRIPT UNLESS YOU *MUST* CLAIM THE CREDIT HOURS. There is no law stating that you have to list all of your past experiences in college. If, for example, you attended a local community college after high school and flunked out because you didn't care and were too busy partying, forget about it. Even though the application will ask you to list all of your former college programs, you are *perfectly within your rights* to withhold this information. The only time you need to present a transcript is when you are asking for credit hours. Remember, there is no national database that will catch you, and you're not lying anyway. You're simply keeping unnecessary information to yourself.

If you have an early, poor transcript that contains some credits you wish to transfer, get into your new university first, on your own merit. Then approach a counselor *after* you have completed at least one successful semester. The university may or may not approve your request, but you run less risk of being hurt by the earlier transcript if you get in first. At most colleges, credits transfer as hours only, so you can receive at least partial credit for every grade of C or higher.

3. VISIT THE UNIVERSITY'S WEBSITE TO OBTAIN A CATALOGUE AND TO COLLECT KEY WORDS THAT YOU WILL USE IN YOUR APPLICATION. Each university has a distinct personality. The more you reflect that personality in your application, the more likely an admissions officer will consider you a good match. Be especially aware of a university's religious or philosophical heritage and its mission. You don't have to pretend to be a gung-ho Catholic, Quaker, feminist,

or some other identity in order to get into a particular school, but a basic awareness of and respect for a university's ideological foundations will make your documentation look better.

You can use the university's website and catalogue to find this information. Good places to look for keywords are in statements by the departments that interest you, and in the admissions office's own literature. Can you name any professors with whom you might like to work? Are you aware of the research going on in the university's laboratories? Do you know which majors the university offers that intrigue you? Are you aware of the university's mission, its history, and its role in the community? By reading first and reflecting that knowledge later on your application, you will seem not just well-informed, but like a potential member of the university's culture.

4. APPLY ONLY TO UNIVERSITIES THAT YOU RESPECT. Remember that there are no penalties in life for aiming high. Especially when you are considering universities, you should always reach above your head. Choose the best programs in your region, and the ones that match your needs and interests most closely. Even if you don't get in on your first try, you can always drop back, take more continuing education classes to improve your record, and then try again. Colleges will even let you report your highest SAT scores if your most recent ones happen to be a bit lower! They have an interest in accepting the highest scores a student earns, so don't be afraid to repeat the test, since you risk nothing except your time and a bit of cash.

5. APPLY ON PAPER, NOT ON-LINE. Many universities offer on-line application options, but I don't recommend them yet. Many on-line applicants go through a computerized general sorting process that weeds them out by SAT scores and grade-point averages before a human ever sees their applications. As an adult student, you are by definition a special case. You want someone to consider

your application packet carefully. Let the traditional high-school-to-college crowd go through the Internet application door. Instead, you'll mail or even hand-carry a beautifully typed, perfectly formatted application package that asks an officer to think about you as an individual.

6. VISIT THE CAMPUS TO UNDERSTAND WHAT MAKES IT UNIQUE, AND WHETHER YOU WANT TO FIT IN. You'll have the best perspective on whether you even wish to apply to a college or not if you make a campus visit before investing the time and application fee in a carefully prepared package. However, many prospective students are afraid to make campus visits because the environment is so unfamiliar. Some worry that universities will treat them in a second-class manner for not being traditional-age students.

If you are intimidated by a campus's unfamiliarity, you are not alone—even to veteran students and professors, each campus is like a little kingdom, with its own rules, hierarchies, and layout. However, admissions officers and tour guides are usually quite friendly to prospective applicants, no matter what their ages or backgrounds. After all, a university's selectivity ratio improves as its number of applicants increases: it will then be able to reject many more than it accepts. If you show up and look interested, admissions officers will treat you just like any other prospective candidate and try to entice you to apply.

Visit a university's website for up-to-date information on tours. Be sure to reserve ahead and to follow the university's advice about when to visit. If you can, try to visit a campus while school is in session, but not at exam time. You can check with the admissions office to select a time that allows you to see the campus in full academic swing. Visits can range from a one-hour get-acquainted stroll around the campus to a formal tour that might even include a night in one of the dorms or a visit to some classrooms.

You may fall in love with a particular campus, and your tour guide may encourage you to apply. That's fine, but please don't believe everything that you hear about your chances of getting in. After all, Ed McMahon and Dick Clark say that you have an excellent chance of winning the Publishers Clearing House sweepstakes. *Everyone's* a potential winner on tour day. Instead, gather whatever information you can, follow the instructions here, and then brace yourself for the typical entrance challenges.

Once you have taken your tour and heard the standard lines about challenging programs and happy students, dig deeper. Talk to the students themselves whenever you can. If there is an adult readmissions office on campus, wander over there and strike up conversations with the students. You'll get different and interesting answers based upon whom you speak to, so ask around.

One woman may glaze over with rapture and tell you about how college is changing her life, and what a gosh-darned joyful person she is now that she discovered the miracle of Higher Education. Another person, a grumpy man, may warn you away from this snake pit and tell you not to believe what anyone tells you. "Watch your back!" he'll murmur as you thank him and say good-bye. You may meet an African-American student who tells you that she finds the campus atmosphere "chilly" and that she didn't really make friends, as she'd hoped. Just as you're about to write the campus off as racist, one of her colleagues may say that he just got hired as a research assistant, that the university offered him an excellent financial aid package, and that he met his fiancée here.

Similarly, your experiences talking to staff may range from heartening to discouraging. Some will make you eager to apply and join the exciting academic community. Others may give you a grunt and precious little hope. In my many campus visits, I have learned to remain cheerful and upbeat, and to keep asking questions until someone with time, inclination, and expertise answers them. Then I ask someone else, and usually get another, often conflicting, set of answers. A university is different things to different people. You will want to collect many opinions and perspectives before deciding how you feel about a school.

Next we'll consider the components of your application and ways that you can improve your prospects from "distant" to "excellent."

COMBINE YOUR RECENT GOOD GRADES WITH YOUR BEST SAT SCORES

Admissions requirements vary from one campus to another, but most of them still accept and respect a strong performance on the SAT I (reasoning) and SAT II (subject) exams. At Dartmouth, for example, SAT scores constitute two-thirds of an "achievement index" and grades make up only one-third. Many other universities use a similar scores-to-grades ratio. Not all adult returning students have to take the SAT. Many colleges have waived this requirement for students over the age of twenty-three. Most do require the SAT, though, and even if they don't, you may well want to take it in order to improve your chances of getting in and receiving scholarship money. Even if you—like many of us—have trouble taking standardized tests, you can learn how to tackle a predictable exam like the SAT and do very well.

Do you remember those high school teachers who insisted that you couldn't study for the SAT? Back in the days when the SAT was still called an aptitude test (the "A" now stands for "assessment"), one counselor at my high school stated that it was an accurate index that measured "brains," or potential. Studying for it, she insisted, made no more sense than studying for an IQ test. Because we were young and didn't know any better, most of us believed her. Our parents, most of whom were born before World War II and had never even *heard* of an SAT, couldn't advise us any differently. We earnestly repeated the conventional wisdom to each other: "It's impossible to get a perfect score. And if you blow it, you can never take it again."

As it turns out, however, none of this was true. Intelligence tests and the SAT's have similar origins; they are both limited instruments that cannot consistently measure brains, achievement, or academic potential. You can *learn* how to take any of them and earn a superior score. Before we discuss your strategies for beating the SAT, let's look at its history to understand why it works the way it does.

The Educational Testing Service in Princeton, New Jersey, isn't affiliated with nearby Ivy League Princeton University, but it would like for you to think it is. It opened in 1948 as a general academic testing service. Henry Chauncey, its first president and a descendant of the second president of Harvard, dreamed of an American academic meritocracy where smart students would be identified as early as high school and nurtured throughout their careers. Chauncey's model presumed that academic potential would be evident early, that testing could uncover it, and that it was a consistent, quantifiable entity, like hair color or blood type. But despite his fondest hopes, Chauncey's dream didn't come true quite the way he'd intended. Just as with IQ testing, the SAT only became an arrow pointing to those students who already had the most social privileges. According to historian Nicholas Lemann,

> The overall results of intelligence tests have always produced a kind of photograph of the existing class structure, in which the better-off economic and ethnic groups are found to be more intelligent and the worse-off are found to be less so. In his book analyzing the results of the intelligence tests that the Army had given recruits during the First World War, for example, Carl Brigham, an early psychometrician and the father of the [SAT] reported that the highest-scoring identifiable group was Princeton students—this at a time when, by today's standards, Princeton was a den of carousing rich boys. ["The Great Sorting," *Atlantic Monthly*, September 1995]

Brigham was more realistic than Chauncey. He was convinced that there was no such thing as general intelligence that could be measured.

But the U.S. government thought otherwise. Back when college educations were still reasonably rare, the Selective Service used the SAT to identify which young men should be sent to college instead of being drafted. Lemann notes that college enrollments subsequently more than quadrupled between 1951 and 1970, partly due to this draft exemption offered to college men. If you could prove yourself worthy of a deferment by scoring high enough on the SAT, you could spend four years behind the books instead of behind a gun.

Colleges still rely heavily on the SAT to rate applicants. Besides using it as an index for basic admissions, some offer financial aid only to those students with exceptional scores. The most famous financial aid program, the National Merit Scholarships, is for students whose combined SAT scores are in the top 5 percent nationwide. As usual, students from privileged backgrounds tend to perform better, as they do on any standardized test. Those in the top 5 percent in terms of advantage and quality of childhood education often turn out—surprise—to be among the "smartest," according to the SAT's internal logic.

This partially explains why top college students go on to get better, higher-paying jobs. Corporate America seized on this routine sorting process as early as the 1950s as a way of identifying potential executive material. After all, the Selective Service was already using the SAT to identify what were then presumed to be our country's smartest men. Why shouldn't corporations benefit from this free weed-out? Of the enormous jump in college enrollment, and subsequently in degree-holders, Lemann writes: "This growth was unmatched in any other country in the world, and it made higher education into something it had never been before—the personnel office for white-collar America."*

*"The Great Sorting," ibid.

Gradually the process came full circle as colleges, eager to send many of their graduates on to top corporate positions, began to rely increasingly on the SAT as an indicator of whom they should accept. Ultimately, the SAT became a number attached to an already privileged group who then fulfilled expectations by completing college and going on to run companies.

Some of my graduate school friends worked for the Educational Testing Service, writing the questions that you see on standardized tests. ETS has a voracious appetite for new questions, since repeated or predictable ones make the test easier to beat. Akim described his ETS experience as a sweatshop atmosphere where question writers had to produce a quota of exam nuggets supposedly free of gender, racial, and socioeconomic bias. The work was boring and demanding, and the workers were underpaid. He quit as soon as a better job came along, and he reported that most of his fellow quizmasters did the same. If a test is only as good as the questions it asks, then the SAT is probably only as sharp as Akim's average ability on a boring Thursday when he had two hours left and six questions to produce.

As an adult returning student, you are likely to do better in school than even the highest-scoring undergraduates, simply because you have a combination of maturity and discipline that eighteen-to-twenty-two-year-olds tend to lack. But maturity and discipline don't show up on an easy-to-quantify grid. Admissions officers have to sort through too many applications to consider each individual until *after* applicants get past the SAT hurdle.

The ETS obviously wasn't thinking about adult students when it set up this system. That doesn't mean the system will go away, however. With race- and other quota-based admissions declining nationwide, universities will rely *more* on standardized testing to sort new students, not less. The better you become at taking these specialized exams, the more likely it is that you will continue to break the admissions barrier, not just for college, but for graduate study as well.

CRACKING THE SAT's CODE:
PROFESSIONAL COURSES
ARE THE BEST WAY TO PREPARE

So how do you learn to take the SAT? Who can teach you to deftly untangle the test's logic while the timer ticks away? The best and most reliable method is to spend approximately $500 on a test preparation course. Your money won't be wasted, since higher test scores will significantly increase your chances of getting offers of financial aid. You can save money later, after you are in at the college of your choice. At this stage, it makes no sense whatsoever to skimp on the cost of a good test preparation service.

Remember that you should always present recent SAT scores to a college when applying for admission. If you have already taken the SAT and your scores are still valid but not really spectacular, resist the temptation to send them on to a university as is "just to see what happens." Even if you do get in, you may miss out on thousands of dollars in potential financial aid and scholarship money reserved for students with test scores above a certain level. Instead, consider a test preparation course to see just how high you can nudge your scores. The two biggest test prep companies in America are the Princeton Review and its archrival, Kaplan Educational Centers. I recommend them over their smaller counterparts because they have each spent a fortune over the years competing with other developing rival systems in cracking the SAT's code. Both companies claim to help students earn high scores on almost any standardized test.

Kaplan will focus on practice tests that teach you how to take different sections of the SAT, such as those on critical reading, analogies, sentence completion, math, and quantitative comparisons. Princeton Review will address these as well, but it will also concentrate on teaching you how to beat the test by understanding its internal logic. Both companies will guide you through the exam in a reasoned way, but Kaplan will linger on the straight test content, while Princeton Review will offer more tricks and surprises. Of course, there is a great deal of overlap between the two systems.

My suggestion is to follow your own personality type. If you are slightly more conservative and linear, you may find that the Kaplan method respects your focus and thoroughness. If, however, you have a more liberal slant, you'll probably enjoy the Princeton Review's "let's beat them at their own game" attitude and its irreverent, energetic style.

I took the Princeton Review's test preparation course for the GRE and watched my scores soar, even in math, in which I am traditionally quite weak. I gained over 150 points there, and also in the analytic section. My verbal score was already quite high and didn't change much. But overall, my scores improved by nearly 300 points, and I got into some highly competitive programs because of them. Since fellowship offers are often tied to test scores, I figure that my $500 investment in the Princeton Review not only got me in the door at the University of Virginia, but also earned me about $5,000 in early fellowship offers. Other students report offers of $10,000 and more, based on a combination of superior test scores and strong grades.

Even if you don't get an immediate fellowship offer, your SAT scores will follow you through college, and some later offers of assistance may be based on the category into which your scores place you, along with your current grades. You can also check catalogues for schools that interest you. You'll learn that as few as 10 points overall can make the difference between the thin rejection envelope and the Fat Boy that says, "You're in."

Princeton Review instructors were energetic, entertaining, and unfailingly patient. All of them had repeatedly scored over 700 on the test sections that they taught, and they took the test numerous times under actual conditions. Many of them routinely earned perfect scores. They taught us the design of the test, gave us strategies for identifying the easy, medium, and harder portions, and helped us decide when to answer a question and when to leave it blank. After initial practice tests divided us up into different groups, we were drilled over and over again in the areas in which we were the weakest. By the time I sat down for the real exam, I was calm, prepared, and thoroughly knowledgeable on the potential content of every section.

It may be tempting to save money by purchasing test preparation books or software instead of signing up for an expensive, time-consuming course. While these methods are certainly popular, I have yet to hear of an applicant who improved his or her scores by the same wide margins just by working alone with books and a kitchen timer.

What's more, the added pressure of taking the test repeatedly at the prep center's site can get you psychologically ready for actual timed conditions. You'll sweat almost as much as if it's the real thing, and that kind of experience is very helpful. I learned, for instance, to bring aspirin, since I tend to get headaches under stress. I also packed a snack and a bottle of spring water, since a growly stomach and a dry mouth can also hinder progress. You might not discover this important information if you're working in the relatively relaxing environment of your own home, with water, the refrigerator, and a bathroom readily available.

If you sign up for the classes, both Kaplan and the Princeton Review promise a full refund if your scores don't go up by at least 100 points. With that kind of low-risk guarantee, I think it makes sense to give yourself the best advantage and let their test-taking professionals help you personally.

That said, however, you can give yourself a big advantage before your course begins by purchasing one of the test preparation software packages and practicing on your own. *The Princeton Review's Inside the SAT, PSAT & ACT Deluxe* offers full-length practice tests, financial aid and scholarship information, a college guide, and much more. *Kaplan's Higher Score on the SAT and ACT Deluxe* covers essentially the same information, but with a uniquely Kaplan approach and tie-ins to the college rankings of *U.S. News & World Report*. Each package costs less than $50 and could significantly enhance your study experience. Addresses and websites for both companies are in Appendix B. Once you visit their sites and try some of their interactive tests, you'll probably be able to decide which approach works best for you.

HOW TO DEAL WITH ADVISORS AND COUNSELORS

Now that you have dealt with the two parts of the application—grades and test scores—that are somewhat under your control, you are ready to consider the bureaucratic side of college admissions. As an adult learner, you may be steered to an advisor who is paid to talk with prospective students and give them information about the university. Some of these are wonderful, caring professionals. Many of them, however, can be unnecessarily discouraging to adult returning students. To keep you from encountering a setback, and to help you enjoy your campus visits and your talks with advisors and admissions officers, I offer the following advice.

If returning to college were just about sitting in a classroom, taking notes, and passing tests, it would be simple. What makes the prospect more challenging is the maze you have to navigate before you ever go to class. The first layer of the maze is emotional: you have to decide that you're ready to attempt college again. The second layer is social: you usually have to discuss your decision with people (bosses, a spouse, your parents, your kids, even friends) who are likely to view you differently because of it. The third layer is technical: you have to organize yourself enough to identify a potential program, obtain and fill out an application, request transcripts, and submit the completed package. So far, so good. If you have made it through these layers, you have really defied the odds, social prejudices, and all of those other vague barriers that tend to keep smart grownups out of college.

The fourth layer, however, can be tricky and cruel. It is a social *and* technical layer, one that operates on an arcane set of rules that vary from program to program, and from state to state. Your success with this layer will depend upon your own determination and clear focus, and your ability to deal with people who may not care about you or like their jobs, and whom you may have to satisfy in order to get into the university system.

I don't mean the receptionists and administrative assistants. They usually consider you and your application just part of the daily routine, so they will probably treat you predictably and fairly unless you ask for something out of the ordinary. Some of them may be annoying, especially if they are work-study students who don't seem to care about their jobs, but few have the power to disrupt your academic career.

I'm talking about the counselors and academic advisors you may encounter when you approach a university to ask about its programs and your chances for admission. That's right: the employees who are rumored to be there to *help* you. Over the years, I have learned that some of the thorniest challenges for adult returning students can come from the one group which claims to have the students' best interests at heart.

Many advisors and career counselors dislike their jobs. This may seem baffling, since their task is to help you find the profession you love. One would think they'd have taken their own advice if it was all that good. But I have talked to advisors who started out with the best of intentions, yet eventually withered under the paperwork burden, the unrealistic student caseloads, and the thanklessness of their duties. There are also wonderful advisors out there, and I'll tell you how to find them, but the sad fact is that even the kindest of them are often overworked, and the advice that they dispense may not always meet your particular academic needs.

Remember your high school guidance counselor? If your experience was like most, your counselor was overworked, underpaid, and trying to help hundreds of students. I went to a public high school with thousands of students. Most of my guidance counselors were aloof, or even adversarial.

When you arrive on campus for a visit, you may find advisors who resemble the high school version. On many campuses you will need their signatures in order to enroll in continuing education courses, to be accepted for readmission, or to take certain courses under what may very well be special circumstances, depending on your age and your desired schedule. If you are fortunate, you will meet someone with bright eyes and a warm handshake who wants to help you. But the chances are very good that you may also meet at least one person who is unhappy with something and who won't mind taking it out on you. However, you can be forearmed. If you approach a university with an upbeat attitude but with your armor on, you'll survive and get the information and signatures you need.

For example, when I called the admissions office at the University of California at Berkeley, a cheerful woman said they had an adult re-entry office on campus. She suggested that I walk right in and talk to an advisor in person. But I never asked where the office was located, since I assumed (wrongly) that it was in the regular admissions building. When I showed up in the admissions office, nobody seemed to know who my helpful telephone friend had been, or where I should go next. Some of those state employees gave me prickly rebuffs and hoped I'd leave. I kept insisting, politely but quite firmly, that there had to be information on adult re-entry hiding around there somewhere, because the young woman on the telephone had sounded so certain. The responses I received ranged from civil to bored to hassled. Finally, when it was clear that I wasn't going to go away, somebody looked in a booklet and found—surprise!—that there *was* an adult re-entry office, after all. She did not offer me directions or even the phone number, but instead looked over my shoulder at the man behind me and said, "Next?"

Then a woman standing behind him in line spoke up: "Excuse me, but I couldn't help overhearing. I'm an adult re-entry student. Is there something you need to know?" Relieved, I chatted with her for a while. She offered to walk me over to the program office, which was halfway across the campus. Once there, I met a friendly, knowledgeable assistant named Ken who also happened to be a recent adult graduate. He suggested that I talk to the director, who didn't have anyone in her office at the moment. He buzzed her, and she waved me in.

How many prospective students, I wondered, made the mistake of going straight to the admissions office because it seemed like a logical first stop? Had I been a hesitant woman with no bachelor's degree trying to find out what UC Berkeley could offer, I might have left defeated. But by pushing a little harder and working with the helpful, competent adult re-entry staff, I ended up learning much about their program. I also collected many firsthand stories from the adult students there.

Here are six great strategies for navigating the shark-infested waters of college counseling.

1. MAKE A TELEPHONE APPOINTMENT WITH THE PROPER OFFICE BE-FORE GOING TO THE CAMPUS. Navigating a new campus is hard enough without not knowing where you are supposed to be. Let your fingers do the walking by calling ahead and asking questions until you find the *exact* advisor who can help you with your re-entry quest. This may involve many phone calls, but it will still be far easier than wandering around in a strange place while your parking fees mount. If anyone is unfriendly or brusque on the telephone, keep trying until you get a friendly voice and a helpful response. Don't forget to ask for a visitor's parking pass, if the college offers one, and specific instructions for parking legally. If you are pregnant, disabled, or prefer not to walk too far, find out if there is a shuttle-bus service from any of the parking lots. This will save you a great deal of frustration when you arrive.

2. KNOW WHAT YOU WANT FROM AN ADVISOR BEFORE A MEETING. Never go into an advisor's office without a clear, obtainable goal. Remember that you control the meeting: the advisor sees far too many students to know what you want, or to have any idea how

to suggest what's best for you. Read the catalogues ahead of time—carefully—and come prepared with a short list of questions. Also, read this book thoroughly and decide what you are looking for. Do you want to try a continuing education course first? Are you asking for formal admission? Do you just want some general advice about programs?

Take responsibility for your own choices and your own future. Don't make the mistake of being helpless about life in general and asking the advisor for direction. No advisor in the world knows what you should do with your life. If you ask something specific, however—such as "What are the advantages of majoring in economics at this university rather than at the private college down the road?"—you are more likely to get a useful answer.

Most counselors will offer you suggestions. By all means, listen to and consider them carefully. But remember that you'll probably get one-size-fits-all suggestions, which may either suit you or represent poor choices. It doesn't cost you anything to nod, listen, and glean whatever useful information you can. But you must also remember how you want to live and not let someone's well-intended but wrongheaded advice change your personal plans and dreams.

3. IDENTIFY GOOD ADVISORS, AND STICK WITH THEM. Finding a good advisor in the university system is like finding a pleasant, helpful officer at the bank. When this happy event occurs, don't let that professional get away! Reward her with a thank-you note after your interview. Keep him informed of your progress.

Here's how Heather found the right counselor. She remembers letting the bureaucratic process discourage her the first time she tried to return to school:

> I remember being so overwhelmed. There was so much red tape, *what a nightmare!* Just trying to find a place to park where I wasn't going to get towed was horrible. Then there was the application process, requesting transcripts from pre-

vious colleges, placement testing, financial aid applications, and on and on. I can't remember how many money orders I had to get for under $5 or $10 for all of the little things. Then, of course, I had to pay for baby-sitters while I was at the college trying to do all of these things.

Heather gave up after encountering one too many hurdles when she had to juggle moving into a new home, caring for her children, and dealing with an eventual new pregnancy. When she approached college again, however, she was prepared for the hassles. She now knew how to ask for help, and where:

> I made an appointment with an academic advisor at the two-year college about forty miles from where I lived. The advisors and student services people held my hand throughout the entire process.

What Heather learned the hard way is that sympathetic, knowledgeable counseling is a must. You can usually find dedicated professionals on any campus. The secret is to *keep looking* until you find the person that you need. Cultivate that friendship over time, and be sure to pass on a good word to the advisor's boss, preferably in writing. Someday you may need a red-tape cutter, and your advisor friend might be just the person to help you.

Similarly, make a habit of befriending the administrative assistants in all the offices you deal with. They are often the best-informed members of the staff, especially if the university has a high advisor turnover rate. You can casually ask the assistants which advisors are the best and get your name transferred to their rosters. I have found that a consistent pattern of treating the administrative staff with friendly respect makes my paperwork zip through the system like an otter on a waterslide. They are usually happy to accommodate my special requests once they get to know me and understand that I am on their side.

4. IF YOU NEED A SIGNATURE, GET ONE, NO MATTER WHAT THE ADVI-
SOR SAYS. You may need to visit a campus in order to obtain an advisor's signature on a form that you need to submit *before* you
can complete your application. Stay focused on what you want out
of the interview, and persistently redirect the conversation toward
that goal. This is especially important if the advisor discourages
you from returning to college as an adult. Listen politely (even if
you're furious) and nod a lot, but continue pushing for that John
Hancock. If the advisor refuses to sign, leave the advisor's office
cheerfully and ask another advisor for a signature, without mentioning that you were turned down before. Working the system
often means ignoring setbacks and pretending that they never
happened while you try the next advisor, and (if need be) the next.

Do not, under any circumstances, unburden yourself or divulge
emotional personal information. If the advisor is brusque and rude
and you feel your anger rising or the tears starting, *politely* terminate the interview and leave. You can pull yourself together
outside and then try again, or ask for a new advisor.

5. DON'T LET ANY ADVISOR STEER YOU OUT OF YOUR PREFERRED MA-
JOR. We'll talk more about your choice of major in Chapter 9.
Along the way, however, you will meet people with a vested interest in steering you into or away from a particular life choice. Remember that the advisor is paid to serve the university, not you.
She may try to redirect your interests into a program that needs
more students. Or she may insist that your chosen major isn't
employable, that the field is overcrowded, and that you'd be better
off getting a tried-and-true degree in something practical that you
don't like. Don't try to argue with her, because you'll just get frustrated and lose her cooperation. But don't react with too much
credulity, either. Remember that you are the one with the final au-
thority to decide your major.

6. PREPARE YOURSELF TO HEAR NEGATIVE STATEMENTS OCCASION-
ALLY, AND TO TAKE THEM IN STRIDE. When I first tried to enter

George Mason University in Fairfax, Virginia, I learned that an advising session was required before I could apply as an adult student after so many years out of college. Since I was already on campus for a visit, I stopped by the advising office and saw the counselor who spoke to all students with last names A through K. He took one look at my transcript from undergraduate school six years earlier and told me that I probably wasn't college material. Then he yammered on about how I could still have a fulfilling life, even without a degree, and how my secretarial job might be the best I could do. I staggered out of his office after this emotional assault and returned to the parking lot, where I sat on the hood of my car and cried.

Instead of attempting what I was certain would be a failed admissions bid, I followed the advice I am now passing on to you. I took an English course through continuing education at that same university and earned an A, plus a recommendation letter from the professor. Later, a much more understanding admissions officer let me in as a probation student on the basis of that grade, my SAT scores, and my successful work experience, factors the advisor never even bothered to consider. I made the dean's list in my first full semester back.

Had I known then what I know now, I would have been prepared for the advisor's acidic speech. In fact, I would have guessed that he had seen twenty students before me that day, one after another. Many of them would have had poor transcripts or GPA's so low that they shot sparks every time they scraped the curb. He was tired of being Mr. Happy Answers. So instead, he smoked a cigarette on his break, took a deep breath, and resolved to start telling *someone* that his university couldn't solve their problems. I was probably number one on his new list, before he had perfected his bedside manner.

I should have ignored him and terminated the interview. (My scathing letter to the dean's office could have come later.) Then I should have requested a different advisor. If the front office computer-clickers insisted that I had to see him because he dealt with all students with last names A–K, I should have politely and firmly stated that we did not get along. Most universities will accommodate your request to speak to a different advisor if you insist upon talking to someone else. If the university refuses, then ask to meet with a dean in private and tell the dean what the advisor said.

Above all, resolve not to believe anything negative that anyone says about you during the advising process. Disregard any harsh words as soon as you hear them. If someone says, "You may not be college material," walk away. If you're up to it, a clearly worded rebuke will usually stun the speaker, especially if you deliver it in a calm, concerned fashion. Pretend you're Barbara Walters on national television as you lean over with a puzzled expression and ask: "What would make you say something like that? Have you had a difficult day?" Sometimes you can change the whole tone of the encounter by such responses, and (if you're lucky) your advisor may even break down and admit that life *has* sucked of late. You could even get an apology. If not, then simply gather the required signature, if you can, and get out, shaking the dust from your sandals as you go.

Of course, the quality of on-campus academic advising will vary, depending upon the school you approach. Meredith College, an all-women's college in Raleigh, North Carolina, is geared to adult returning students, and its advisors range from very good to excellent. But Meredith is also a small, well-funded private school. At most it may face a prospective pool of seventy or eighty adults for its re-entry program each session, not many hundreds. You'll find the most egregious offenders in the bad-counseling category at state universities that find themselves forced to offer some sort of advising, even though their internal bureaucracies aren't set up to accommodate such personal services. If you steel yourself, however, and if you identify and reward professionals when you find them, you can learn your way through even the most heartless system.

HOW TO ASSEMBLE YOUR APPLICATION PACKAGE INTELLIGENTLY

Now that you have identified the colleges that interest you, you are ready to make your final school selections and put together your formal application packages. There are several excellent books on college admissions and applications that can help you through this detailed process. Rather than repeating their advice here, I'll focus on those aspects of the application that are unique to you as an adult student. If you'd like a good general guide to filling out college applications, I have listed some useful titles in Appendix B.

Before we move on to advice about recommendation letters and personal essays, here are a few questions that adults commonly ask about the application process:

1. SHOULD I APPLY FOR LIFE EXPERIENCE CREDIT? Not necessarily. Many universities offer life experience credit as an incentive for adults to return to college. I don't recommend this path, however, because it allows you to avoid fundamental classes that may be very important to your intellectual development. Why should you go to all the trouble to document your reasons for not taking Sociology 101, Basic Anthropology, or Greek and Roman Classics? One of the beauties of the traditional bachelor's degree is the breadth of study that it offers. You also might discover a lifelong academic love in one of these "gateway" classes.

Rebecca signed up for Introduction to Archaeology reluctantly, since she thought it had absolutely nothing to do with her linguistics major. Her professor turned out to be an expert on ancient Middle Eastern languages, however, as well as a scuba diver who studied underwater archaeological sites. They became friends, and he invited her to join his graduate students on a dive in Israel the following summer, exploring a seaport built by Herod at the beginning of the Christian era. She spent a month on a boat, gofering for the graduate and professorial staff and for some journalists from *Outside* and *National Geographic* and having a wonderful time. She earned a scuba certification, a modest paycheck, and three hours of advanced course credit. Now she is considering graduate study in underwater archaeology and using her linguistics background as an important credential.

2. WHAT ABOUT THE CLEP EXAMINATIONS? Taking a national standardized test can help you opt out of classes in such basics as freshman composition or college algebra. However, I do not recommend it. I have taught many students who "clepped out" of freshman composition and therefore thought they were talented writers. Few of them were even *competent*, though, causing me to wonder just what the exam actually measures. Instead of telling you how to evade required courses, I'm going to encourage you to take as many as you can, work hard, and learn as much as possible. Even if requirements add a year to your schedule, they will be well worth it if they build your fundamental skills and lead you into potentially fascinating new fields.

3. SHOULD I EARN AN ASSOCIATE'S DEGREE AT A COMMUNITY OR JUNIOR COLLEGE FIRST AND THEN TRANSFER TO A TRADITIONAL PROGRAM? While this is certainly one alternative, it seems like a lot of extra work for nothing. These degrees carry very little weight in academia, and they are meaningless in the business world. If you do very well at a community or junior college and also present excellent standardized test grades, you can usually transfer to a mainstream program after one or two semesters. Why waste the extra year when you can jump right into the program you want?

4. IF I ASK THE UNIVERSITY TO WAIVE THE APPLICATION FEE, WILL I HURT MY CHANCES FOR ADMISSION? No. You should *always* ask for a fee waiver if you think you might qualify. Most colleges charge an application fee—typically between $30 and $50—for the courtesy of processing your paperwork. From their standpoint, this fee serves two purposes: it cuts down on frivolous applications to uni-

versities that you have no intention of attending, and it helps
defray the high costs of printing and mailing thousands of catalogues and admissions packets.

You may qualify for a fee waiver if you are over fifty-five years
old or if you meet certain financial aid criteria such as earning less
than $14,000 per year, being a member of certain ethnic groups,
raising children on your own, or being unemployed. Most experts
say that requesting a fee waiver makes no difference in the han-
dling of your application. Check university websites under "Admissions" to make certain that you qualify for a waiver. If you do,
it won't hurt your chances of admission if you take advantage of
it.

Next we'll consider two important items in the standard application: letters of recommendation and the personal essay. Both of
these components are tiebreakers, and they will help admissions
officers see you as a potentially excellent student. A university
may take your application seriously on the basis of SAT's and
grades alone, but your letters and essay will help the officers see
you as a person and consider you for offers of financial aid.

OBTAINING OUTSTANDING LETTERS OF RECOMMENDATION

Your recommendation letters are the more important of these two
components. Your recommenders should be (in order of preference):

1. *Professors at the university, offering a detailed analysis of
   your successful performance in the classroom.*   The single
   best recommendation for any college applicant is a letter
   from a professor at the university to which you are applying. While high grades may be your primary goal in con-

tinuing education or extension courses, your secondary
goal will be to earn a letter of recommendation from one or
more of your professors.

2. *Professors from another university who can vouch for
   your abilities.*   If you know a professor at another university—even a family member—who is acquainted with your
   work and believes in your abilities, a letter from her or him
   can't hurt. It might not carry as much weight as a letter
   from someone on the university's own staff, but it will still
   carry more weight than a letter from an employer.

3. *Alumni of the university who know your work.*   A present or former boss who graduated from the university to
   which you're applying might be able to write you an excellent letter. For example, a letter from a present or former
   boss who went to the University of Michigan would be
   useful in an application to that college. That same letter
   would probably be of only limited use, however, in an application to the University of Wyoming.

4. *Present and former employers.*   I place these last because
   you should seek out recommendations from professors and
   alumni first. Remember that a university's standards are
   not the same as those of the workplace, and some universities won't have as much respect for your boss's opinion as
   they will for that of a faculty member, a professor from
   another campus, or an alumnus.

Do not ask for recommendation letters from high school teachers, former athletic coaches, friends or family (unless they are
very famous), or anyone who does not have an intimate knowledge of your recent academic work. If you're reading this section
and despairing that nobody knows you, take heart. You can sign
up for one or two continuing education or extension courses at
your favorite campus right away and work hard for a semester to
earn those all-important professorial recommendations. Remember that a professor can also write letters on your behalf to other

programs. Don't be afraid to ask your professor for a letter to go with each of your applications. Writing recommendation letters is part of being a professor. If your work is outstanding, most of them will be happy to assist you.

THE ART OF THE APPLICATION ESSAY

Universities generally ask you to write a 250- to 500-word statement about why you wish to attend their fine institution of higher learning and what makes you an appropriate candidate. Your first instinct may be—as mine was—to blather on about how brilliant you are, what a great university Whatsa Matta U is, and how the two of you were meant for each other. Resist it. Other students fell into this trap before you, and many received the thin envelope wishing them good luck in applying somewhere else.

Another common impulse is to apologize for or attempt to explain earlier low grades and lack of focus. Never do this. Remember that the admissions officers will only notice what you ask them to. Use your application essay to draw their attention to the *best* things about you.

This strategy particularly paid off in my graduate school application. I had included a poor early transcript from my first try at undergraduate school, since it represented fifteen credit hours that I had later transferred for undergraduate credit. But I never mentioned it in my essay or apologized for it in any way. Years later, a staff member let me look at my file. To my great surprise, I noticed that the earlier transcript had never been opened. If I had mentioned that bad record, they might have scrutinized it. But because I presented it and said nothing, they let it go and never knew about my problematic past.

To write the most effective application essay, sit down and ask yourself why you want to go to college. Be honest. Is it really because you simply want a better job? Or is there another, more important reason lurking behind your hunger for more education? Perhaps you have always believed that you were intelligent, and your experience at work has proven that to you. Maybe you watched your kids go through school and even tutored them, and now you know that you can succeed as much as they can. Did you work for years to put a husband through college and law school, and is it your turn now? Or maybe you dropped out to "find yourself," and all you found was that you had had a pretty good deal in college the first time, which you didn't appreciate at the tender age of nineteen. Many woman, especially those who attended college in the 1950s and 1960s, went for an "M.R.S." degree, dropping out as soon as they met a college man and received an engagement ring. Now they want to go back and finish what they started. Whatever your reasons, they are probably more personal and complex than simply wanting a promotion or needing a degree for its own sake.

As you ponder your real reasons for wanting to return to college, make notes. Do you remember the day you decided to go back to college? What happened? Why did the urge strike you at the age of forty-eight? Was that the first time you had considered higher education? What kinds of things do you do in your personal life that feed your intellect? Are you a reader? A filmgoer? A political junkie? Do you tutor underprivileged children or volunteer at your children's school? See how much of yourself and your personal story you can jot down on paper. How could you rework these facts so that they would make an admissions officer interested in you as an individual?

When I went through this process, I realized that there were many times over the past decade when I had considered returning to college. But there was one particular day, in one specific place, where I remembered actually feeling a sense of loss about not having an undergraduate degree. That was the day I made a resolution to change things. I closed my eyes and pictured myself on

that day, back in England, chatting with a man about academia.
Here is how I used that story to begin a successful admissions essay:

> I wish to study English Literature at the University of Vir-
> ginia to continue an educational process that began three
> years ago, at a pub in the High Street in Oxford.
>
> That year I was twenty-six, an aspiring young writer
> backpacking in Europe on the few dollars I had saved. It was
> Easter weekend, and an Oxford student and I had a conversa-
> tion about William and Dorothy Wordsworth, Lewis Car-
> roll, and, eventually, universities in America. My friend was
> surprised to learn that I had not yet earned my bachelor's
> degree. He encouraged me to complete what I had started.
> When I came home two months later, I applied to George
> Mason University.

The key to this essay is artful honesty. I didn't try to present myself as the greatest student who'd ever lived, but I didn't apologize,
either. Many admissions officers can identify with taking a cir-
cuitous route in life and then feeling inspired to try again. The
presence of a friend and a fortifying brew added to the universal-
ity of the story. I hoped that someone reading the essay would
smile and think, "I've felt that way before." I didn't use big, unfamiliar words or try to sound erudite. This gentle, evocative opener
worked.

Similarly, if you can take your reader into your world by including something specific from your own journey, you may succeed in earning that person's empathy and respect. You don't want
pity, but you do want someone to understand just how unique
your adult path toward college has been. By remembering a specific moment and helping the admissions officer to see your story
through your eyes, you will elicit a feeling of camaraderie and encourage that person to cheer you on.

Remember that the admissions officers are just as worried

about making the right choices as you are about getting in. They *want* to select students who will succeed. Sidonia M. Dalby, an admissions officer at Smith College, writes about how important the selection process is to her and her colleagues:

> There is enormous pressure from all sides. Admissions directors get canned, just like college coaches, for not having winning seasons. Trustees, college presidents, alumni, legislators and the media have insatiable appetites for statistics, reports and the bottom line. The bar is often raised for the number of applications, test-score averages, a particular type of student (lacrosse players, Native Americans, physics majors), and there is intense competition for good ratings in college guidebooks and magazines. Sometimes it seems as if what we do is never enough. We may not be up there with air-traffic controllers, but we suffer a lot of stress-related illnesses in the admissions office. ["An Insider's War Stories," *Newsweek*, April 20, 1998]

Adult returning college students have an excellent reputation for earning top grades and graduating with honors. Consequently, they have become increasingly popular with admissions staff, even when saying yes seems like a bit of a gamble. Give admissions the information it needs to accept you by presenting your brief personal story and your unique qualifications (your expertise in business, your success as an entrepreneur, your abilities in carpentry, your skill at rearing perfect children) for approaching academia later in life.

Now that you have a group of notes on yourself, set them aside. It's time to consider another vital aspect of your personal essay: the university itself. What do you know about the campus? What does the university mean to you symbolically? Did you grow up knowing about its reputation? Have any of your family members gone there? Why is that particular university more important to you than, say, another one right down the street? Do you share a religious or philosophical outlook? Is there something you feel the university offers, such as a particular program, interesting professors, or a certain national reputation, that you can't get anywhere else? This part of the essay is where you will convince the reader that you *know* about this college. It is also where you will explain why you believe that you belong there. Here is what I wrote:

> As a native Virginian, I grew up with the tradition of the University of Virginia, and I have been a frequent guest on the grounds. I believe the rigorous discipline necessary to obtain a degree from Virginia, and the superb reputation of the University's English Department, will stand me in good stead with the literary and academic communities to which I hope to be admitted.

Notice here that I took the time to learn how U.Va. refers to itself. I said "grounds" because U.Va. does not use the more common term "campus." I referred to it as "Virginia," or "the University," which it does in its own literature. I acknowledged the national standing of the English Department without adding a lot of smelly, obsequious filler. By reading through the college's documentation and referring to it in its own insider terminology, I made myself sound like a natural fit for its unique culture.

The key to this step of the admissions process is research, as we noted earlier. Read a university's own materials and pay attention to the language it uses to describe itself. Also read as many excellent examples of admissions essays as you can before you try to write your own. Remember that your voice is important and that you should sound like yourself, but that there is also an elegant, winning formula that tends to succeed.

There are many collections of college essays you can consult to give yourself a sense of what has been considered good. The best books are usually written by former admissions officers and include actual examples of essays that worked. I have listed a few in

Appendix B. Like the titles mentioned earlier, these books focus on the traditional student, usually a high school junior or senior. Your essay should emphasize your greatest asset: your adult status. By presenting yourself as someone who has lived and learned, and by stating in an engaging way why you want to return, you stand an excellent chance of impressing even the most jaded admissions officer and getting into a great university.

Be Cheerfully Persistent, and Don't Take No for an Answer

If you research universities well and apply carefully, you will probably get into a good college. But will it *necessarily* be the college of your choice? Maybe not in the beginning. You might have to start out at a lower-level school to prove yourself, and then transfer once you have enjoyed one or two successful semesters. If you receive a rejection letter, however, and you really believe that you belong on a certain campus, don't be afraid to try again. As salesman Chester Grant (Danny Aiello) said in the film *The Closer* (1990):

> If you took things at face value, then no means no. But *no* means *maybe*. And if you think any other way, you're not a closer.

In college admissions, "no" often means "maybe."

You also may be put on a waiting list at a school you've applied to and then never hear back with good news. Don't be discouraged! Most waiting list students remain on that list. Instead, enjoy a successful semester or year somewhere else, and then reapply to the campus of your dreams. Your earlier waiting list status may give you an advantage the second time around. After all, college admissions is an imperfect process. Give it your best try on your first application, but don't be afraid to restock your arsenal with higher grades and improved test scores and try again next semester, or next year. Persistence pays off, in academia as anywhere else. If you consistently aim for where you want to be, you will make it somehow.

BALANCING THE DEMANDS
OF WORK, FAMILY, AND SCHOOL

Now that you have been accepted into a program that you respect, congratulations! You're in, but the real maneuvers have only just begun. You still have to construct a schedule that you can live with for the next few years. Let's start with your financial lifeline: your job.

Recently, a company in the U.K. called More Balls Than Most made headlines when it taught busy executives how to juggle. *Really* juggle. Apparently employers were getting criticized for asking their employees to take care of too many responsibilities at once. Soon it became popular for them to offer their employees real juggling lessons as a kind of humor and stress-relief break. I don't know if it worked, but it certainly pointed out the degree to which companies acknowledge that they often force their employees to try to keep too many professional and personal balls in the air at once. If you work for a company like this, you might logically wonder how you'll *ever* find time to go to college and handle the demands of your full-time job.

On top of that, many adult returning students have families who expect such societal luxuries as regular meals, live conversation, and kisses before bedtime. If you have a partner and/or children, you may well think that you can't handle your busy life *now*, let alone in connection with an academic schedule. Adult students do it all the time, however, and a vast number of them manage it without getting divorced, downsized, or sued by their own offspring for parental neglect.

How? Well, most of them make their bosses and families partners in the academic quest. After all, there are benefits for everyone at work and at home if you finish college. All you have to do is convince the people around you that it will be in their best interests to help you get ahead. Adult students also find extra study hours hiding in a seemingly full schedule when they intelligently reorder priorities. By questioning habits such as television watching and cooking elaborate meals, you can find extra time where you previously thought it simply didn't exist.

EXTRA STUDY HOURS MAY BE HIDING IN YOUR TELEVISION SET

Most adult students say that finding enough enthusiasm for their studies is easy, and they're eager to get started. But where will you find enough hours in the week to accomplish your goals?

We can start with television. Most people harvest extra hours every week when they crawl out from in front of the TV. As you may already know, the average American watches over three hours of television daily, or about one full day out of every seven. Of course, this statistic includes people who sit at home and click channels while popping bonbons, but even if you put yourself in the category of infrequent television viewers, you probably watch about seven hours of tube per week. If you exchange just six of those viewing hours with study hours and save the seventh for programming you feel you can't miss, you may already have your main problem of "When will I study?" solved.

I cut back on my television time and realized that watching less television wasn't enough of an answer. TV tapped my brain into a shared culture that was neither intelligent nor witty. By watching television for even one hour a week, I was essentially having a conversation with a dim-bulb buddy and letting him teach me everything he knew. Television episodes crept into my analogies, for it was easier to talk about social complexities in terms of well-known sitcoms than it was to come up with my own, more original examples. I found myself talking and thinking in TV shorthand and assuming that people around me knew what I meant.

Taking matters a step further, however, yielded remarkable rewards in my academic life. I confess that one night in 1988 I "killed" my television, unplugging it and relegating it to a top shelf in a closet. The change was astonishing. In just a few months, I stopped borrowing words and images from television culture in order to make assertions when I spoke in class. I began to forget the simple vaudeville model upon which most situation comedies are based, and I developed an appreciation for more complex and subtle forms of humor, such as satire, and for metaphor. My vocabulary changed as I drew my lexicon from books, film, and radio rather than from rapid-fire advertisements, overly laugh-tracked sitcoms, and crude medical dramas.

By the end of a year, my experiment had become a way of life. Now, over a decade later, I can point to academic degrees, books I have written, and hours I have spent absorbed in a life that never would have been possible if I had let my cultural influences be dictated by *Felicity, E.R.,* and *Ally McBeal.*

Although you may not have to take such a drastic step in order to find enough study hours in the week, I encourage you to give it a try. Take a complete vacation from all forms of television for one academic semester and see how it affects not only your grades, but your thinking patterns as well. If your family loves television and won't give it up, keep a quiet place all to yourself in another part of the house where you can slip off to do your work while they watch. If your house or apartment is too small for this, then try my favorite trick from graduate school: buy yourself a box of earplugs. You'll be surprised how much noise they filter out so that you can work at the dining room table while the phone rings, the golden retriever barks, and your kids and spouse marinate in the light of the tube.

Before compromising, though, try asking your family to simply quit along with you. It may not be as difficult as you might think to get them to cooperate. After all, television viewing is dropping, largely because of the number of hours people now spend on the Internet. Also, many people find it a surprising relief to turn off the TV and just talk or read. Television is loud and insistent: its absence can often feel like a peaceful break. Even children who have been raised on television can be cooperative when, say, Dad puts on some quiet music and offers to play a board game instead of sitting silently with them in front of a situation comedy. You may broach the subject with trepidation and then be surprised when your family likes the TV turnoff trick as much as you do.

THERE ARE OTHER HOURS
HIDING IN YOUR SCHEDULE

I found many more hours in what I thought was a "packed" day when I adopted the following habits.

1. IF YOU HAVE A NOVEL OR OTHER BOOK TO READ FOR CLASS, CARRY IT WITH YOU. When you have a book always at the ready, you can read a chapter on the subway and another one while waiting in the dentist's office. If you also carry a pad of paper or some sticky notes, you can jot down discussion points as you go. When you're finished with the book, spend an hour or two retyping your notes and filling in any knowledge gaps. Then, at exam time, study your notes rather than returning to the book itself.

This kind of piecemeal reading can actually be more effective than a straight-through session of several hours. You will remember more of the book if you read a bit and then write about it, and the book won't feel nearly as long. Doing this also "spackles in" those previously wasted portions of time spent on the subway or bus, or sitting in a waiting room. Reading one book in bits when you can may give your day a comforting sense of continuity, and may even improve your overall sense of well-being.

2. LEARN TO USE YOUR UNIVERSITY'S INTERNET RESOURCES. You will be amazed at how much faster your research goes when you are an expert at electronic resources. Many of these will be available at home and can save you hours of travel time to the library. Your university probably offers an assortment of articles, indexes, databases, on-line dictionaries, and other helpful study aids that are free to students. Don't just glance over the instructions, either. Slow down and learn how each website operates. You will learn how to perform effective searches with Boolean operators (constructing search phrases using AND, OR, NOT, and other delimiters), and you'll begin to understand how the research hierarchy works at various academic and research sites such as the Library of Congress, the National Institutes of Health, and other institutions. Check with your university's research librarians and with the academic computing center to find out what's available. If your school library offers introductory courses on computer research, take them.

3. LIMIT YOUR E-MAIL HOURS. When I have lots of work to do, I check E-mail only twice a day: once in the morning before 9 a.m., and again in the evening after 5 p.m. By reducing your on-line hours, you'll free up lots of study time. The only exception I make to this rule is for on-line research, which can be much faster than the slower, paper-based kind.

4. PLAN MEALS AND OTHER FAMILY ACTIVITIES AHEAD OF TIME, AND LEARN TO DELEGATE RESPONSIBILITY. Sometimes habit can lead to

doing much more work in a family than is necessary. The busiest adults usually assume most of the responsibility for running a household. I have watched in astonishment as friends with children stop to cook and serve snacks to fourteen-year-olds who are perfectly capable of serving themselves. Some moms and dads, like Maggie, say that they can't deprive their children of full-course, sit-down meals every single night, even though these meals require many hours to prepare. Once they try a more casual approach, however, many find that children don't really mind an adjusted schedule. As Maggie recalls:

> There were days when my kids wondered why we had a quick meal and why I had to spend so much time on homework, but we learned to manage and cope with the new situation. We coined a new term, called "group clean," and we did our homework during the same times. Mine usually lasted for several more hours, but it was fun to prepare for the next day by packing our book bags together. I think my children began to develop a different perspective toward education, commitment, and their mom.

Most kids are flexible, and they all prefer happy parents. If you are fulfilling your goals and dreams, they will appreciate that much more than a hot dinner every night at 6:30 from a grumpy adult.

5. TRY A PHILOSOPHICAL PLANNER SYSTEM—IT COULD CHANGE YOUR LIFE. All may be well when you start school, but as time goes by, you may find your boss expecting you to skip class or even drop out of school if work demands become too great. Or your family may get tired of making compromises that early on seemed manageable. How can you avoid this typical trap?

The first step requires a bit of an investment from you up front, but it will probably be the smartest gift you ever gave yourself. Invest in a planner that's more than just a place to write the date your work is due. Find a system that offers you a proven philosophy for getting more out of each day without sacrificing such important things as your family life or good job performance. You will probably find, as most students do, that you become much better at managing your time. After starting school and adopting a planner system, you may actually have *more* time for your career and your loved ones than you did before.

While writing this book I tested several systems and attended numerous time-management seminars. The one that worked best for me was a day planner from Franklin Covey. In a one-day seminar that I highly recommend, a time-management professional taught us how to reorder our priorities so that life consists of much more than just busily putting out fires. We learned to revision each day so that it becomes a well-functioning unit, with plenty of time for life's demands—such as business presentations and math tests—but also for spending hours with families, playing sports, attending church, or doing whatever it is that makes life worth living. We also learned to use every section of the planner in a specific way so that no items are ever lost or mistakenly transcribed. These courses cost about $200, but they include a complete planner book, extra supplies, and personal coaching that really will save you a great deal of time and money down the road.

In a session known as "Planning and Solitude," I now spend about thirty focused minutes each morning deciding how to divide my busy day. That half-hour investment saves me many hours later, because it gives me a visual map of the best and easiest way to navigate. I have scheduled regular exercise, reading, and leisure time into each of my days so that I seldom have that "overbooked" feeling. Now not only do I accomplish more, I also have more leisure time than ever before.

Franklin Covey was formed in 1997, when Franklin Quest merged with Stephen R. Covey's firm, the Covey Leadership Center. Covey is known for his 1994 bestseller *The Seven Habits of*

Highly Effective People. His system, also available from Franklin Covey, brings a different focus to the time-management concept, with a longer planning session on Sundays designed to map out each week as a unit. Covey also breaks up tasks differently. Whereas the Franklin system teaches you how to cut up an enormous job into manageable daily bites, Covey envisions large tasks as groups of rocks, which you order from biggest to smallest. Covey is also more assertive. He sees everything from corporations to families as having the potential to be "highly effective," which strikes me as a bit harsh. Franklin focuses less on efficiency and more on quality of life.

The two systems sound similar, but they are quite different in practice, and Franklin Covey offers both of them in separate planner materials that you can purchase at one of their stores. You might need to experiment a bit to find the one that's best for you. I find that the subtle, consistent touch of the Franklin system is much more to my personal taste. One of my attorney friends likes the assertiveness of the Covey line, however, and can't imagine structuring his life any other way. Other competitors, such as the manufacturers of Day-Timers and Planner Pads, also offer excellent systems that may be perfect for you. Just be certain to select a system that is more than just a place to jot your notes. Pick one that teaches you in carefully led steps how to really make the most of what can feel like a fragmented life.

Whichever system you choose, I strongly encourage you to work with it on a daily basis. Your college career will try to conflict with your job and your family every chance it gets. By sitting down at the start of each semester and mapping out tasks carefully, and then by working your plan daily, weekly, and monthly, you'll give yourself a chance to get ahead once in a while and actually enjoy peaceful lulls in the middle of what has the potential to be a stressful life. We'll talk more about task mapping in Chapter 8 when we discuss study skills.

GOING TO CLASS WITH ASSERTIVE STYLE

Now that you have extra study hours each week, when will you find time to go to class? And how will you get there without angering your boss or alienating your family? Although some classes meet early in the morning or in the evening, many meet during the day, and they all require regular blocks of time that you can't simply reschedule if something comes up.

Going to class became less of problem for me when I made it a priority, and when I announced this change to everyone who was affected by it. For example, your boss needs to know in advance, preferably before the beginning of each semester, that there are certain times when you will be out of the office. But she also needs the reassurance that there will be corresponding blocks of time when you are all hers. This may well turn into a personal exercise about establishing boundaries around your time and understanding which blocks are nonnegotiable (class time, for example), and where you can give a little.

At some level, you may have to be willing to risk your job for this, because the minute you start compromising on school time, your boss will most likely begin to try to drag you away from school for work duties. Despite the feeling of risk, however, you probably *won't* lose your job over school, and you might even get more respect.

Even though they grumbled a bit, none of my bosses really resented having to work around my schedule, mostly because deep down they appreciated the value of a good education and the sacrifice it requires. My bosses would have made the same choice in favor of school if they had been in my position, so most of them understood my insistence that class time was a strict priority. The more I focused on my identity as a student and an intellectual without apology, the more they noticed me and my abilities. It is ironic but true that the more you sacrifice for your job, the less your employer will value you and your time. But when you set limits and focus on your education, your employer will appreciate you more.

The only people in the office who gave me a hard time about school were those who had never gone to college. The office manager, for example, deeply resented my student status, and she made it clear that she wasn't about to give me a break just because I had such a tough schedule. Instead of complaining about her lack of support, however, I took her seriously. I listened carefully to her concerns, and I respected her enough to schedule in a bit of extra time when I took care of her personal requests. She appreciated this. Even though I didn't really sympathize with her, just by listening and trying to, I gave her the impression that I found her opinions valuable. Although she never became fully supportive of my college quest, she eventually got out of my way.

It may occasionally be necessary to miss class because the attorneys you work for have a big trial coming up, or because the office manager has been giving you grief. This is not as terrible as it may seem at first. Studies show that adult students miss more classes than their traditional-age counterparts, yet their grades *still* remain consistently higher. My advice here is to assess the individual class and then decide what's best for you. If the course is in an enormous lecture hall with two hundred students, the professor never takes roll, and you feel you can miss a class and keep your A, then go ahead. But my "A" students are almost always the most regular attenders as well. Remember, too, that if you skip class once to take care of work duties, your boss will feel comfortable asking you to do it again. You can prevent this if you carefully plan your schedule each semester and then stick to it, with only rare exceptions.

If Your Job Won't Bend,
Consider a Better One

Most bosses are reasonably well educated and will understand why you want to earn a bachelor's degree. Lawyers are particularly responsive to a student's needs, since they all placed a high value on education in order to get where they are now. When you return to school, many will respect you and your time more.

But if you have trouble getting your boss to accept your new schedule, take heart. You can find employers who like hiring students, since they know how motivated and efficient they are. Glenda was an administrative assistant who had trouble getting her boss to let her leave in time for evening classes. She had told him about the big exam coming up at the end of the month, and even reminded him about it the morning of the exam, but he still asked her to work overtime that night. Glenda refused, and he threatened to fire her. She surprised herself by saying, "Don't bother, I quit!" Although she felt empowered and enormously relieved at the time, Glenda became terrified when she realized just what she had done. She spent the weekend frantically searching the want ads, wondering how she'd ever find a job that paid enough to keep her in school.

When I met her, however, she was enjoying a new career that meshed perfectly with her academic ambitions. As a certified professional organizer, she earned a living helping others become as productive as she'd had to be all those years. She worked for a company, but kept her own schedule and managed her own clients. Glenda was now free to book her daily appointments around her school requirements, and even to take her daughter along on jobs when the client didn't mind or had children too. She was able to switch from a part-time to a full-time academic schedule and to work fewer hours, since her hourly wage was higher.

You can even look for a job on campus that will allow you to walk a block from work to school instead of driving across town. Besides having a more convenient schedule and understanding bosses, you may earn tuition remission as an employee benefit.

WHY NOT GIVE UP YOUR FULL-TIME JOB AND LIVE LIKE A STUDENT?

Too many books tell adults to hang on to their jobs and their old ways of life when they go back to college. Instead of living in the manner to which you have become accustomed, why not break free and return to full-time student life? You'll be amazed at what kinds of expensive creature comforts you can live without if you adopt a traditional college lifestyle.

Before moving to Charlottesville, Virginia, and embracing student life at U.Va. I thought that I "needed" expensive cars, lots of makeup, new furniture, a private home, restaurant dinners, and membership in a health club. Soon I learned, however, that comfortable used cars (I favor old Volvos), shared housing with other students, and free workouts at the university gym made me just as happy. I learned how to make a variety of inexpensive rice-based dishes—ask me about my curried eggplant—and I experienced the joys of share-purchasing bulk foods with neighbors and friends to save money. My cost of living plummeted, and my quality of life soared.

Rhoda, a divorced mom with two small children, decided to return to college. She moved out of her comfortable suburban home into cramped college housing. She feared that her economic adjustment to college life would feel like poverty. Instead, it felt like freedom:

> I had managed to save enough so that my kids could have beds. I had my computer, but no bed or couch. Eventually, things shaped up, but it was tough to leave it all, move to a new town and new schools, deal with divorce and how it im-

pacted my children. But I did it and did it well, and I believe that anyone can. With the support of the traditional students as well as other returning women, I was able to enjoy my first year, join a women's rowing crew for a year, win the college's athlete-of-the-year award for novice rowers, work every weekend waitressing, and still keep a respectable GPA.

Generations of students have been making college towns inexpensively livable for a long time. If you decide to *really* go back to college by living on campus or near it, you will find creative housing options, cheap restaurants with menus designed around student budgets, co-op health-food stores, and plenty of people your age, *whatever* it happens to be. Many adults live on or very near campus and structure their whole lives around the academic culture. Some colleges, such as Smith and Mount Holyoke, even have a house on campus for their adult undergraduates. The residents range from their twenties and thirties to their fifties, sixties, and even beyond.

Couples can request married-student housing and live together, often far less expensively than they did in their home cities and towns. When Arnie began his studies at the University of Arizona, his wife, Jess, enrolled as well, and they trundled their three kids into the cramped married-student quarters. It was a squeeze, and they had to learn to save on everything from groceries to clothing. Fortunately, most of the kids in the neighborhood wore clothes from the same thrift shops, so the children didn't suffer socially— and they had plenty of playmates. Arnie and Jess both earned master's degrees at the end of it all.

You may still decide to work, but college-town jobs can be far more accommodating than the career-focused kind. For several semesters I worked in a Charlottesville attorney's office, answering phones, filling out bankruptcy applications for low-income clients, and researching legal cases. Later, I worked for a local politician, Mitch Van Yahres, who was also an expert on historic trees. The hourly wages were high enough to cover my modest rent in a group house near the grounds. I worked only fifteen to twenty hours a week instead of forty, and I spent more time worrying about my grades than office politics. My bosses, some of whom were U.Va. graduates, were completely supportive of my academic schedule and never argued when I put school first. In Chapter 10, we'll discuss campus life in depth, and you'll see that there are many advantages to cutting your ties to a stressful job, an expensive home, heavy car payments, and a consumer-based existence.

YOUR FAMILY AND YOUR BOSS ARE DIFFERENT

Working relationships respond to one set of rules, and families to quite another. After all, you have to live with these people, and you can't just "quit your family" and find a more accommodating one if it doesn't go along with your academic schedule.

Some parents, particularly mothers, wonder how they can justify neglecting their children by not being home in the evenings. "What," asked Pam, "am I supposed to tell my fourteen-year-old? That she can run around like a wildcat every Thursday because I'm at school and can't keep an eye on her and her budding libido?"

Of course not. But happily for all adult students who are parents, campuses are remarkably child-friendly places. Why not bring your gangsta-rap-craving ninth-grader, who thinks she wants a tattoo, *with* you on Thursday nights? She can do her homework in the library, or read in the lounge with the undergraduates, and feel very grown-up. Then the two of you can have a soda together at the student union before you go home. Children and teenagers love campuses and being around college students. They will gradually absorb the message that studying is important, especially if you do it together before or after class. And campuses usually offer cheap or free movies, many of which are suitable for young viewers, and which are often of much better quality than the average Cineplex fare. You can also check out videos for your children to watch in the library's private viewing rooms.

If your children need adult supervision, consider hiring college students to keep an eye on them while you're in class. To make certain you get a safe, reliable person, ask some of your professors to recommend their best former students. You can request that the sitter stay with your child in a nearby study area so that you can be on the scene in the event of an emergency, or you can wear a pager with a vibrating feature that can notify you of a problem while you're in class. Many college students would love the opportunity to earn even a modest amount of cash once or twice a week for an easy on-campus job. Some of them will be creative, taking your kids to the college radio station, for example, or helping them with school projects and homework. You may also find student help by putting up a notice on a bulletin board in the education building or running an ad in the college newspaper. Be sure to leave some of your notices at the laundry or community rooms in married-student housing, where more parents are likely to congregate.

Some campuses even have early childhood education programs with on-site care centers. The Molly Michie Preschool next to the University of Virginia charges $135 a month for a five-day program from 9 a.m. to noon, offers options for two- and three-day programs. The University of Chicago has a laboratory school for children from prekindergarten through high school that offers after-school and evening care options. East Tennessee State University has a year-round laboratory school. Although some of these schools are expensive, many offer partial or full scholarships to the children of parents who are receiving financial aid.

Try teaming up with another adult student or a professor and starting a "your night/my night" system. On your night, you go to class while your friend takes all the kids, perhaps in conjunction with another helper. On his or her night, you can take the little darlings.

You can also benefit from the advice of veteran college parents. Here's how Deborah, a mother of two small children, describes her experience at Mount Holyoke College:

> Never underestimate the power that sharing your personal goals, setbacks, fears, and concerns with others whom you respect can have on your life. I cannot begin to enumerate all the times that I shared what was going on inside my head, and others always said something I could use or gave me a lead that proved invaluable. I think the old patriarchal expression "I came, I saw, I conquered" could be modified to "I came, I shared, I conquered" for the way that parents can network to share valuable resources with one another.

Once Deborah stopped hiding her status as a single mother and started asking for help, she found many other parents at the college who were more than happy to assist her.

Professors' attitudes toward children vary, but many won't mind a quiet child who sits in the back of the classroom and draws or reads. Even a Lego set, a few dolls, or some modeling clay can be enjoyed peacefully. At Aquinas College, Penny observed other parents who took their children to school with them:

> I was in a Business Case Study class last semester where one of the moms in my class brought her ten-year-old son with her. He brought his own schoolwork, quiet games, and a lot of junk food. He did very well, I thought.

As a professor, I make case-by-case decisions. I usually will allow children in the classroom as long as the parent agrees to take a crying or disruptive child out of the room at the first sign of a disturbance. "It's not a problem unless it becomes a problem" has settled a lot of judgment calls like this.

Lynn, an adult student at Bryn Mawr College, remembers receiving support from professors when her child-care responsibilities conflicted with class: "I once took a kid on an IV antibiotic to class with me, and my professor was fine with that." She added that being at a women's college helped, since so many of the returning students had similar family duties.

Heather, a thirty-one-year-old mother of four, one of whom has a disability, is a student at the University of Wisconsin–Eau Claire. She agrees that it can be tough to go to school with children, but she still recommends it:

> I attended the spring semester pregnant and returned to classes in the fall with a three-week-old, breast-feeding infant in tow. I arranged all my classes with professors that would allow me to bring her into class with me. Everyone from the new dean to professors, staff, and custodians were more than supportive. I am told that because I opened the door, other students are finding that they can return to school soon after having a baby instead of missing a semester or having to drop out.

Of course, that doesn't mean every day went smoothly. Heather is especially talented at recounting horror stories, "everything from four children with chicken pox in the middle of the semester, to having to rent a car to get to school because the two-year-old threw away my keys." You'll need to increase your flexibility and bolster your sense of humor, but it is still possible to finish college with children.

Lawrence, a graduate student whose wife, Elaine, is also in college, reports how life in married-student housing at the University of Tennessee is easier than he expected with an eleven-year-old. He took his son Parker trick-or-treating and found that the students enjoyed joking with him, sword-playing, and treating him like one of the group. Even if you have a child with physical or emotional challenges, campuses can be among the most accommodating of places. Students and professors will usually go out of their way to help you adjust to campus life while caring for a child with special needs.

Some adults solve their child-care problems by asking for as many independent study courses as possible. During an independent or directed study, you work one-on-one with professors, meeting in their offices several times a semester instead of attending regular classes. This alternative helped Penny, whose challenging schedule at Aquinas College took her away from her daughter Dakota more often than she wished:

> Initially, when I returned to Aquinas, I tried to take a night class. My husband, Vern, stayed with Dakota. I had to run home at 5 p.m., make sure she was bathed and fed and ready for bed, and then be back to class by 6:30. But I felt like I wasn't seeing her for a day and a half, which essentially I wasn't. I would drop her off at day care in the a.m., spend about an hour of rushed (not quality) time with her that evening, and then get up and take her to day care again the next a.m. and not see her until the second evening.
>
> This was not acceptable to me, and Vern wasn't very supportive of it, either. Consequently, I completed the last two years going to school on Saturdays, taking advantage of Aquinas's directed study format. In this format, you are only required to attend class one to two Saturdays a month, or roughly one Saturday every three weeks. Classes are from 8 a.m. to 12:30 and 1:00 p.m. to 4:30. I would take a morning and afternoon class.

While this option may work during some semesters, it has some of the same drawbacks as distance learning. You won't bond with your professors and fellow students in the same way, and eventual discouragement can be a real problem. It is far better to aim for the traditional classroom and try to fit your children into the lively world of the American college campus.

Every family is different. You may need to try a number of creative options before finding the method that works best for you. As more couples accept dual responsibility for child care, however, and as parents become more comfortable bringing their children on campus, academic opportunities for moms and dads will greatly increase.

Heather's husband got a wonderful new education in being a father after years of spending too much time away from the family when he was stationed on submarines. As Heather puts it:

> I have learned how to be assertive and communicate my needs without coming off as a whiner. Before I started going back to school, he honestly could not make an appointment for the children with the pediatrician. Now I have learned how to prioritize my life, let go of the little things, and force my husband to take more responsibility for the children.

Heather's education created an opportunity for her husband's reintroduction to their children, an experience no father should miss.

Take Your Partner to School with You

Children may not be your only concern when you go back to college. Husbands and wives can report feeling neglected on your school nights. If this happens, then consider it a fine opportunity to involve that spouse or significant other in your quest as well. If your husband complains that you're never home, convince him to sign up for a class and come to school with you. He'll be amazed how much more interesting history is if he writes a paper on the Civil War rather than sitting at home falling asleep in front of the

History Channel. Or, if he wishes he had more time to work out, sign him up for the university gym and take him along to pump iron while you're in class. Many universities have full-scale health centers with pools, weight rooms, and state-of-the-art equipment, and most offer substantial discounts to the domestic partners of registered students. At many of the major state universities, gay and lesbian couples usually enjoy the same privileges as married couples when it comes to "spousal" benefits. At the University of North Carolina at Chapel Hill, for example, students can sign up their domestic partners for full gym benefits at a cost of as little as $40 per semester.

If your wife misses you on Tuesdays and Thursdays, convince her to take an economics class that might help her at work, or perhaps an aerobics course through the athletic department. Your partner can learn to paint in oils, program a computer, or speak Italian while you're in another class. Sure, it costs money, but domestic harmony is nearly always worth it. Such cooperative learning also minimizes feelings of jealousy that might arise when one partner gets all the academic attention while the other one "slaves at home."

Some partners—even old-fashioned ones with more traditional gender-role expectations—will surprise you by being perfectly supportive from the beginning. Colleen found that her new schedule gave her more time with her husband rather than less, simply because they now had to make an effort to see each other:

> He changed his work routine to make the weekends free, and actually we spent more time together than anytime in our marriage of thirty-five years. He enjoyed the topics I talked about from classes, and he put my art and color projects up in his office. Several of our friends were very supportive and cheered us on. I did find it stressful to get my house cleaned and the laundry done on weekends, but we cut back on entertaining and simplified our lives quite a bit. My husband even took over paying the bills!

Through cooperation and simplification, Colleen found herself with a stronger marriage than she had before she "challenged" it by going back to school.

Try to Keep College, Work, and Family Separate

Compartmentalization can help you keep the various areas of your life focused. Try to keep work at work, and school at school, to minimize complaints from people who might not understand. For example, I found that most bosses did not want to see textbooks at the office. It wasn't that they resented my academic pursuits but that they wanted 100 percent of my attention when I *was* at work. The presence of textbooks, even if I never opened them, made my employers feel as though my attention was divided.

The same holds true at school. Very few professors will understand your work demands, because they expect you to make school a priority. They sacrificed for years to earn their degrees, and some of them may have little patience with your dual existence.

You can maintain greater focus if you keep these two worlds as separate as possible. For example, if you schedule in an extra thirty minutes after each class to review your notes and copy out sections that aren't clear, you won't have to study them at home that night, and you'll drastically reduce the amount of cramming you need to do at exam time.

Let's say your religion professor asks you to make a list of potential works to be cited for a major research paper. Instead of planning to do it later in the week, stop by the library on your way home and do the assignment immediately. Then you can go to work with a mind ready to focus on the office rather than feeling pressured by an extra school demand.

Try to complete all schoolwork on "school days." For example, take care of everything for your Tuesday–Thursday class on Tuesdays and Thursdays. That way, you, your boss, and your family will feel that Mondays, Wednesdays, and Fridays are clear for other work- or family-related matters. You'll soon find yourself thinking in sync with this schedule. You'll find it easier to put your classroom worries aside until it's the proper day to think about them. Posting your schedule on the refrigerator at home and giving a copy to your boss will help, too. Bosses are especially responsive to prearranged schedules, since most live by their calendars or day planners. They simply want to know when you are available and when you're not. The more consistent you are, the happier they will be.

Students who commute long distances to school and stay overnight recommend getting all schoolwork done during the time away. Colleen commuted over two hundred miles round trip to attend classes at the University of Minnesota and Iowa State University:

> I left home either late Sunday evening or Monday morning and returned Friday every week. I always took a *full* load and tried not to bring homework home on weekends . . . I had a tiny bachelor's flat in St. Paul and a small apartment in Ames where I "kept my nose to the grindstone."

By keeping schoolwork at school and preserving her weekends with her husband and children as family time, Colleen thrived.

FIVE SCHEDULING TIPS THAT CAN SAVE YOUR SANITY

If you keep these five principles in mind throughout your academic career, you will have a useful set of tools for avoiding traps and maneuvering out of one when you hit it.

1. START SLOWLY, AND GIVE YOURSELF TIME TO ADJUST. You need to learn how to be a student, and you'll best accomplish this by giving yourself an easy first semester. Many adults read the course catalogue, get excited, and sign up for biology, economics, medieval literature, and Spanish all at once. Instead of doing this, try an easy semester that interests you and emphasizes study skills. This will give you a nurturing nudge back into a curriculum. Here's how Ina advises her nontraditional students at Aquinas College:

> You ask what advice I would give a forty-year-old contemplating college. I just got off the phone with a prospective new student in that age bracket. I told her to take a course that looks interesting to her, not to tackle a course like statistics at the outset. I also told her she will find that the wealth of knowledge she brings with her into the classroom will translate into academic reality once she is exposed to theories and application of theories in the academic setting.

Diane, a thirty-four-year-old undergraduate student in the Ada Comstock Scholars program at Smith College and a full-time employee there, emphasizes the importance of selecting a first class that complements your natural abilities:

> I was cautious in the beginning, which worked for me. I started with one class and chose something I already loved—computer programming. I aced that class, though I sweated out every assignment and exam. I would not let myself relax until I had my report card in hand. I sent it to my mother, and she had it on her refrigerator for months!

Like Diane, I took only one course during my first semester while working forty hours a week at my job. It was an English class that met on Tuesday and Thursday nights. By focusing on one class and carefully learning how to take notes, perform research in the library, and write papers, I built a "skills base" for the next semester. It is far better to take one class and earn an A, and then add another class next time, than to try to juggle three with mediocre or low grades.

2. STOP SPRINTING AND ADOPT A STEADY MARATHON PACE. If you rush before papers and panic at test time, chances are that you're sprinting through your work rather than loping along at a steady, measured, long-distance trot. A hurried, stop-and-start pattern will eventually exhaust you, especially when you get into the second or third year of your studies. You'll gain more from a daily half hour with a textbook than a three- or four-hour block of reading at the end of the week. The time may add up to the same amount, but with daily half hours you'll be less stressed, and you'll learn the material better. Smaller blocks of time are also easier to schedule around the needs of children and other important commitments.

Schedule at least one study hour per week outside the classroom for every hour you spend in it. Work in some additional hours—up to twice as many—when assignments are due. That's how much time your professor usually assumes that you will devote to the class. If you spend an on-campus hour directly after each class quietly reviewing your notes and clarifying fuzzy concepts, it won't feel like much work at all. That extra hour after class may actually be a calming break, especially if you buy a cup of coffee or a soda and sit somewhere peaceful. You probably won't need any other study time except just before tests and when you write papers.

This kind of as-you-go studying blends in with your daily routine so seamlessly that you may not ever feel as though you formally study at all. At the end of each week, you might want to devote fifteen or twenty minutes per class to reviewing basic concepts, drilling yourself on vocabulary, and testing yourself on new skills. If you are taking a study-intensive course such as economics, philosophy, mathematics, one of the sciences, or another notorious time-eater, then this policy of managing a small bite every day will be especially useful.

Remember that study is like exercise: it is much more effective in smaller, more regular sessions. If you went to the gym and tried to get a week's worth of weight training done in seven straight hours, you'd collapse. But an hour a day will make you strong. Dennis liked to stop off at a university computer lab immediately after class to type his notes, review material, and draft his papers. He carried extra computer disks with him just in case he wanted to write something. By steadily logging an hour after every class without even thinking about it, he seamlessly wove his study time into his daily life.

This is a great policy for working parents who are trying to finish a degree. There usually isn't much time left in your busy day to hit the books. But if you reserve extra time after each class to go over your reading and notes, you'll excel. If home and work make too many demands on your time, develop the early morning coffee or juice habit. Get up just one hour earlier and get into the office before everyone else is there. Over your morning beverage, review your class notes for the week. Don't try to get fancy and cram in many weeks' worth of upcoming material. Just review your past notes, especially the most recent ones. This is an excellent substitute for the daily newspaper, and it will take about the same amount of time. If you have small kids and you can't find another hour in the morning, try switching to an evening schedule and reviewing your notes during the last hour before bed instead of watching a late-night talk show.

3. PRACTICE SAYING NO AND YES IN A CREATIVE WAY, AND TAKE FUN BREAKS SOMETIMES. What if your father-in-law surprises you and your husband with a pair of tickets to see *The Lion King* on Broadway? Will you be happy and excited? Not if the show is a week before finals and you also happen to live in Kansas City. Instead of panicking, however, think of this as a great time to encourage your husband to take his mother or your oldest daughter

instead. Or take your books along and study in the hotel room while your spouse goes sightseeing. You can still enjoy the play at night as a welcome break.

Perhaps the friends in your Thursday-night book group resent your continued absence. Instead of constantly saying "I have to study," why not invite them all to a campus literary event and then join them for coffee after your class? If the group at the corner pub begins to wonder what happened to you, make a point of going there once a month on a regular night (say, the first Friday), and holding court. They'll enjoy knowing when to find you there and having a beer as in old times, even if you're available far less often than you used to be. Remember that you need friends to keep your sanity. You may not be able to see as much of them, but regular, scheduled downtime is important for your continued success in school and for your general happiness.

4. ASK FOR HELP FROM PROFESSORS *BEFORE* YOU NEED IT. Almost every semester, a student comes to my office teary-eyed and upset because school and work demands are simply too much. Rachna, for example, was working thirty-five hours a week to pay her way through Georgetown. When she explained this to me, we went over her schedule carefully and I adjusted her due dates so that she wouldn't have three papers to turn in at once. She completed some work for me earlier than scheduled and other work later, but overall we worked out a fair distribution. Although some professors can be difficult about this, most will try to work with you and help you succeed.

If you approach your professors *before* the semester begins, you can head off a lot of this emergency pressure. Many departments ask professors to be available the week before classes start to answer questions and greet students. Schedule a meeting with each professor during this week. Professors are more relaxed then, and they can give you personal attention. Start off by saying that you want to do very well in school. Briefly explain your adult student status and say that you are looking for success strategies. Talk about your harried schedule, and how important it is that you devote enough time to schoolwork. Ask your professors for advice about how to approach their classes.

You'll be amazed at the kind of information people share. One professor might tell you that she is a stickler for careful, close reading and writing. Another may say that he doesn't really care whether you come to lectures or not, as long as you pass his exams (you should go to the lectures anyway). You will hear some things that seem alarming, and other things that seem quite encouraging. Some professors may say things that will convince you to switch to another course. This, too, is valuable information that can prevent you from making a mistake by staying in the class.

Above all, however, you will get the professor thinking about you as an individual. Try to avoid scheduling your meetings during exams and times when papers are due, when other students will be trooping through your professor's office, often for the first time. If you make a habit of visiting professors for no more than ten minutes two or three times per semester, just to make certain that you are both in sync on performance and expectations, you will have a much easier time meeting their individual expectations.

5. Learn to strategically drop a class when necessary. Sometimes, despite your efforts, you may find yourself in a class that just isn't for you. What if the professor you thought would be great is actually terrible? Or maybe the course material is way over your head. If you make a mistake in choosing a particular class, don't be afraid to drop the course. You can usually tell if you're in trouble if you are still completely lost two or three weeks into the semester. Visit your professor often and try to catch up, but don't berate yourself if the course is just too difficult or confusing.

I have "hung in there" with problem classes, trying to prove something, and all they did was damage my self-esteem and my GPA. It is much more important to keep your grades up and enjoy your studies than it is to prove that you can tough out a semester in the wrong class.

You may hear a nasty rumor that colleges penalize you for withdrawing from classes and then repeating them later. Colin worried about dropping philosophy, since he thought that graduate schools looked unfavorably on strings of withdrawals even when followed by A grades later on. It just isn't true. All anyone will ever check is your overall GPA and your completed transcript, to confirm your reported grades. Few students withdraw from more than two or three courses in an academic career anyway, so you should not let any rumor of a tainted record prevent you from dropping a class.

If you take a class that you want to drop later in the semester and you hesitate because of the forfeited tuition, think again. You'll lose the money, but you just might regain your sanity. And you'll save your all-important GPA.

ACCEPT THE FACT THAT YOU WILL MESS UP OR FEEL FORLORN SOMETIMES

The band Drivin' and Cryin' made its radio-station debut just in time. It began to get some airplay in the late 1980s, when I was busy trying to juggle a full-time job and a full-time load at college. Had it not been for its name—taken from the title of one of its early club tunes—I might never have known that other people besides me have clutched the steering wheel and wept. Since then, however, I've conducted an informal poll of adult returning students to find out that many of us have cried in our cars. Several men reported punching a wall, or occasionally looking and feeling like the frustrated, overworked guy in those antacid commercials.

If you try to juggle work, school, and your personal life, at some point you will probably feel overwhelmed. The students I talked to agreed that school was both rewarding and demanding, and that some days they didn't keep all the elements in balance. You will have semesters when you accidentally take one class too many. Or you will have to deal with your son's broken leg, your mother's surgery, the loss of a loved one, or an irascible boss who seems to keep piling on the pressure. *Something* will happen—because something always does—to make you wonder why you ever decided to try such a crazy thing as college.

Maggie at the University of Wisconsin encountered problems during her sophomore year. She was weary of dealing with a painful disability, and she felt overwhelmed by the number of obligations she had as a student, wife, and mother:

> Sometime during my sophomore year, I started questioning my ability (or sanity) to put myself through the rigors of academia. My focus began to waver. After speaking to a close friend and fellow student, Michelle Young, I realized this was a common experience for a majority of students. I'll always value her friendship and understanding.
>
> After regaining some focus, I was able to seek the assistance I needed at that time. Every once in a while, I still question my sanity, and my abilities to meet the pressure of deadlines, or the mounds of reading and writing assignments—but I know I can find the strength to continue. There are times when I have to consciously remind myself that my commitment means an obligation—to myself and to others. With a clear understanding of this, the challenges of higher education seem less overwhelming.

For Maggie, one secret was allowing herself time to relax. "Good mental health is a big factor at college," she learned, "and if students lower their stress levels, it shows in all they do."

Cynthia, a student at the University of Arizona, remembers that her path was not always an easy one. She overcame substance abuse and worked for years to raise her three boys, often alone. Now that she has been sober for eight years and is on the verge of receiving her bachelor's degree in substance abuse education, she looks back on her undergraduate path with appreciation:

> There have been times that I have been overwhelmed with schoolwork and have had a very difficult time balancing time for school, homework, job, and time with my children. At times I felt I was not as available as I could have been for my children. There were times I wanted to just stop and throw my hands up in the air and scream, "I can't do this anymore." But I've gotten this far, and I am so glad I have stuck it out. I can't believe I'm so close to my degree. I will definitely get the cap and gown and invite everyone I know to attend my graduation ceremony. I especially want my three teenage sons to see Mom get her diploma, which she worked *very* hard for. I have no regrets, despite the stressful times I have endured.

Cynthia concludes that "the benefits far outweigh the problems that I have encountered."

Helen, a sociology student at the University of Wisconsin–Madison, agrees:

> There are times when I am working so hard on papers and trudging up Bascom Hill that I wonder what I am doing. However, there are more up days than down days, and I feel like a kid in the candy store when I get the new course schedules . . . I feel sorry for the people who spend their time between golf and bridge. A friend asked me how long I would be going to college. I told him forever!

Occasional Setbacks and Even Depression Can Be Normal, Even When You're "Supposed" to Feel Happy

College may force you to face a past from which you tried to hide. Helen remembers how strange it felt to gather together her application paperwork: "It was quite a memory trip to contact my high schools and get those old records."

For Lynn, although returning to college was the best choice she could have made, she couldn't avoid the challenges that she faced back when she first dropped out in the 1960s: "Whatever caused you to leave or avoid school in the first place at eighteen will crop up again to be processed." Like Helen and Lynn, you may have to confront earlier images of yourself as imperfect, and either accept or modify them. This is an important process and, as Lynn points out, a "golden opportunity," but it can also be confusing and even make you feel depressed for a while.

Important studies have linked the stresses of adult student life with an increased risk of clinical depression. Researchers Patricia L. Dill and Tracy B. Henley examined psychological studies of adult students dating from 1983 to 1998. They noted that adults who return to college after an absence of at least two years, with an average absence of ten years, score twice as high on scales of depressive symptoms as their younger counterparts. The most typical causes of this depression were too many time and role demands. Women with young children reported the most strain. All adult students, however, were susceptible as they tried to balance jobs, domestic roles, and their emerging identities as scholars.*

Talking to an academic advisor who has juggled school and family can help. Ina, who has four children, was a stay-at-home mom for years before returning to college at age forty. As Director

---

* "Stressors of College: A Comparison of Traditional and Nontraditional Students," *Journal of Psychology*, January 1998.

of Adult Student Recruitment at Aquinas College, she counsels some candidates who are definitely college material but who need to focus on their families for a few more years before committing to a college schedule:

> I think we all know when the time is right. I have engaged in an ongoing E-mail relationship with a young mom who worked outside the home and really wanted to pursue a degree in education. We talked extensively about financial issues and time management. In the end, she came to the realization that the time was not right for her. Since then, she has had another child and her husband was transferred to another location. Things just wouldn't have worked out for her.
>
> I also believe that I have an ethical and moral obligation as a recruiter to help prospective students find the right fit. Our programs are not always going to fulfill everyone's needs. I know when to suggest starting at the community college to test the waters and when to recommend other colleges/universities in the area that offer curricula more in line with the individual's goals.

Ina doesn't counsel anyone not to go to school. She just helps people decide whether now is the time and, if so, whether her college is the place.

The good news is that on the same tests that measured depression, nontraditional students scored *much higher* than younger ones in such important areas as confidence and academic satisfaction. Women who were students scored higher on self-respect and respect from others than women who worked in the home. Overall they gained much more than they lost, but that didn't mean that the road wasn't bumpy sometimes.

If you start feeling down, your relationship with fellow students will be crucial. "Veteran" adults on campus will give you advice, comfort, and friendship at a time when you most need it. If reaching out to friends doesn't feel like enough, consider professional counseling as well. Most universities have a counseling center as part of the student health program. You will qualify for a range of services if you are a registered student, so be sure to check with your university and find out what is included in your health plan. Even if your university charges for its private counseling, it is generally offered to students at a far lower hourly rate than on the open market.

Periods of depression or frustration are a normal part of the adult student transition, so don't let them intimidate you. Learn to ask for help early and to inquire about personal counseling, stress management, and mental health wellness options.

SLOW DOWN IF YOU MUST, BUT DON'T DROP OUT!

Remember that you can always drop an individual course that is making you miserable. You can even get another job. If a family crisis arises, you can take a brief break from school to handle it. When school demands become too much, you can lean on friends and adjust your priorities. But you can never go back and relive a life that was made less full because you missed out on your college education.

The secret to excellent scheduling is to remember what matters most in life. Your education is enormously important. So is your family, your house of worship, your job, and your goofing-off time. Learn to ask yourself daily, "Am I spending my time wisely, or am I running around at the mercy of the clock, dousing blazes and feeling harried?" If your personal and professional life seem to suffer at the altar of academia, slow down. If your academic life suffers because of demands from your boss or your spouse, slow down.

Jay, a husband and the father of three, has rearranged his sched-

ule so that school is a priority, but his children's growing-up years
are even more important:

> Never put your schoolwork ahead of your children's or fam-
> ily's needs. I am never too busy to help my oldest stepson—
> a sophomore in college—with proofreading his papers. I
> listen when something is troubling him . . . girls, mainly.
> My middle stepson—a senior in high school—is rather
> aloof, but I always went to his basketball games, and he
> knows that I'll always be available whenever he needs me.
> My thirteen-year-old daughter also needs assistance with
> school projects, has band concerts, and provides me with the
> trials and tribulations that any young teenage girl gives her
> father. The bottom line is that your children are your first
> priority. You will always be able to find the time to get
> schoolwork finished. You can't make up missed basketball
> games, concerts, and those times when the kids need advice.

Focusing on your children more may mean slowing down your
academic progress, but that's okay. Twenty years from now, it will
not matter whether you graduated in 2005 or 2007. What *will*
matter are the relationships that you maintained with the people
that you love, and who care about you.

But this doesn't mean, of course, that you should stop because
of your family, either. As you learn to adjust for their needs while
focusing on your own academic goals, you will probably strike the
kind of balance that everyone in your family can live with. Barb, a
student at Wisconsin, offers this advice:

> Listen to what you really want, and make it a priority. But
> with priorities come commitments. Do not try the super-
> woman syndrome that I attempted. It is possible to be stu-
> dent, parent, and worker all at once, but the balance has to be
> monitored and you have to demand time for yourself, even
> if it means TV dinners at night and letting the laundry go. It

is a lot easier if your family understands your reasons for college and supports you. Make them your cheerleaders in life, and teach the kids how to fold towels.

Remember that there is no grand prize for finishing college quickly. But there are many rewards for top grades and excellent work over time. You can easily decide to take one extra year, or even two or more, in order to maintain a pace that makes you happier and keeps your family and your sanity intact.

8

WHERE THERE'S A WILL,
THERE'S AN "A"

If you pay your bills, manage your finances, or succeed at your job, then you've already got what it takes to earn top grades in college. You don't have to be a genius, or even strikingly above average, to do well. I have learned from years of teaching that my "A" students are not necessarily the smartest ones. In fact, with only a few exceptions, I seldom have the opportunity to award the A grades to my most intelligent students. Why? Because many bright kids don't work hard enough. It is easy for them to be moderately successful with little effort, so they just do enough to get by.

Instead, strong grades tend to be a measure of considered diligence. Students earn them in direct proportion to the degree to which they work hard and demonstrate a grasp of the principles in my courses. If you are willing to delve into a topic beyond mere memorization of vocabulary words or regurgitation of abstract statistics, then you are capable of earning an A in most college classes.

You don't need to worry about how smart you are, as if college were some sort of high-IQ contest. Instead, concentrate on cultivating excellent study skills and your grades will shine no matter where your measured intelligence falls on some arbitrary standardized scale.

On your job and in your daily life you have already gained many of the skills you will need to succeed at college. In fact, you'll find that much college work is generally easier than the kinds of tasks you have to master to run a household or work in the typical business office. Successful office workers make the best students because they have learned how to type, file, organize materials in a manner that others can understand, and work to a tight deadline. Note-taking in class is really no different from jotting notes in meetings with a boss or during business telephone conversations.

Studying will also be easier for you than it was when you were a teenager or young adult. Hormones aren't raging within, you're not busy rebelling against your parents, and you're years away from your first drinking binge or your first heartbreak. In fact, almost nothing that constitutes a typical tragedy for an undergraduate will mean as much to you. Emotionally and physically, you will be much better suited to the academic task.

What if you've driven a delivery truck, catered weddings, worked in a day-care center, or fixed cars for a living? You'll have great classroom skills, too. As a professional, probably the most crucial thing you've had to do is the one most young undergraduates don't yet understand: you've budgeted your time. Every adult, from stay-at-home moms to telephone line workers, budgets time every day in order to function in a complicated world. Most students haven't learned how to do this yet, mostly because it hasn't counted very much. They've always had parents or guardians to guide them. You've already lived apart from that guidance, however. You've had time to get better at doing it yourself. You'll be surprisingly good at managing a basic school schedule.

AS AN ADULT, YOU HAVE A BETTER
CHANCE OF SURVIVING MINOR
SETBACKS AND COMING OUT ON TOP

Most adults are astonished at how easy some college courses really are and how little most undergraduates have to work to succeed in them. The challenges that felt insurmountable when you were nineteen may feel like a brisk morning's work twenty years later. There will be tough times and daunting assignments, but not every semester, and not in every course. After all, you already know how to please a boss, so you should have little trouble pleasing most professors.

How can I be so certain? Well, when a boss gives you an assignment, you do it, right? And if you don't do it, what happens? You're fired, of course. But most younger students don't understand this yet, since they haven't worked for a living. They often hand in the *first assignment* late. This creates a terrible impression in the professor's mind, and although she can't "fire" students, she can certainly think less of their skills and abilities. Eventually, if the student has a borderline grade, the professor will usually choose the lower one, simply because the student didn't understand the importance of timeliness. You, on the other hand, will quietly do your work when it is assigned and hand it in on schedule. If you stumble, you will repeat your lessons until you succeed. Consequently, you will stand out as a mature adult in an inexperienced crowd.

Even smart, hardworking younger students frequently show up for class with excuses and lamentations about computer problems, alarm clocks that wouldn't go off, power failures, and general stress. "We've had a death in the family" has become such a standard refrain that another professor and I once joked about setting up a chart. We'd put up a skull for each reported demise, just like World War II fighter pilots. Then we'd have a contest to see whose class came in first with the most "kills." Grisly? Only if you haven't just listened to fifteen tearful, choked reports of dead grandmothers, uncles, and other dear departed next of kin, all of whom conveniently passed on during finals week.

Meanwhile, you will work steadily along, wondering if you are doing enough. If a death in the family does occur, you will attend the funeral without burdening your professor with your woes, and you will get your tasks done anyway. While the eighteen-to-twenty-two-year-olds congratulate themselves on dreaming up a new disease ("Tell her you have scrofula and that it's very contagious, so you *have* to take the final a day late!"), you will be taking and passing the exam for which you carefully studied. You may worry and fret about your grades only to discover that, by consistency and reliability, your work naturally moves to the very top.

If you still don't believe me, try this little test. Let's say it is the first day of the new fall semester and I hand you a syllabus. As you read it over, you see that there will be a quiz every two weeks on the material we cover in class. Then I go to the board and say, "Remember this, it's going to be on the next quiz." What do you do? Obviously, you write down what I say. If you do, congratulations, you just moved to the top 20 percent of the class.

I'm not exaggerating. Every time I go to the board and write something down, I notice out of the corner of my eye that about five or six of my twenty-five students write down what I say. Another 60 percent listen to me, ask questions, think about it, or even comment to one another, but write nothing. And then there is always the plankton in the academic food chain: that bottom 20 percent that doesn't even bother to pay attention.

If you read through your notes when class is over to make sure you understood everything, you just moved into the top 5 percent. Most students close their notebooks and assume they got it right. If you take a few minutes after class to clarify a point with me that you didn't understand, then you are in the top 1 percent or less, because I only get students like this every few semesters or so. Now, if you top this off by reviewing your notes after class while the material is still fresh in your mind, you're golden. There is almost no way that any of that material will take you by surprise on the upcoming quiz.

FOURTEEN WAYS OF LOOKING AT A BLACKBOARD: STRATEGIES FOR EARNING HIGHER GRADES

Many of your keys to academic success involve taking steps long before you enter the classroom. You can accomplish a lot by planning first and selecting your courses with high achievement in mind. Here are fourteen excellent strategies for earning higher grades:

1. START CLASS WITH A POSITIVE ATTITUDE, AND ACT LIKE YOU BELONG. You're not the first adult to sit in a standard undergraduate classroom, and you won't be the last. Here's what admissions officer Joe Carver reminds his nontraditional advisees:

> Typically, I begin by advising a student that she is not alone; that although most classrooms look to be filled with nineteen- and twenty-year-olds, indeed there is a mounting population of students who have not been in school for the last ten years. Then I encourage them to relax, buy a pair of designer jeans or whatever else it takes to look like a student, and get started. Most, of course, want to start gradually, but after a good semester become impatient and want to go around the clock.

2. SHOP CAREFULLY FOR ENTHUSIASTIC, ACCOMPLISHED PROFESSORS. Every department has its shining stars: those professors who consistently invest in students and do an excellent teaching job. If you take the time to study your prospective professors and choose the best ones, you will enhance your undergraduate experience.

In Chapter 11, we'll talk about your personal relationships with professors, and how they can affect not just your academic performance, but your whole future career and life. You can identify these superstars by talking to the heads of departments, by contacting the university's press office (which keeps track of professorial awards and commendations), by checking the archives of the campus newspapers, and by talking to students who are majoring in the fields that interest you.

Only sign up for courses taught by professors you have handselected, and with whom you have personally met for a one-on-one interview. Do not take courses taught by graduate students, since they do not have the experience or the departmental political power to help you at this stage in your life.

3. PLAY A BLACK CARD AGAINST A RED, OR ELSE LINK CLASSES TOGETHER. Whenever you have to take a difficult class, try to pair it with one that emphasizes your natural gifts. Also, try to take right-brained classes with left-brained ones so that you don't get overwhelmed. Matching a traditional toughie such as firstsemester accounting with a much different course, such as public speaking, will give you natural study breaks. When you're tired of crunching numbers, you can practice your speeches, and each discipline will provide a mental rest from the demands of the other.

The reverse strategy also works: you can take two classes that complement each other. A course in eighteenth- and nineteenthcentury English history, for example, will go well with one on English poetry. Other natural pairs are statistics and sociology, or Middle Eastern politics and Arabic. Your research and reading for these courses can do double duty. While you can't submit the same paper in two different classes, you can certainly write two different papers from the same body of research! I once paired a course on the American 1950s with one on twentieth-century masculinity. My semester's research on *Esquire, Playboy,* and the rise of the midcentury literary men's magazine worked well in both classes.

4. READ AHEAD BEFORE EACH SEMESTER, AND BE SURE TO INCLUDE THE PROFESSOR'S MOST RELEVANT BOOKS AND ARTICLES. If you use summer breaks and the winter holiday to read ahead for the next semester, you'll start each course with a strong advantage. Not only will you have lightened your workload, you will also better understand the professor's lectures. From the first day of class, everything will make better sense to you than it would have otherwise. You'll find yourself needing less time to prepare for tests, and you'll come up with good ideas for papers and projects earlier, while there is still plenty of time to complete your work.

Economics professors Munir Quddus and Marie Bussing-Burks at the University of Southern Indiana in Evansville asked some of their straight-A students about their secrets for higher grades.* Most said that they studied each day's textbook chapter *before* class. Consequently, they understood the lectures better and took fewer but more focused notes. If you are familiar with a chapter before the lecture, you'll be able to recognize new material that the professor offers and concentrate on that. Remember that your job usually isn't to learn the whole textbook, but rather to learn what the professor focuses upon, one lesson at a time.

You can also read "around" a subject by consulting other important books in the field. Spend a weekend afternoon at the library browsing a basic text or two before the semester begins. Learn the precise meanings of field-specific words, especially those that the professor uses in describing her interests. For an overview of general issues, read a few articles in respected magazines and journals, or watch related videos. Your in-class comments and your written work will begin to take on new, intellectually broad dimensions as you grasp the principles behind your required courses.

5. TREAT HOMEWORK AS AN IMMEDIATE MANDATE. Homework should begin as soon it is assigned. As soon as you know that a pa-

---

*"Students' Study Tips Help Others in Economics," *College Teaching*, March 22, 1998, p. 57.

per or problem is due, it's time to start. Learning to move straight from your classroom to the library or the computer lab for an hour of work on a new assignment will vanquish it quickly and painlessly. Even if you only jot a few sentences that first day or read just one related article, you have done something, and that is a beginning. You will have put new ideas in your mind so that you can think about your assignment even when you are driving, taking a shower, or weeding your strawberry beds.

Schedule assignments so that you can complete them days before they are due. Then put them away for a few days, and reapproach them "cold" for revisions. You will catch many spelling, grammar, math, and logical errors this way, because the material will seem fresher. By using all of the time between the day an assignment is given and the day it is due, you will give yourself time to think about your work and refine it in a considered, intelligent manner.

6. STUDY WITH OTHER TOP STUDENTS. Students consulted in the Evansville project also stressed the importance of study groups. If you form a group with two or three other top students, you will be able to share notes, work together, and fill in points for one another that you might have missed individually. Don't make the mistake of working with a friendly but mediocre student, however. You will end up contributing much more than you get from the experience, and that student's misinformation and poor grasp of the course's principles may drag you down. Instead, ask the professor for names of students who are doing well, and introduce yourself to them. E-mail is an excellent, nonconfrontational way to approach fellow students about potential study groups and sessions. Nearly every student has a university E-mail account, and you can look up your classmates' E-mail addresses on-line through the university's web page.

7. USE VIDEO WHENEVER RELEVANT TO ADD DEPTH TO A COURSE. Some of the finest scholarship in the world is available on video, if

you know where to look. Shakespeare's plays, for example, are meant to be performed on stage, not necessarily read. When your class studies *Hamlet,* most of your fellow students will simply read the play at home. You'll master the play, however, if you rent a few videos. Try comparing the 1964 version—directed by John Gielgud (who also played the Ghost) and starring Richard Burton and Hume Cronyn—with the BBC's classic version starring Derek Jacobi, with Patrick Stewart as Claudius. If you really want to be an expert, round out your knowledge by watching some of the twenty-five other versions of *Hamlet* filmed in the twentieth century, going back to the earliest days of cinema. Actors as varied as Laurence Olivier, Kenneth Branagh, Mel Gibson, and even the great nineteenth-century actress Sarah Bernhardt have played the starring role on the screen.

Be sure to keep your printed text with you and make notes as you watch. This way, you can observe dramatic departures from the original work. These wonderful performances will fix the characters in your mind and show you interpretations of them through the craft of many gifted actors. By the time you have watched just two or three performances, you'll be a near-expert.

This method also works if you want to see and hear famous people describing their work in their own words. Many names in your reading will come to life when you see them on video. Alice Walker, Jean-Paul Sartre and Simone de Beauvoir, Albert Einstein, Joseph Campbell, Aldous Huxley, Joan Didion, Malcolm X, and thousands of other writers, painters, poets, actors, philosophers, mathematicians, and scientists are the subjects of documentaries or have made their own films about their lives and work. You may find many of these at your university library. Ask a research librarian how to limit your keyword search to video recordings only. You may also locate recordings at other libraries that you can obtain for free through interlibrary loan.

8. USE ON-CAMPUS STUDY RESOURCES. Most colleges hire graduate students to work in their writing centers. You can bring drafts of

your research papers and get help with structure, grammar, and writing style. Some colleges even have academic development centers where professors volunteer a certain number of hours to assist students in various disciplines, such as math, accounting, and the sciences. You usually need to make an appointment for these services, and they are *very* busy around exam time. Stop by early in the semester and ask the center's directors how you can best make use of their resources.

9. LET GO OF THE LAST-MINUTE-ADRENALINE MYTH. Every semester, I ask students to turn in drafts of their final papers three weeks before they are due. I spend most of my time marking these drafts and handing them back. This is much more helpful than making in-depth comments on the final paper, which can't be revised. Many students complain to me that they don't want to go through this process because they think better under pressure. They insist that they "need" the end-of-semester stress to produce good work. "I'm smarter at the last minute!" they announce. "Too many rewrites and too much time will mess me up!"

This is one of the most naive and yet persistent myths in academia. I have read hundreds of examples of these so-called last-minute miracles, and they are *always* of poorer quality than the well-thought-through work. I have graded so many papers that now, almost without fail, I can smell one that's fresh from a 4 a.m. writing session. One key is the improbable reach of the argument. I can almost hear the author chuckling as he sips his stale coffee, takes a drag on a cigarette, and pops another No Doz, saying, "This is brilliant. She's gonna love it." Quite the opposite is usually true, however. These one-draft wonders are generally so immature and ill-considered that they can make a highly intelligent student seem far duller than an average person who starts earlier and revises her work over time.

Palma began her studies at Sarah Lawrence College in her fifties, after raising two children and welcoming five grandchildren. She remembers having "cold feet" before her first big paper;

she almost wanted to give up. But she worked faithfully and diligently over time, and achieved surprising results:

> My first academic writing assignment in more than thirty years was a comparative piece on Eugen Herrigel's book *Zen in the Art of Archery* and four articles by Brother David Steindl-Rast, a Catholic monk. It was exhausting and excruciating. At precisely 10:48 p.m. on October 2, 1997, I telephoned a friend and encourager, and wearily announced: "I have just given birth to a 7-page, 14-paragraph, 1,516-word expository essay. I thought I was going to die."
>
> One week later, after examining my writing, the professor handed the essay back to me. Imperfect perfectionist that I am, I braced myself for the worst possible news. To my absolute astonishment, she proceeded to read and critique each paragraph of my paper to the class, and concluded with, "In short, excellent." It was precisely at this point that my feet were no longer cold.

If you begin writing papers the day they are *assigned*, rather than the week they are due, I guarantee you will enjoy a corresponding uptick in your grades and a comforting drop in your stress level. Like Palma, you may find yourself producing distinguished work. My greatest reward at the end of the semester is the student evaluation comments: "She made us turn in drafts early, which seemed like a pain, but in the end it really helped after all." One student happily reported that his ten-page paper "almost wrote itself" because he followed my guidance on research and early assistance with drafts.

10. TAKE PLEASURE IN YOUR STUDIES. Studying can be fun if you do it right. You should be majoring in something you love, anyway (see Chapter 9 for a fuller discussion of majors), so your core classes will emphasize your natural interests. Beyond this, however, you can learn to enjoy a course by approaching your studies

with a sense of anticipation and vigor. Instead of asking what minimum amount of work is required for a good grade, test yourself to see what happens when you consistently shoot beyond the mere requirements. By trying to understand concepts instead of abstract facts, and by embracing areas of study, you will find yourself getting excited by the prospect of visiting the library and doing your homework.

Think of any college course as an opportunity to approach an entire field of study. For example, don't just take Biology 101 with the goal of passing the class. Instead, consider yourself a student of the biological sciences for a semester. Walk into the classroom with the same attitude as the majors. By declaring yourself a novice scientist, you will approach each day's lecture with a subtle difference. Instead of thinking, "Will this be on the exam, or can I ignore it?" you will be more likely to consider all material as potentially relevant to the field.

11. Befriend a research librarian, and learn what your libraries have to offer. Research librarians are among our universities' most underused resources. If you schedule time with them early in the semester, when they're not as busy, they can teach you research skills that will make all of your studies easier and more productive.

You may have to hunt around in your library to find them, though. If you wander up to the front desk, you will usually find a graduate student, or even a work-study undergraduate, who is unlikely to give you the professional help you need. Instead, ask to see a list of the library's staff, and find out which ones specialize in helping students learn to conduct professional research. You will find these librarians at various reference stations, including ones in such often-hidden rooms as Periodicals and University Archives. Seek them out, and ask questions regularly. Many of them will patiently teach you what they know.

Bring the syllabus from each of your classes and ask the librarians for assistance with specialized databases for your field, indexes of articles, reference works, and computer resources. You may well get more information than you can absorb in one day, so plan several meetings, giving yourself time after each session to practice, explore, and learn how your university library works. Ask several librarians. Their specialties frequently differ, and some are more people-oriented than others. Once you find friendly ones who can explain things in a way that you like, stick with them. Some of them teach free classes in the library, which you should take as soon as you can.

If your research library is small, find out if you have reciprocal privileges at larger libraries nearby. For example, Georgetown University is part of a research consortium in the Washington, D.C., area. Students at Georgetown can also use the libraries at George Washington, American, Howard, Catholic, and George Mason universities, among others. Also familiarize yourself with smaller specialized libraries right on campus. There may be a medical library near the university hospital, for example, or a law or music library. Once you are familiar with the main library, you can use these specialty libraries for access to field-specific databases, books, and journals. In Appendix B, I have listed some useful books on conducting college-level research.

12. ACCEPT CRITICISM OR CORRECTION, AND MOVE ON. You'll stand apart from the crowd if you accept helpful feedback and suggestions from instructors. Instead of being defensive about your work or acting crushed, you'll seem much more professional if you simply revise it.

As tempting as it may be sometimes, especially in a private office, to argue with a professor, try not to. Remember that in the microcosm of the classroom, the professor is—however temporarily—God. By bending to her point of view just for the duration of the course, you will learn how to approach an academic discipline in a new way. You don't have to retain that perspective, and someday you may go on to publish an important paper and refute it, but you are temporarily in that professor's world, and it will serve you well if you learn to adapt.

Try not to panic if you get an early paper back with a low grade on it. Remember that most professors are harder on students in the beginning in order to encourage then to work up to their standards. Also, strict grading early makes it easier to establish a realistic curve. If everyone gets a mushy, softball B and a "Very promising!" as a sop to self-esteem, they'll all expect A's in the end. Instead of getting upset, make an appointment to discuss the paper. You'll pleasantly surprise the professor if you don't try to contest the grade, but instead ask how you can improve.

Most professors welcome questions like this and will try to explain how you can do better. If you get one of those unfortunate souls who don't want to talk about it, then find another caring professional (a sympathetic former professor, for example, or one of the tutors in the university's writing center) and find out what went wrong. Brace yourself to hear negative feedback in a positive way, and see every setback as an opportunity to learn. Even if you don't like the critic, learning to accept criticism can still be constructive in the long run.

You may find yourself in a situation where the professor is younger than you are. It may be tempting for you to say, "I've worked in advertising for twenty years, and that's simply incorrect." You will lose much more than you gain with a strategy like this, however. Remember that professors are not infallible, but that most know more about the academic aspect of their fields than you do, since academics and practical applications often differ. And yes, sometimes your work *may* be judged unfairly. By separating yourself and your self-worth from your work, however, you will be able to examine the situation dispassionately and meet your professor's expectations, even if they seem unreasonable.

13. LEARN TO QUESTION ASSUMPTIONS AND DIG DEEPER FOR THE FACTS. The mark of real scholarship is a willingness to look beyond

simple answers and search for actual data. If a history book says that Richard M. Nixon was paranoid, investigate that by looking up examples of times when he acted contrary to that characterization. Try reading his own words or looking up conflicting newspaper articles about him during his presidency. Can you offer historical examples of a trusting, statesmanlike Nixon? If you read that many African women writers have been treated as elitist for writing only in French or English instead of in their native languages, challenge that by finding examples of authors who had different experiences. Or seek out the criticized authors in their own words in order to defend or explain their positions.

The habit of pressing every assumption to see if it holds true will help you think more critically and improve your grades. It means moving beyond a sophomoric need to argue the opposite position simply for the thrill of playing devil's advocate. It also means easing away from old debate-team strategy of "Resolved: That the New European Currency Is a Threat to the Global Economy" and arguing that position for all you're worth. Instead, you will want to learn how to view an issue in all its complexity by considering several sides and then arriving at a reasoned, informed conclusion. As you learn how to assess the opinions of pundits and do your own research using primary sources (the actual words and original documents or artifacts surrounding an event rather than books referring to them), you will become adept at investigating generalizations and learning to be focused, specific, and factual.

14. DON'T BEAT YOURSELF UP FOR NOT BEING A WHIZ KID. This means silencing the negative chatter that may go on in your mind. When you attempt something new, do you ever hear a voice inside saying you can't do it? Many of us do. I once made a list of the negative messages that marched through my mind like stock quotations on a Wall Street ticker board. Here are some of the most persistent:

- "I'll never finish this."
- "I'm rushing, and it won't be good."
- "I've gone in too many directions already."
- "I should have done this weeks ago."

The secret to being a good student, a fine employee, a productive writer, or anyone else of accomplishment is to keep going despite these messages, and to learn to quiet them down.

Some people use affirmations ("I'm good enough, I'm intelligent, I'm diligent") in order to see themselves as more powerful, capable people. Affirmations are fine as long as they work for you. But to me they smack of self-importance, and I resisted their aggressive cheerfulness as they beamed at me from my refrigerator door every morning. By the third morning, I stuck my tongue out at the chirpy list and said, "Oh, hush up." In my world, there was only one way to overcome the negative messages: I needed positive experiences.

When the magpie chatter of negativity starts in your head, try shrugging your shoulders and saying, "Okay, fine. You win. This *should* have been done weeks ago. But I'm doing it today." By acknowledging the guilty, nagging voice, you may be able to pacify it long enough to get something done in spite of it. Eventually, your successes will outweigh your setbacks, and the voice will quiet down. Nothing quiets them more effectively than a well-earned A or B in a difficult course.

Concentrate on Keeping an "Inner 4.0" in Your Major

Your first good grade report will change how you feel about yourself forever. There is no self-esteem program that can quite match the simple boost that comes from staring at a list of courses with excellent grades following them, and then seeing the additional notation "Dean's List" at the bottom.

But I am also going to give you some advice that may sound counterintuitive. Instead of playing it safe and taking only easy courses so that you can have perfect grades, I encourage you to try challenging classes for majors, even outside your field. The best professors teach the courses for majors. You'll stand a much better chance of falling in love with your studies if you take these exciting classes rather than the campus equivalent of "Physics for Dummies." You can read more about this strategy in Chapter 9, "Declaring a Major." Sometimes you may not do as well in these classes as you will in the ones in your major. However, this may work to your advantage if you strive for what I call the "inner 4.0." Although you should try to aim for such Latin distinctions as "cum laude," "magna cum laude," and "summa cum laude," you probably won't earn an A in every class, every time. A 4.0 in your major, however, will impress people just as much as if you'd gotten an A in everything you ever tried.

Cecilia's undergraduate G.P.A. missed the "cum laude" mark by 1/100th of 1 percent; she graduated with a 3.489 overall, and a 3.5 was required for "cum laude" status. Universities don't round up, either. What were her options? She could have taken another class in summer school for an additional A and bumped her GPA up a notch. But that would have meant delaying graduate school applications, which she didn't want to do. Instead, she emphasized her 4.0 grade point average in her major. This "inner 4.0" can help you seem like a superstar in your field, which is all your bosses and the graduate schools care about anyway. They want assurance that you were a strong scholar overall, but they are particularly interested in the GPA in your major.

You should fight like a tiger for top grades in your major. If a demanding course threatens a grade and you don't see any way out, drop the troublemaking class if you can. Should the unthinkable happen and you perform poorly in a class in your major, don't hesitate to take it again with another professor, or to sign up again with the same professor for round two. Some universities will substitute the second, higher grade for the lower one, and others will make a notation beside the lower grade saying that you repeated the class and succeeded. Either way, you will be perfectly justified in telling a future boss that you aced the course. There is no need to say that you repeated it. After all, the point is that you took the class and succeeded. Nobody cares how quickly you learned the material, but rather that you eventually mastered it.

How to Recover from the Setback of a Low Grade

Some courses work harder than others to challenge your GPA. Foreign languages, mathematics, accounting, chemistry, and many other disciplines that measure an unfamiliar and quantifiable body of knowledge have notoriously high failure rates. While most class performance can be linked to effort and capability, you may "bomb" a course simply because high achievement is meant to be difficult. You may have overreached, or underestimated the amount of concentration a particular course would demand. Whatever the reason, you will probably find yourself baffled in at least one major college class. It will help if you let go of the patently false notion that high achievers never fail. Ina, who eventually graduated summa cum laude, remembers her first low grade:

> As is the case with most adults in school, I worked hard for straight A's . . . [But] the best thing that ever happened to me was getting a C in statistics. It took the edge off. I was just happy to get through that nightmare of a class.

Ironically, instead of making her overly upset, the C calmed her down. It wasn't the end of the world, and it didn't destroy her GPA. Troy likens the stress and subsequent relief of getting through a tough class a tad scathed to driving a new car: "Sometimes you have to put a tiny scratch on it yourself, just so you stop worrying about the inevitable."

To be good, the success myth goes, you must never stumble. You can't overestimate your abilities on a term paper, or misunderstand an assignment. You must never falter in your presentations, give a less-than-brilliant speech, or (heaven forbid) go through a hard-knocks learning process that teaches you a set of skills over time while you offer up buckets of sweat and intellectual bloodshed. Even though all great scholars work hard, suffer, sometimes fail, and learn how to succeed by correcting their own mistakes, the myth grinds on that perfection, first, last, and always, is the only acceptable answer.

It's just not true.

If you run into grade problems, remember that these are situations where your adult status will come in especially handy. While other, younger students clutch their miserable grades to their sunken chests and bemoan a world that brought forth such idiots as themselves, or while they blame their professors for their own missteps, you will understand that grades do not always equal capabilities. You'll simply try again, creatively, and succeed wherever you have determined to do so. By understanding that occasional failure is a universal malady, you can get over it more easily and continue working toward sustained success.

Did you know that many students, even those who go on to become doctors, fail organic chemistry on their first try? It is so common to flunk the first pass at "o-chem" that it has become a rite of passage. The question among pre-med students usually isn't "How'd you do?" but "How bad was it?" Here's how Kevin, now an industrial hygienist working near San Francisco, remembers it:

> I came to Florida State as a National Merit Scholar who had pretty much skated through everything I ever took. True to form, I sailed through freshman year, convinced that I had

the whole thing wired. So, in perhaps the ultimate act of sophomoric hubris, I signed up for genetics *and* organic chemistry (both, of course, with labs) in the same semester. I had heard organic was a total bitch, but I was sure that wouldn't apply to me.

For the first time in my life I really, really tried at something and failed miserably. I studied incredibly hard (for me) and got a 42 on the midterm, and it was all downhill from there. I somehow passed first semester, but if they gave out F minuses, I think my final average of 39 percent in Organic II would have received one. Needless to say, I learned a lot about my limitations and the need to plan ahead for a realistic workload. Next time through, I just set aside huge blocks of time for studying and arranged a light load otherwise. That time, I aced it.

Many students take o-chem early in their undergraduate careers in order to learn the terrain of the course. Sometimes they strategically drop the course just before the deadline, but stay on anyway to expose themselves to the material. Then they take it a second time, often working with a paid tutor, and pass.

If foreign languages give you GPA nightmares, then consider yourself a proud member of the Tongue-tied Americans Club. Public schools in the United States have a history of starting foreign-language instruction way too late. Instead of introducing languages in preschool and kindergarten, America throws beginning French and Spanish grammar books at bored, hormone-frazzled seventh-graders. There is probably no *worse* time to introduce a child to foreign-language study than junior high school. Most students are too busy applying makeup and reading *Teen People* magazine to give a particular damn about the past tense of the verb "to be." Yet universities consistently wonder why foreign-language majors are less popular than others and why college freshmen struggle through—and often despise—language classes.

If you garble German, for example, don't despair. It doesn't mean you're stupid, it just means that German is difficult for Americans and you tried to go too fast. I have a spectacular suggestion that will not only solve your grammar problem, but possibly change your life. Get thee to the university's foreign study office and find out about spending a summer in Europe studying intensive German, and perhaps even earning an extra three hours of credit in another discipline like political science in the bargain. You'll improve your résumé and gain more credit hours.

Yes, I mean you. I know it sounds crazy and wildly unaffordable, but if you work through your university's travel office, it will probably be within your reach. Universities enjoy deep discounts on travel, and many of them finance much of the cost as part of your student fees. When Theo studied Spanish at Skyline College in California, he found that travel enhanced his ability to become fluent:

> I was excited to not only rush home and complete assignments, but to become actively involved in the work itself. For example, instead of reading about Mexico or Venezuela, I boarded an aircraft and visited these destinations. When my Spanish teacher was stuck in Caracas, I flew from San Francisco to assist her at the U.S. Embassy. Learning Spanish became a burning desire, and even though I faced major hurdles, I focused intensely on learning to speak this language.

In Chapter 11 we'll discuss foreign study in detail, including advice on going abroad even if you have a job or kids. After a few weeks of total immersion in the language, including plenty of evenings speaking to friends and enjoying some rounds at the local bar (a.k.a. "liquid Berlitz" because alcohol loosens your tongue), you'll return to the States speaking better German than some of the graduate students.

Scholarly Organizations, Honors, and Extracurricular Activities Will "Make" Your Résumé

We have already discussed the importance of top grades. A superior GPA matters more to future employers than the name of your degree or the speed with which you earned it. Beyond this, however, you should also join academic societies and try for honors if you really want to boost your credentials and make your degree mean something special.

Although many of these societies are by invitation only, they have to know who you are before they can invite you. You can increase your chances of getting into a scholastic or honor society if you know which ones are available and what their requirements are. Your membership in one won't require that much extra work on your part, and it will impress future employers for the rest of your life.

Even if you begin school at a community or junior college with plans to transfer, there are usually honors organizations available to you. Here's a checklist of nine ways to find out what your campus offers.

1. Consult the college catalogue. Many students make the mistake of looking at only the course requirements section. If you read the catalogue cover to cover, however, you will learn about all sorts of hidden treasures, such as honor societies and annual awards and prizes. Make a list of the groups for which you might eventually qualify, and find out which professors serve as advisors for them.

2. Talk to the dean's office. There may be awards or groups that aren't mentioned in the college catalogue, either because they are specialized or because they are new.

3. CHECK WITH FINANCIAL AID. As we noted in Chapter 5, you should be a regular visitor here anyway, and everyone should know you. Read the bulletin boards, and ask the financial aid officers for suggestions. They are usually delighted to help you identify honor societies and programs, since your membership in these will help them justify you as a top scholar and qualify you for particular awards.

4. INVESTIGATE EVERY DEPARTMENT THAT INTERESTS YOU. Check with your major department first, and keep reminding professors once per semester that you are on the lookout for opportunities to excel. Also visit related departments that might offer specialized awards. For example, some departments offer an "Outstanding Major" award, which you should try to earn. But you can also earn an "Outstanding *Non*-Major" award, especially from departments like math or one of the sciences. There are awards for the best undergraduate research paper, the best essay, and the best lab work. Many departments post notices about these awards on their bulletin boards.

5. ONCE YOU IDENTIFY AN HONOR THAT INTERESTS YOU, NOTIFY YOUR DEPARTMENT. Don't make the mistake of approaching an honor society on your own. The value of membership in such an organization depends upon its exclusivity. Instead, let those professors who have awarded you top grades know that you have a strong record and that you are trying to distinguish yourself, if possible. The most subtle way to do this is to ask the professors for whom you have already earned top grades for advice. You should probably wait until your grade in a class is final. If your grade was good, schedule an appointment with that professor shortly after classes end, and ask for personal suggestions on earning honors and other distinctions.

There are some societies, such as Phi Beta Kappa, that you can join only if a professor who has already earned the honor recommends you. This is where your networking skills will come in handy. Make certain that your past professors know about your present successes. Make a habit of visiting former professors for a five-minute chat and an update on your progress. Don't be shy about letting professors know how well you are doing and how much you owe to their encouragement and great teaching. They'll feel flattered and rewarded that you have considered them partners in your academic growth. As they grow to know and respect you, one of them might decide to nominate you for one of these honors. You usually can't come out and ask for the nomination, but you can certainly make yourself visible to someone who has the power to help you in this way.

6. Take honors courses as soon as you qualify. Always seek out advanced-placement and honors classes, since excellent performances in them will bring you to the attention of the "right" societies. Look particularly for courses with competitive enrollment requirements. Most of these aren't much more difficult than regular undergraduate classes, and they are generally taught by the better professors.

7. When you earn an honor, let important people know. Make certain you notify the chair of your department, your favorite professors, and your best friends over in financial aid. Don't make the mistake of thinking that they'll notice what you've done. Too many pieces of paper snow down upon too many desks for that. Take a minute and write a brief, handwritten note on excellent paper to each professor who helped you. Write something like "I want to thank you for your past encouragement and great teaching. This semester I was inducted into the Alpha Chi Omega honor society, and I never would have made it without your support!" These notes are enormously rewarding for professors and administrators, and they will make those people want to help you even more in the future.

8. Never let honors get in the way of top grades. The most important thing you can do for your future while in college is

earn the best possible grades. Honors are important, but not if chasing after them lowers your GPA. If your grades suffer because of honors coursework, slow down. Consider going to summer school or taking honors courses during a less-demanding semester.

9. INVEST TIME IN THOSE STUDENT ACTIVITIES THAT WILL ENHANCE YOUR RÉSUMÉ. If you want to be a journalist, be sure to contribute an occasional article to the student newspaper. There is no need to get so deeply involved that your schoolwork suffers. But don't ignore such opportunities, either. Take advantage of such on-campus luxuries as the radio station, the literary magazine, and other student organizations and publications. Find out if there are any awards or competitions for essay writing, journalism, science reporting, or other achievements.

I volunteered for two years at U.Va.'s student-run station, WTJU, as a classical and jazz radio announcer. The work was great fun, I didn't need past experience, and they let me choose hours around my schedule. Some radio stations will let you invest as little as two or three hours a week! I received excellent training in radio announcing and basic studio production. Later, when I approached WUNC in Chapel Hill, North Carolina, the home of National Public Radio's Southeastern Bureau, I got a paid announcing job became of my WTJU experience. From there, it was a short hop to contributing occasional pieces to NPR. On-campus opportunities can translate into real-world benefits very easily. Don't miss the chance to turn your degree into a wonderful new job by taking advantage of them.

OVERCOMING COMPUTER ILLITERACY AND OTHER TECHNOLOGICAL FEARS

Computer culture in academia may take you by surprise if you don't use a computer in your daily life. Fortunately, a college campus is one of the best places to learn new computer skills. Paul had worked for years as a security guard, police officer, and volunteer firefighter before he went back to college. None of these occupations involved computers. Then he decided to attend the University of Wisconsin and earn a B.F.A. in graphic design. He was taken aback when he realized just how much the field had evolved over the years since he'd first tried college:

> I arrived at first with the old tools of the trade—the ones I remember using the first time I was in school (T square, technical pens, etc.), and quickly felt like a fool. Most of the younger students looked at me as if to say, "What are you going to do with those? Start a fire?" I was amazed at the influence of computer technology on the field! It seemed as though a person couldn't use the restrooms without a floppy disk! Since then, I have worked forty to fifty hours per week at my job and have attended school full-time also. I have been selected as a member of the university's dean's list each semester, and don't feel quite so helpless with computer technology.

If you feel technologically unsophisticated, you're not alone. Many adults, especially those who grew up with slide rules and calculating tables, find computer culture a bit baffling.

There are two big secrets about computers on campus, however. First, most college campuses lag far behind the business world in terms of technical expertise. If you have ever used computers on your job, you will know enough to get by, at least in the beginning. Second, many old-school professors, deans, and administrators are more afraid of computers than you are. Because these academics tremble every time they have to touch a computer mouse, universities have developed some *very* rudimentary classes to get them started. You can usually take introductory computer courses for free through your university's academic computing or information technology department. I promise that you won't be the slowest student in the room. That world-famous professor across the aisle who squints and scratches his beard while trying to read the screen will be way behind you.

If you are on one of the few campuses that don't have a formal training program, then check the directory of a nearby community college, or sign up for a class at your local public library. You shouldn't have to resort to this, however. Nearly every campus in America has resident experts who can help you understand what you need to know.

I do suggest buying your own home computer eventually. But before you spend your money, learn about computers from the classes on campus. Most universities have free computer labs where you can gain experience on your own. If you watch the bulletin boards or read the want ads in the student newspapers, you might even be able to buy a less-expensive used computer. Students frequently receive new computer systems as gifts and sell their perfectly good older models for very little money. You can benefit from their lack of concern over the sale price and pick up a real bargain.

Your college or university will probably give you a free E-mail account and access to the World Wide Web to get you started. Take some introductory workshops and learn to use E-mail and the Web first, and then gradually master the skills of computer-based research in the library. Be sure to learn about word processing software, and gain at least a basic introduction to simple graphics for your papers. Soon you will have all the skills you need to work effectively on a typical college campus.

BELIEVE IN YOUR ABILITIES, BUT DEVELOP A LIGHT TOUCH

Concentrate on good grades, but try not to let yourself turn into an ultraserious study grind. If you practice the principles in this chapter, and if you adopt the scheduling suggestions in Chapter 7, then your academic life should proceed at a manageable pace and your work should shine. You won't have to grunt through, because your efforts will naturally pay off.

If stress begins to wear on you, however, take specific steps to relax and slow down. My favorite stress-reducer was a professional full-body massage at a local New Age medical center, followed by a long nap. Regular exercise also helps, preferably at the university's well-appointed gym. Instead of allowing yourself to get progressively more upset and ineffective, learn to stop, rest, and regroup before moving on to the next task. Remember that your self-worth comes from a lifetime of goals and accomplishment and that no single class can bring you down. Approach each day as a fresh opportunity to delve into scholarship while also enjoying it.

9

DECLARING A MAJOR

When it comes to your major, everybody will seem to have an opinion. Your father, whose intellectual life consists of occasionally watching bears mate on the Discovery Channel, will become an academic expert, telling you to ignore fluffy subjects and major in something "real," like engineering. Your mom, who dropped out of college to get married, will recite statistics about dropout and hiring rates and inform you that a pre-law major followed by law school is really the only responsible choice. Your next-door neighbor will offer hot tips on the hireability of information systems specialists while you clean the oak leaves out of your gutters. You'll catch yourself smiling and nodding while relatives, friends, and even casual acquaintances mention that genetic counseling is the latest trend in medicine, or that you'd be crazy not to try to land one of those cushy government jobs with the Bureau of Land Management and earn a full retirement package. Ever since "Plastics" became the most-quoted line from *The Graduate,* self-styled experts have been giving college students of all ages unsolicited advice about majors and careers.

But how wise are the counselors who offer this bounty of suggestions? Think about it: the average person gets up in the morning with a scowl and trudges off to a job he doesn't enjoy. Is this someone you want choosing your life's direction? Instead of worrying too much about what anyone else says, use your college experience as a rare opportunity to discover your own interests.

If you shop around and discover what you really enjoy in college, you'll usually find that it has little to do with identifying a specific career and then trying to maneuver your coursework to fit it. Instead, take your time and explore a bit before deciding on a major. Then you can major in your first love—no matter how esoteric or self-indulgent it may seem—and work to distinguish yourself in the field. Just by loving your studies and devoting yourself to them, you will put yourself in a tiny, elite group of college students. This process takes time and patience, but it will pay off for the rest of your life.

Yet there is often an organized push from within and without to force you to *decide something* before you necessarily know who you are or what you want. Don't let this influence you too much. Instead, I encourage you to wait until you have enjoyed at least ten varied courses, taking some fun risks and finding out where your interests and intellectual hungers lie before you select your major.

INTELLECTUAL PASSION IS THE REAL RATIONALE BEHIND THE BROAD-BASED BACHELOR'S DEGREE

Ideally, undergraduate school should be an opportunity to sample many disciplines and learn what you love. You will cut yourself out of this important process if you declare a major too early on the basis of what someone else told you would lead to a job. If you fight for dubious "life experience credit" and rush yourself through a no-frills program that only focuses on core courses, you might miss the intellectual love of your life. But if you slow down and earn a traditional degree, you will have a rare opportunity to investigate new areas, many of which you may never have considered before.

Diane, an adult student at Smith College, explains how a basic European history course introduced her to her present major:

> I finally became familiar with the entire map of Europe. It sounds silly, but my last geography class was in seventh grade, and I considered myself someone who did not know geography. Now I can tell you where Estonia and Latvia are. I'm majoring in British history, which I find fascinating . . . My colleagues at work will tell you how enthusiastic I get about architecture in London during the Middle Ages or during a discussion about Hadrian's Wall.

The traditional bachelor's degree at a top university was designed to stretch your vision in just this way. In Diane's case, it meant developing the confidence to major in something that she absolutely loves.

Grace, a registered nurse who lacked a traditional bachelor's degree, tried this approach and changed her whole career focus later in life:

> My first thoughts turned toward getting a degree in nursing, and I briefly explored that approach. However, to my amazement, despite my extraordinary experience, I found I would have to take basic nursing courses, even though my accomplishments were far above those of the professors involved and at one time or another I had actually taught those courses to aspiring nurses.
>
> So, on second thought, I realized a degree in nursing was really rather meaningless, because already I was at the top of my profession. Accordingly . . . I decided to enroll in the "Adult Experiential Program" at American University, taking evening classes. My first history course was enough to convince me that history was *it*.

Grace was in her seventies when she began her studies and is in her eighties now. She would have missed out on a fulfilling major if she had let age and expediency dictate her choice.

COURSES FOR MAJORS ARE USUALLY THE BEST INTRODUCTION TO A FIELD

To find out what you love, you'll want to get into as many academic departments as reasonably possible during your first thirty hours of undergraduate study. You'll get the best sense of how you really feel about a discipline if you try the courses designed for majors. These classes are usually taught by the top professors, and they typically attract a stronger group of students than the easier options for nonmajors. Yes, these courses are challenging, but ironically, the more a course demands of you, the greater the likelihood that you will succeed. Courses designed for nonmajors can encourage lazy, generalized thinking and a lackadaisical approach. No one will care whether you thrive in the field or not, as long as you pass the class. Classes for majors, however, may spark your intellectual interest, and even your competitive drive.

Here are some ideas for tackling a variety of courses that seem unfamiliar or even beyond your skills level. If you take the following steps, you may enjoy these classes much more than you expect:

1. PREPARE YOURSELF FOR DIFFICULT MATERIAL BY BRUSHING UP A SEMESTER OR MORE AHEAD OF TIME. For example, many fledgling science students encounter problems because they aren't ready for the math required in labs. Before you take a science course for majors, talk to the teaching assistants who run the labs and find out what level of math you will need. Take a placement test, if necessary. If you need an additional lower-level course that your university doesn't offer, you can go to a campus tutoring center or

even attend a nearby community college for a remedial class or two. By assessing the requirements for unfamiliar fields early and preparing yourself specifically for those challenges, you will enter the classroom prepared.

2. TEAM UP WITH TALENTED STUDENTS AND SHARE YOUR SKILLS. As a nonmajor, you may bring skills to a course that the majors need. Ellen's Korean biology lab partner, Yong-Sun, didn't speak great English, but he had superb math skills. Ellen, on the other hand, wrote beautifully, but she didn't know how to use the most basic piece of lab equipment. By teaming up, they aced the course together. Yong-Sun taught Ellen how to use light and heart-rate sensors, how to work out the math formulae, how to use a scalpel, and how to perform accurate dissections. Ellen taught Yong-Sun a basic English lab vocabulary, and she edited his prose until he could write more fluently himself. She wrote up all of their lab reports. By joining forces with others and asking for help, you may be more of an asset to any field than you may have initially guessed.

3. BECOME AN HONORARY MAJOR FOR THE SEMESTER. Pretend, just for the semester, that you are considering a prospective major in the field, even if you probably aren't. Learn about the field as well as the class, and talk to professors about the requirements for a major. Speak to some experts outside the university as well. You may find out interesting things that can change your mind about what to major in.

Professors and colleagues will generally treat you differently if they think you have the potential to join them in the field. You'll find that there are two levels of interaction: one for insiders, and one for everyone else. Once you're an insider, you'll start to see why people choose the fields that they do, and what motivates them to spend their professional lives there.

For example, many anthropology and archaeology students

travel with their professors, spending semesters and even whole academic years in the Middle East, Europe, Asia, the American West, and other places. If you've ever daydreamed about the life of Indiana Jones, then why not take one of these courses and see if the field suits you? Or you may learn that the university has a prestigious internship program for junior-year journalism majors that sends them to top newspapers and magazines for hands-on experience. If 80 percent of the graduates who intern find good jobs in the field, doesn't that throw a whole new light on a major you heard had "low employment potential"?

4. SCHEDULE CAREFULLY, PLACING RISKY COURSES ALONGSIDE EASIER ONES. If you sign up for something challenging and new, be sure to enroll in other courses in which you know that you are strong. Also, be careful not to schedule unfamiliar and potentially difficult courses in overload semesters. Some universities offer required courses that are relatively undemanding, such as large, introductory lecture-hall classes with basic textbooks and predictable syllabi. Take one of these "easy A" classes when you face your biggest challenges.

After ten classes of introductory work in various disciplines, you may develop a whole new assessment of yourself and your skills. The best way to break down barriers is to quietly alter the statistics by following your tastes and gifts rather than the path society has laid out for you because of your gender, your age, or your ethnicity. Once you have given yourself the opportunity to roam freely on campus, exploring the offerings in religion, science, communications, fine arts, and other disparate fields and working with the best professors in many departments, *then* you should select a major in something that you love, where you have proven yourself capable of earning your best grades. This is traditionally done during the first semester of sophomore year, but you can wait until the second semester if you still want to shop around.

CONSIDER A MAJOR IN WHAT
YOUR UNIVERSITY DOES BEST

If you're torn between two or more majors because you have varied interests, you might consider selecting the major that represents the best of what your university has to offer. If you like a
variety of scientific subjects, for example, and you make friends
with a top chemistry professor, it can make sense to work with her
and even switch your major to her field. If you know that you
want to teach high school and would be happy teaching history,
social studies, or English, then direct your major to your college's
strongest department. Is your college nationally ranked in history
and only mediocre in the social sciences? Does it boast several famous authors and scholars in the English department, but no one
of particular note in history? Does it have a top school of education but a weak English department?

By examining your college's strengths, you may discover a
number of places where you can logically fit in. When well-known
professors from these top departments write you letters of recommendation, your future employers in your chosen field are bound
to notice you favorably.

SHOULD YOU RELY ON
ACADEMIC ADVISING?

I caution all students to be very careful when they seek career
counseling or academic advising. In some cases, academic advising
can be helpful for the confused student. But there are always administrators within the university who will have an interest in
pointing you toward specific majors and away from others. Remember that although they usually mean well, *you* are the only
expert on your own interests and abilities. Advisors can be helpful
when they encourage you to try courses or think about majors

that you haven't considered before. But when the push is away from your declared interest and toward a field that supposedly has more job openings, the line between help and hindrance can blur.

Many advisors will cry foul here and defend their assertive redirection of students toward alternative, employable majors. As one advisor told me about majoring in English: "*Somebody* has to warn them away from this absurd field!" He had grown discouraged trying to shoehorn too many English majors into too few teaching jobs. He concluded that none of them—not even the best—should be encouraged.

Was he just being realistic? For the bottom half of his advisees, perhaps. But the most talented *will* be able to find jobs in their fields. His routine discouragement sent many students into other fields where they might not demonstrate the same commitment. The advisor felt that he was doing the profession, and his students, a big favor. As an English major who didn't listen to him, and who found a great job in my field, I heartily beg to differ.

There is nothing fundamentally wrong with assertive academic advising as long as it is done in a spirit of open-minded communication about options and goals. But some advisors have too much psychological power in these one-on-one meetings. What starts out as a well-meant suggestion can end up guiding a student's choices in the wrong direction. The business world boasts many information systems specialists who don't like their jobs but who claim that a career counselor steered them there during the recent hiring boom. Just because certain jobs are plentiful doesn't make them right for you.

IS YOUR GOAL AN "OCCUPATIONAL FANTASY" OR A BRILLIANT CAREER MOVE?

If your stated goal in college is "sexy," that is, if it represents what many people consider a daydream rather than a practical career, you may encounter opposition based on subtle jealousy. Students majoring in fine arts, theater, film, radio and television, and other fields with a lot of perceived glamour run into this negativity from advisors all the time. In fact, advising experts sometimes informally refer to these types of majors as "occupational fantasies," which reveals a deep bias against them as viable life choices.

Vincent wanted to be a film director. His advisor informed him that very few fledgling film directors make it, so he encouraged him to study physics (his strongest "serious" academic subject) instead. Since Vincent believed the advisor, he went through a period of upheaval, during which time he questioned his goals and doubted his talents. He graduated with a bachelor of science degree that meant little to him. Then he pursued his film goals anyway, after college. If Vincent had trusted his own instincts, he could have gained valuable experience in school by taking film-editing courses and screenwriting workshops. The world didn't need another disgruntled science major with a B-minus average who really wanted to be the next Spike Lee.

Students who want to be writers also hear the argument about sexy careers. Advisors will tell you again and again that writers don't make money and that you won't be able to sell your books. Someone usually comes up with a statistic demonstrating that only a small percentage of all manuscripts are ever published. The next time you're tempted to let that stop you, walk on over to the nearest bookstore and have a look around. Every book you see, especially on the display shelves in the front, represents at least one author proving that the field is viable. You'll hear that athletes, dancers, poets, musicians, and painters are also unemployable. As someone who happily earns her living as a professor and an author—*two* careers my advisors cautioned me against—I recommend smiling and walking in the other direction when someone tries to warn you away from your dreams.

The push toward so-called employable majors may come from

several other sources as well. Your company's personnel officer may inform you that certain majors are "hot" and hireable. She may say that your company will pay for one major and not another because of this. Your parents may also place pressure on you, especially if either of them works in a degree-based profession. Children of lawyers, for example, tend to receive more encouragement and monetary support when they think about law school. Physicians' children often drift toward medicine, perhaps with a helpful nudge (or an overt shove) from Mother and Dad. Even if your parents had never envisioned college for you, they can try to influence your choice of major, encouraging you to major in something that they perceive as practical to justify "wasting" all that money and time.

Naturally, my own parents were worried about my choice of writing and teaching as a career. I sat them down one afternoon and said, "I love and respect you, but I'm also going to do this." Even though I was scared about confronting them like that and saying the words out loud, there was really nothing to be nervous about. The roof of the house did not collapse, and nobody had a cerebral hemorrhage after hearing the news. All my parents said was "Let us know if you run into trouble." When my grades proved strong and my fortitude lasted for the long term, they became not just helpful, but enthusiastically supportive.

If you take responsibility for your own choice of major, no matter how risky it may seem, you will feel better about yourself. Also, by not giving others around you too much power over your life, you'll minimize their ability to upset or dissuade you. Some people may offer you genuinely helpful advice. It will be easier to listen to these well-intended suggestions, and to take them for what they are worth, if you feel personally responsible for your own final decision.

IT'S OFTEN EASIER TO SETTLE
FOR YOUR SECOND LOVE
THAN TO GAMBLE ON YOUR FIRST

Oddly enough, your first love can feel like a risky major even if others *are* supportive of your goals. It is often easier to major in something that doesn't put you emotionally "on the spot" in terms of life choices. Majoring in mathematics, for example, when your first love is logic, can be a subtle way of not testing yourself at the level that feels riskiest but also most exciting for you. While math and logic may *seem* similar, one path may divert you from the very discipline in which you suspect that you are most talented.

Redirecting your academic focus to your primary interest will challenge you to live up to your secret dreams. It can be scary, but it can also make the difference between a professional life that challenges and fulfills you, and one that merely pays the bills.

Here's an irony, however. When you declare your major in an area you love, life may also humble you about your choices. Once you decide that you want to be a professional photographer, for example, and that you are going to major in art or photojournalism, you may encounter a professional setback. April had trouble with her first photography course, and she lamented that an orangutan pushing buttons randomly on a camera probably had more talent than she did. This self-doubt is commonly expressed as "I've got no business being here," and it is a close relative of the imposter syndrome we discussed in Chapter 2. Flaws and human foibles have a way of coming to the surface as soon as you declare your intentions in a given field.

Ignore these setbacks. In fact, if you can, try to welcome them. After all, if you are aware of your mistakes, you are on the road to true professionalism. Self-criticism and a balanced perspective without unnecessary self-flagellation is a valuable attribute, and part of true humility. Remember that even the most accomplished professionals felt a little wobbly at the beginning of their careers. The key to becoming successful and effective in your first-love major is pressing ahead and building skills so that you eventually become good at what you enjoy.

No program expects you to be accomplished at the beginning of your studies. That's why they call it school: you are there to learn. Soon, however, through diligence, you will develop the kind of confidence that grows out of true competence.

As you consider your own potential major, we'll examine two typical mistakes that many adults make. The first is thinking that business is the only practical major, and that responsible adults *must* pursue it. The second is avoiding traditional toughies such as accounting, math, and science because you are afraid of them. Either of these mistakes—forcing yourself into a business degree just because you think it's the right thing to do, or avoiding "hard" subjects like accounting, math, and science because you have a dubious background in them—can be easily corrected by rethinking the conventional wisdom.

The perceived opposition of business and the humanities persists as one of the oldest rifts in academia. It presumes a great deal: that businesspeople can't love history or rhetoric, that artists can't be fiscally responsible, and that the names of students' majors somehow define who they are as human beings. In reality, you can easily major in the humanities and yet become literate and capable in business, just as you can major in business and still enjoy a rich background in the liberal arts. We'll examine each of these areas in detail. Then I'll offer you some excellent reasons why you should stop worrying about what other people think, and major in what you love.

IS BUSINESS *REALLY* THE
MOST PRACTICAL MAJOR?

The myth that only business majors get jobs is so persistent that many adult students continue to force themselves into some form of a business degree. Applications to universities' schools of business have soared. Many of the night and weekend programs at universities emphasize business degrees over the arts and the sciences. Today, over 25 percent of college graduates earn some form of a business degree.

Of course, if you love business, you should major in it. I am a huge fan of the involved, devoted student, and some of the most passionate are in business school. If you know that you enjoy marketing, investing, business analysis, finance, and other exciting fields, then please enter them and succeed.

But don't try to force yourself there if you don't really belong just because you think business is more practical than astronomy, exercise physiology, linguistics, education, medieval history, psychology, or dance. As Thoreau pointed out in his 1849 essay "Civil Disobedience," if you follow society's imaginary rules even though your heart urges something else, you're in for some "very steep marching indeed."

If you're really worried that only the business majors will get jobs, then put yourself on the other side of the hiring desk for a moment. Let's say you're the head of personnel at a Fortune 100 company. You have two résumés on your desk. You need a new entry-level manager in marketing. The first résumé is from a liberal arts major at the University of Michigan. She joined an honor society, and also wrote a senior thesis that won a medal for excellence. She enclosed two letters of recommendation, even though you didn't require them, from former professors who couldn't say enough good things about her motivation, creativity, and spark. The second résumé is from a marketing major at the University of Wisconsin. He did nothing much to distinguish himself except graduate. His résumé includes the standard (and much overused) line "References available upon request."

You're not certain which of these two would be better for the position. You also know from experience that transcripts tell an interesting story. Personnel officers, hiring partners, and other employment professionals have been relying for years on transcripts rather than mere major descriptions because they show a different side of various job candidates. So you open the envelopes and examine their grades. She had a 3.4 overall, and a 4.0 in her major. She had only one grade that wasn't an A or B: a lone C in astronomy her sophomore year.

Then you open the marketing major's transcript. He earned solid B's with occasional C's, including one C in his major, and had a 3.1 average. He had only one A, in music appreciation, and one D, in linguistics. His application comes to you with no honors, no letters, nothing else to make you believe that this man is a stand-out. But of course the job *is* for a marketing manager, and he *did* major in marketing at an excellent university.

What would you do?

If you're like most personnel officers, you'll ask to see both candidates. Then you'll try to assess whether the superstar liberal arts major has any aptitude or perceptible interest in marketing, which can be, after all, a highly creative field. If she does, Mr. Middling Grades may get a thanks-but-no-thanks letter, even though he selected the right major for the field.

Even when undistinguished business students do get jobs, how happy are they? Compare them, if you will, to outstanding philosophy majors or stellar literature students who make the dean's list, earn their place in honor societies, and graduate at the top of their classes.

Edward used his return to college to make a transition from business to his first love, social science. He had enjoyed a lucrative career in sales before he went back to the University of Massachusetts, Dartmouth, to earn his bachelor's degree. However, although he had been happy with his job and his salary, he felt that something was missing. His life seemed one-dimensional:

> After much success in business, it wasn't about money any more, but about finding my inner self. I went back to college to prove to myself that I could do it and become a more well-rounded person. I expanded my intellectual capacities and reached a goal that I had wanted since high school. I became a teacher of social studies . . .
>
> Material things that had high priority were now replaced by feelings that what I had accomplished intellectually was far more important than a new car or fancy clothes. I can always replace a car, but my mind cannot be replaced . . . I worked two jobs, am a single parent, and maintained high grades because I wanted to make the most of this last chance.

For Edward, the rewards were worth the risk because business, while important and interesting, wasn't his first love. But no career counselor would ever have said to Edward, "Hey, why not give up your big salary and go earn half as much teaching high school social studies?" Most of them would have steered him into a business degree and a sure shot at promotion in the sales field, which wouldn't have made him happy.

Even if you're sure that you do want a career in business, you should major in the subject that will earn you the highest grades with the greatest amount of pleasure, not the one that sounds most like what you think you will be doing someday on the job. After all, if you struggle for C's in something that you think is "employable," you won't be much good to anybody. But your future boss will happily place you in a variety of positions if you show talent and accomplishment in undergraduate studies that suit your particular gifts.

Don't Rule Out Accounting, Science, or Math Because of Past Difficulties

The same holds true in reverse as well. Some adults, particularly women, "hide out" in the humanities because they erroneously believe that they aren't suited to the challenge of business, math, or science. Many discover that they enjoy finance, accounting, engineering, chemistry, and statistics once they master basic skills, and then try these disciplines at a higher level. Even if they fared poorly as children because of a culture that often allows girls to lag behind boys in math and science, they may find a natural aptitude hiding within after all.

Please don't judge your taste or talent for a field by your past history with the subject, even if you had low grades. You may believe that you are "no good" at science because you never earned anything higher than C's and D's in high school chemistry twenty-six years ago. Because of this, it would be very tempting to try to dodge science in college by putting it off as long as possible, and then taking a course for nonmajors with no lab requirements. But what would happen if you prepared for your science requirement by learning the necessary math? And what if you took a science class early, choosing a course for majors taught by a famous professor who is known for inspiring his students? You might do well in the class and find out that you love the field now that you're old enough to appreciate it and focus on it.

Maggie was certain that she would hate college math, since she had done so poorly at it in high school years before:

> I had a non-traditional-age math tutor who helped me overcome my lack of confidence with this subject and helped me understand the difficult concepts. My third semester, I passed Math 110 with a B plus, and I was elated because I had fulfilled the requirements.
>
> The following semester, both my math instructor and tutor recommended me as a math tutor. I did tutor this level of

math for the next three semesters. I had worked hard for this knowledge, and using it in this manner helped me retain it. Even more surprising, I eventually ended up taking two semesters of physics to meet my science requirements.

Maggie attributes her increased confidence and much of her comfort with difficult subjects today to this unexpected success in mathematics.

Sue took a risk and majored in engineering, even though she had no examples of other adult women trying the same thing. However, she stuck it out and earned the respect and comradeship of her peers:

> In the fall of 1992, I began making the weekly commute to the University of Minnesota–Duluth. I was fully prepared to be the oldest person there. Instead, what surprised me was how alone I was as a female student in so many of my computer engineering classes. Two hundred twenty-four students have graduated from this program, but only fifteen of them have been women. But by the time I was wholly in the upper-division classes, that sense of isolation was gone. There was more mutual respect among those students that remained in the program.

If Sue had let her first feelings dictate her choices, she might have left engineering during those early isolated days. Instead, she remained, made friends, and was even elected to Tau Beta Pi, the national engineering honor society. She enjoyed two consecutive summer internships at an electronics corporation that eventually hired her when she graduated.

Another adult student, Veronique, is now doing graduate research in physics at Dalhousie University in Nova Scotia. She never considered such a thing until she did well in her first undergraduate math course—at age thirty-eight! She started out in an adult re-entry program, and then entered Dalhousie for graduate study *by invitation* after impressing her instructors with her unique combination of creativity and intellectual rigor. She did it by challenging one long-held belief. As a teenager, she accepted an image of herself as incapable of even basic high school algebra. She wasn't, of course, but her public school experience, which routinely taught math as if it were beyond the capabilities of little girls, convinced her that she was math-impaired. If she had stuck with what she wrongly believed were her only strengths and taken a predictable degree with no surprises, she would have missed out on the career of her life.

MANY EMPLOYERS PLACE A SURPRISINGLY HIGH VALUE ON A BROAD-BASED EDUCATION

No matter what your major, if you strive for the top, you will probably find a job in your chosen field. If you plan to work in the nine-to-five business world, you will have an easier time landing a good job if you major in the field that will earn you the highest grades and the most recognition. Most employers will respect your choice. After all, they have learned over time that candidates with a broad-based background including humanities and science bring valuable skills to the business world.

Want proof? How about this: Researchers Judith Scott and Nancy Frontczak asked 97 top advertising executives about their hiring of new college graduates. Oddly enough, the majority of the new hires (53 percent) hadn't majored in advertising. They'd studied journalism or English, or received broad-based liberal arts degrees with no specified major.

Of course, the vast majority of these bosses insisted that college *itself* was highly important, and 86 percent of the respondents said a bachelor's degree was mandatory for hiring in their field. Beyond that, however, they encouraged a broad-based curriculum as

an excellent background for advertising. They were certainly
happy with students who took advertising courses, but the name
of the major was far less important overall:

> Some respondents commented on the need for a liberal edu-
> cation, and one CEO from Georgia specifically lamented that
> "students are rarely as broadly educated as they should
> be." . . . Even when given the option of other courses, liberal
> arts was a popular choice for at least part of a curriculum.
> Some executives commented on the need for the integration
> of liberal arts into the business curriculum (i.e., the use of
> music and art in advertising). Others pointed out the need
> for graduates to have broad knowledge, especially for work
> in smaller agencies where there might not be a high degree
> of specialization. ["Ad Executives Grade the New Grads: The
> Final Exam That Counts," *Journal of Advertising Research*,
> March–April 1996]

If you're a gifted writer and think you might enjoy a career in
advertising, you could major in advertising and find a job. But if
your first love is literature or philosophy and you'll get higher
grades by focusing there instead, according to this research you'll
be even *more* likely to land your desired position.

Best yet, you could use your liberal arts background to approach employers in a variety of fields. An advertising major pre-
pares you for advertising alone. But a broader grasp of literature,
logic, linguistics, and ethics, among many other subjects, can give
you strengths in any business field that relies on skilled verbal
communication.

These 97 executives also confirmed my earlier emphasis on
grade-point averages. Top grades mean much more to a future employer than the name of your major. Nearly three-quarters of
the respondents said that they were favorably impressed by the
various standard academic honors that accompany high grades.
Choosing a major that also represents your first love may easily

make the difference between you and your competitors. Those who followed the herd toward a predictable, "safe" major may actually be *less* employable than risk-takers who earn higher grades.

Yet the word-of-mouth prejudice against certain majors continues. For instance, biology majors have long listened to routine arguments that their field is overcrowded and that they'll be underpaid. What they don't hear is that many biologists are happy with their professional lives. In my journalistic work with biologists and ecologists on Maryland's Chesapeake Bay, I met dedicated professionals who were challenged on the job and free of many of the pressures that higher-paid workers in cities face. A field biologist doesn't need an expensive wardrobe or a vast expense account for entertaining. She spends most of her days slogging through marsh grass counting snails, or working in the lab measuring salinity in water samples. While this might not sound glamorous if you prefer driving your Lexus to the Four Seasons while talking to your stockbroker on a cell phone, it was heaven for the field biologists I met.

The majority did earn modest salaries as predicted, but some of them went on to become highly paid consultants. Some biologists I know now earn six-figure salaries advising companies about ways to responsibly improve their public image by cleaning up their environmental messes. Yet they and their colleagues had to weather a litany of advice from well-meaning relatives: "Biology? Where's the money in *that?*"

WHY I DON'T USUALLY
RECOMMEND DOUBLE MAJORS

Many colleges and universities offer double majors as a way for students to demonstrate equal interest in two fields. Students come to me every semester asking if they should take on a second major. My answer? Probably not. You'll only stretch yourself in too many directions trying to meet all of the requirements, and you are likely to dilute your overall performance.

If you double-major in art and business to satisfy both your interest in painting and your desire for money, you may appear "neither fish nor flesh, nor good red herring," to quote Dryden. No one will know quite what to make of you. A better strategy is to focus on an undergraduate major in a single subject and do very well in it. You can then go on to graduate study if you have a strong interest in a different field.

There is room for exceptions, however. You may legitimately have two great academic loves. Now and then a student comes along who just isn't sufficiently challenged by a traditional major. If you can keep a very high grade-point average in each major, and if you don't sacrifice one to serve the other or water down your performance in both, then I will concede that a double major may be a good idea. Also, certain combinations, such as political science and Russian, go together naturally and can make an exciting curriculum when joined in a double-major format.

Before you take on a double major, however, why not consider adding a minor, or even just a few "breadth courses" of academic work outside your major that you think may help you in your future professional life? If you're worried about the marketability of your intended major, you can enrich it by adding individual classes in other areas that you feel might expand your experience and skills, or even by devoting whole semesters to other subjects. If one of these disciplines naturally evolves into a formal minor, then by all means let it. But don't feel compelled to take on minors that feel uncomfortable to you, because you can tailor certain courses to your own professional interests.

For example, you may find your calling in classics. You may also legitimately worry about how many classicists get well-paying jobs. At the same time, you uncle the stockbroker may keep nudging you toward a career in the stock market, and he may offer you some financial assistance with tuition for your trouble. Who's right?

Well, maybe you both are, in a way. You could very sensibly

major in classics, which you love, and earn top grades. Then you could add a core of business-related courses that will not just please Uncle Louie but also give you some extra professional options when you hit the streets looking for a job. Even if you do land a job in your field, you will still need to be able to work in a world full of computers, information systems, and financial realities, so your related coursework won't really be wasted. By adding some basic courses in advertising, accounting, or economics, you might make yourself look more hireable, and yet you can still stick with your first love to keep your all-important GPA as high as possible.

How to Make Any Major Look Good on Your Résumé

When you look for a job, you will want to tailor a résumé for each prospective employer. Instead of distributing a one-description-fits-all résumé, you'll point to your specific courses that make you look more hireable to each individual employer. Let's consider, for example, the classics major above who pleased his uncle by taking some business courses. He might tailor his résumé this way:

> *Indiana State University.* Bachelor of Arts, Classics, 1999, cum laude. Additional courses in accounting, finance, and statistics, plus an emphasis in foreign languages (intermediate French, introductory German and Russian) and computing.

> *Honors:* Advanced-placement and honors courses in classics, French history, and Eastern European political structures. Dean's list four semesters. Pi Sigma Alpha honor society. Scholarships from the Newtown Policeman's Fund, the Valley Foundation, the Elk's Club, and two anonymous philanthropists offering merit-based awards.

Notice how this student has a degree in only one major, with honors, and then mentions courses that demonstrate capability in one specific employer's immediate interests. Even though he didn't minor in business, his list of business courses reads almost as impressively as if he had. If he had really loved his business coursework but hadn't wanted to give up the classics major, he could easily have stayed an extra semester and added a formal business minor.

Suppose you were applying for a job at *Condé Nast Traveler* magazine. No matter what your major, you would emphasize your literature and journalism classes, plus your articles for the student newspaper, any freelance work, and your undergraduate study-abroad experiences. If you were applying for a job at the World Bank, you would emphasize your languages and your coursework in accounting, finance, and statistics. Either way, you have managed to put an employer-friendly spin on your basic degree while still avoiding the rigors and dubious gains of the wrong major or a schedule-crushing double major.

Always mention honors in a separate section following the summary of your degree work, and list *everything*, including financial awards, advanced-placement classes, and other distinctions. A résumé is no place to be shy. Include everything of note from your undergraduate experience (class rank, famous professors, outstanding personal performances, speeches, travel) to make yourself look as accomplished as possible. I never advocate inflating credentials, but I do believe that you should point to the fine ones as clearly as possible.

Does this process of approaching a major sound slow? It doesn't have to be. In many cases, it is just as fast as any other way through the university system. But even if taking the scholar track rather than the fast track takes more time, why should that matter? If you love your work, if your studies are the most fun you've ever had standing up, and if you emerge from it all as a hireable candidate with a superb record and the potential to move on to graduate study if you wish, isn't it all worth it?

10

Developing an Intellectual Identity (Without Becoming a Snob)

The 1997 Hollywood hit *Good Will Hunting* insists that inborn genius is admirable but hardworking bookworms are losers. Will Hunting is a streetwise kid with a photographic memory and an instant grasp of complex mathematical formulae. He works as a janitor at MIT and studies mathematics on his own at night. He eventually forces MIT math professor Gerald Lambeau to admit that despite his own education, publications, and carefully built academic career, Will is naturally the smarter, and hence the better, man. Even though Gerald has worked hard for years, Will beats him every time. "It must be heartbreaking," wrote film critic Roger Ebert in his review of the movie in the *Chicago Sun-Times*,

> to be able to appreciate true genius and yet fall just short of it yourself. A man can spend his entire life studying to be a mathematician—and yet watch helplessly while a high school dropout, a janitor, scribbles down the answers to questions the professor is baffled by.

Ebert reflected the sentiments of many viewers who propelled *Good Will Hunting* to the forefront of that year's movie pack. It earned two Oscars, was nominated for seven more, and won many other international honors.

However, while most viewers sighed along with the humbled professor and would have agreed with Ebert's analysis, I hooted with derisive laughter and threw a rolled-up gym sock at the television screen. Will is a brilliant pub crawler who just "knows" math without having to study, who never fumbles a proof, and who makes a mockery of the most brilliant minds of his day. He is also a classic symbol of anti-intellectualism and a figment of the imaginations of two Harvard dropouts, Matt Damon and Ben Affleck, who wrote the screenplay and also co-star in the movie (Matt Damon plays Will Hunting and Ben Affleck plays his best friend, Chuckie). I can almost hear their bar bet now:

> Matt: Those MIT mathematicians are a bunch of pansies. Heck, they didn't let me in, and I'm a *genius*!
>
> Ben: They didn't let me in, either. We both got stuck going to Harvard and being English majors because they're so full of themselves.
>
> Matt: (*Slugs his brewski; belches*) I'll bet their teaching assistants . . . hell, I'll bet their *secretaries* are smarter than they are.
>
> Ben: (*Wipes beer foam from his lip*) Damn straight. I'll bet their *janitors* can do better math than they can!

Damon and Affleck's Freudian fantasy actually began as a short story for a writing class. They then expanded it into a conspiracy thriller, probably (my guess) imagining Will Hunting as an off-hours hacker who discovers that MIT professors are taking CIA money to develop nerve gas and eradicate Saddam Hussein. After the script bounced around Hollywood for a while and went through many so-called creative sessions, the boiled-down tale of simplistic repression hampering extraordinary genius was all that remained.

Anti-intellectualism is Richard Hofstadter's term for most

Americans' discomfort with academic achievement. In his Pulitzer Prize–winning *Anti-Intellectualism in American Life* (Knopf, 1963), he defines the phenomenon as

> a resentment and suspicion of the life of the mind and of those who are considered to represent it; and a disposition constantly to minimize the value of that life. [7]

While Americans claim to value innate intelligence, they don't like stereotypical academics who seem to always have their noses in dusty texts. They love Will Hunting, but they hate the MIT and Harvard boys he bests with such glee.

Foghorn Leghorn, the Southern gentleman rooster from the Warner Brothers cartoons, pretty much sums up how many Americans feel about too much education. Every time he sees tiny, brainy Egghead Jr. running around the barnyard wearing giant spectacles, with his beak in a book, Foghorn gets the shivers: "Ah say, ah say, there's sumthin' a little *yeeeeeh* about that boy!"

Just because of this natural American discomfort with the life of the mind, you may feel uneasy with your own academic success. Your first good grades might make you feel oddly embarrassed. If you struggle, you may give yourself a hard time because you believe that intellectual accomplishment is supposed to come easily. If it doesn't, then you must not be intelligent. If you have to work hard for your grades, you may think that you're slow and that other "A" students were born that way.

It isn't true. Real intellectual accomplishment is almost always the result of hard work. Even celebrated geniuses such as Albert Einstein and Jonas Salk had to work at it. What's more, whether anyone wants to believe it or not, they made their discoveries as a result of collaborative effort. Face it, America, even Einstein and Salk had to study.

Many fans still think of Albert Einstein as a kindly, rumpled civil servant who scribbled at physics in his off hours, perhaps on coffee breaks, and accidentally unraveled secrets of the universe.

They love to recite the details of his failed application to the Swiss Federal Polytechnic School and use that underachiever image to portray him as a free spirit who worked outside academia.

Einstein's collected papers, however, belie this myth and reveal a disciplined, dedicated scholar with a troubled personal life who carefully earned his laurels in the established academy. He got into college on his second try. During 1905, his so-called Miracle Year, when he published three of his most famous papers in the journal *Annalen der Physik,* he also earned a doctorate in physics from the University of Zurich. He collaborated on much of his research with his then-wife, the physicist Mileva Maric.

Yet the myth-making public *wants* Einstein's achievements to be a lonely miracle, and the work of an insightful amateur. They love the image of a humble office clerk who effortlessly scratches out the general theory of relativity on a whim, and then goes home to kiss his wife and read the daily paper. But why should the notion of a hardworking, collaborative, and ambitious Einstein diminish his reputation or contributions? Why wouldn't most people *prefer* the thought that their imaginary intellectual icon and grandfatherly hero was really a disciplined academic who had to think before crafting his theories?

Well, for one thing, people in general, especially Americans, tend to associate intense thinking with wimpiness. It's okay to be smart, but the *effort* of thinking, especially if it takes a long time and doesn't result in swift, decisive action, makes one seem like a vacillating ninny rather than a man. Einstein shouldn't have had to study, or sweat, or labor in the university system in order to achieve the kind of breakthroughs that led him to actually apologize to the memory of Sir Isaac Newton for having overthrown so much of eighteenth-century physics. It is much more appealing to imagine him as a wild-haired bumbler who simply spouted brilliantly whenever he spoke, exhibiting a sort of Tourette's syndrome for bright guys.

Jonas Salk has been similarly misunderstood by fans who want to see him as a lone genius. He worked his way through college and med school, and then served during World War II testing military flu vaccines. The research that led to the polio breakthrough took eight years and was conducted with other scientists. Those researchers who worked alongside Salk have claimed all along that "his" vaccine was the culmination of years of group effort and medical understanding. Many insisted that Salk was a scientist of typical ability for his level. They said that his achievement, while important, was more attributable to diligence than brilliance at a crucial "aha!" moment. Salk himself was always reluctant to lay personal claim to the vaccine. He refused a ticker-tape parade in New York City and turned down repeated requests to patent his discovery, even though he could have earned a fortune. The most commonly administered polio vaccine in the 1960s was not even Salk's original version, but a competing live-virus type that Albert Sabin, Salk's colleague and sometime rival, developed.

Even though Salk's collaborators and his own ethical behavior belie the lone-genius-as-social-savior theory, popular culture insists on something more. Society *wants* a heroic Jonas Salk and an effortlessly insightful Albert Einstein. Society also wants a Will Hunting, a rakish man's man who doesn't let the established university intrude on his intellect, his libido, or his working-class values.

EQUATING SPEED WITH INTELLIGENCE IS PART OF AN IQ-OBSESSED CULTURE

Your academic progress may take time. Yet most Americans still believe that intelligence has something to do with quick results. This fallacy persists partly because that's how our intelligence-testing system is set up. Children race solo to solve puzzles or finish illogical-sounding sentences while psychologists observe them with stopwatch in hand. When Eugenia completes her word analogies before anyone else in the class, she receives a gold star, a compliment, and a high-IQ mark in her file. But what about Trevor, who takes twice as long to finish but whose work is more accurate? Or Margaret, who takes three times as long because there is an underlying double meaning in one set of words that no other student saw, and that stops her for five concentrated minutes? Are these two students dull? Of course not. But in our quickest-takes-all system, Eugenia will win every time. Even the words that we use to describe these children, such as *swift, fast, sharp,* and *bright,* are the same words that describe lightning-speed mental bursts.

This preference for speedy performance also excuses the mass of people for not trying anything difficult, or ever challenging themselves. If you're not the fastest, why bother? If you don't get there first, what's the point? You can easily disqualify yourself from the highest achievement by shrugging your shoulders and saying, "I can't win, so why play?"

PRODIGIES HAVE TO WORK AS HARD, AND AS LONG, AS THEIR ADULT COUNTERPARTS

Society likes to call youthful high achievers "prodigies," as though their ability manifested itself without effort. But *every one* of these so-called prodigies has to work very hard indeed. Each one has to work for the same number of hours as adults to achieve the same results.

But the faithful still believe in miracles, and prodigies. They think, for example, that Mozart and Beethoven understood music without a struggle. Will Hunting even spouts a version of this myth when he tries to explain his own gift: "All right, well, Beethoven, okay, he looked at a piano and it just made sense to him. He could just play."

Never mind that Ludwig van Beethoven's musician father,

Johann, gave him piano lessons before he was five years old in order to parade him about and make money. Although little Ludwig didn't last in the competitive world of the *Wunderkinder*, Johann made him practice for many hours daily, sometimes dragging him out of bed at night to force him to practice even more. Take no notice of the fact that he was socially isolated as a child because he spent so many hours at the keyboard, or that in boyhood he played professionally in daily masses at various churches in Bonn. And please don't be distracted by his position as an apprentice court musician when he was ten. It shouldn't matter that by then the young Beethoven had probably accumulated over five thousand hours of playing time, which is the average that a prospective student practices before being admitted to Juilliard. According to the persistent myth espoused by many of his fans, "he could just play."

So what does this mean for you as an adult returning student? At its most fundamental, it means that you may distrust the very process that you will need to succeed in college. If you didn't do well in high school because you were too busy having fun, or if you squandered your first run at college because of all the enjoyable opportunities to smoke, drink, and never think, you may have concluded that you weren't academic material. Society would have encouraged this conclusion. Hey, really smart people don't have to study, and neither should you. If you couldn't get through school effortlessly the first time, then you probably weren't meant to go to college in the first place, right?

Wrong. Absolutely wrong.

High-Achieving Students Often Make It *Look* Easy

High-achieving students are well-known for downplaying how much they really work to get ahead. They fib for several reasons, the most prevalent of which is their own anxiety about the association between hard work and wimpdom. What happens if you arrive prepared for a mid-term examination after having studied for ten hours, only to hear the swaggering, attractive guy on your left and the pretty, popular woman on your right both say, "Oh, I'm sure I'll flunk, I never studied"? When they each get an A, even if you earn one too, you could conclude that you just don't have what it takes. After all, they "didn't have to study," and you did. Even if they're not telling the truth, the image of top students as effortless achievers prevails.

It has generally been considered rude to arrive for an exam calm, relaxed, and prepared. Campus culture allows a student to show up in a sweatshirt and pajama bottoms, with circles under his eyes from lack of sleep. He can sport a fashionable whiff of caffeine and body odor from having been up for hours popping stimulants and then not even taking the time to shower. This kind of obvious last-minute cramming shows that the student cares about school, but that he also invests many other hours in an active campus life. The other socially acceptable option is for a student to show up for the exam seemingly unprepared, with a wide-eyed concern that she just didn't have a minute to hit the books because she was so busy working on the Homecoming Committee.

Either of these students may actually do well on the exam, the former because he managed to squeeze in enough hours of study time at the last minute and the latter because she actually does study on a regular basis, but pretends she doesn't. She also may not realize just how fruitful her regular habit of opening her books for an hour or so a day really is. If she is consistent, she may keep a high GPA via accumulated hours that she doesn't really notice, since her study habits are so well ingrained.

But what if you're somewhere in between? Suppose you studied for twice or three times as long as any other student admits, and on top of that you held down a job? What if your life doesn't afford you much time to go to any student functions at all, let alone work on the committee for a major event? How will you feel when you walk into that exam knowing that it was all you could do to find enough study hours to feel competent, but not fully confident or solidly prepared?

If you're like many of us, you will probably secretly suspect that you're an academic loser, and that the "superstars" around you are besting you at every turn. While other students claim to breeze through this work, you're reading and rereading, taking notes, and asking your best friend to quiz you on Chapter 6.

So you take the exam with a combination of frustration and trepidation. If you earn anything less than A plus, you conclude that you're a fool who wasted many precious hours only to prove just how impossible it is to educate a rock. I have had students sit in my office holding final exams with strong but not-quite-perfect scores on them, and looking at me through eyes brimful with tears, gasping out quietly, "But I *studied.*" My biggest challenge is assuring these students that yes, they did study, which is why they survived the exam at all. A perfect score of 100 is not the only acceptable one in academia, and an A is not the only respectable grade.

Academic life is not a choice between perfection and failure; rather, it is a walk along a continuum where results will vary, depending upon the material, the presentation, your talent and taste for the field, and even the professor's teaching style. The best way to maintain this important balance is to embrace campus culture and get to know many of the people who represent academic achievement at its most exciting. As you make friends with fellow students and professors, you will make the transition to knowledgeable insider. Campus life and rich relationships with colleagues are the key to developing and enhancing your intellectual identity. In the final chapter, we'll examine campus life and see just how important it is to your overall happiness as a nontraditional student.

11

CAMPUS LIFE:
WHY FELLOW STUDENTS AND
PROFESSORS ARE VITAL
TO YOUR ACADEMIC SUCCESS

New friends and great professors are two of the best things about earning your bachelor's degree. They are also crucially important to your intellectual and professional development. You *need* this network, and it is one of the many reasons why I do not recommend independent, self-directed study, or earning degrees via distance learning over the Internet. Unless you go to actual classes and establish new friendships with like-minded colleagues, you'll miss out on the richest aspects of higher education.

Yet I hear adults dismiss the value of the social side of college. "I'm not at college to party," said George, "so why should I care whether I meet anybody or not? I'm on a deadline." Inge agreed: "I have two daughters in college, so I don't miss the 'campus' thing . . . I get plenty of that at home!" Other students cited their seriousness or their commitment as reasons they avoided spending too much time on campus. A few worried that their families would miss them too much. Others voiced disdain about meeting undergraduates who might be half their age. By avoiding the campus, however, these students inadvertently undermined their own progress, and actually damaged their careers.

If you learn to appreciate campus culture, you will find that some of the most important parts of higher education have nothing to do with credit hours earned or the name of your major or minor. Instead, college is about joining a community of scholars and embracing education for its own sake. You will also need these contacts if you plan to go on and pursue graduate study. As you immerse yourself in campus life, your intellectual identity will naturally emerge.

When an adult returning student tells me that she doesn't need on-campus friends or that she's too busy to make them, I worry. There are many long, lonely periods when you will need the support of like-minded colleagues to get you through. Friends can study together, compare class notes, cover for each other in class, and be there to cheer each other on. The more friends you have on campus, the more likely it is that you will succeed, simply because you will become invested in school as a cultural entity.

Mary remembers the Ada Comstock Scholars' residence at Smith College as an important part of her adjustment period:

> I lived on campus the first year . . . All the women were of nontraditional age or circumstances. I had the pleasure of being the oldest. We ate our meals with traditional-age students in a house just two doors away. From the beginning, I loved being with the younger students; they were wonderful, always encouraging, never making me feel different or unwelcome.

Age wasn't a detriment to Mary at all. Her experience and wisdom were part of her contribution to the group.

If you make friends with other students in your classes, you will learn about financial aid, great professors, study skills, and other important things. You'll also have the priceless memories of *real* college: all-nighters, pizza study sessions, cold beer, foreign films, and final exam panic. Bev, a student at the University of Wisconsin–Eau Claire, attributes much of her present success to the support of her more-traditional-age fellow students:

I think my real intellectual identity switch came a semester ago in a history class when I began to make real friends at college. Even though I was older, the students in the class took a real interest in my opinion and friendship. I felt worthwhile.

College can become a time machine, sending you back to a lost youth that you may have missed out on by working or marrying young instead of finishing a bachelor's degree. When I went back, I didn't always party with the kids or try to act ten years younger, but I enjoyed and appreciated the best of their culture. They taught me the new songs, and they helped me adjust my wardrobe so that I didn't look like such a workaholic yuppie. We studied together over coffee, and I was able to help them with their love crises and their parental problems.

For Evelyn, just being on campus was enough to make her feel like a part of a shared academic culture:

I had such an extreme sense of accomplishment just walking into class. Every class I felt this way, and I still do. The atmosphere is so exhilarating for me, whether it is raining, sunny, snowing, whatever it may be. Just being on campus is actually fun.

Her friendships with fellow students made the difference between feeling as lost and bewildered as she did in the beginning and finally thriving. Campus culture became integral to her motivation. It wasn't just fun: it was part of her formula for success.

It's important not to judge younger fellow students by their backwards baseball caps or mirrored shades. Some of the sleepiest-looking slackers can actually be good students under deep cover. As a professor, I have learned to look in the back of the classroom as well as the front for my brightest students, and to recognize talent in a variety of disguises. Sometimes the cleverest and most pleasant are also the most unconventional. Lenore writes fondly about her traditional-age colleagues at Sarah Lawrence:

> I love to see the students learning, having fun, pierced tongues and all. The more bizarrely they dress, the greater my smile. We are getting an excellent education.

Instead of hiding out at home, she embraced the traditional classroom and found out just how entertaining and instructive younger friends can be.

You'll want to start looking for potential colleagues as soon as you walk on the campus. Here are four simple ideas for finding fellow top students.

1. ASK YOUR PROFESSORS. Let's say you want to form a study group for the midterm. Why not ask the professor for potential candidates from the class? Your teacher will usually not mind saying, "Why don't you talk to Josh?" or "Lisa seems to be working hard." Your professor should have at least a vague idea of who is doing well by about the fourth week.

2. HANG AROUND FOR A FEW MINUTES AFTER CLASS AND SAY HELLO TO PEOPLE. Many adult students bolt out of the room after class and race for the parking lot to get back to the job. Instead, wait a few minutes to see who stays and who talks to whom. Spend a few minutes in your seat, or in a nearby study area, reviewing your notes where everyone can see you as they leave. If you smile at others and offer a few hellos, students will notice you, and good ones will begin to seek you out.

If you ever feel lonely at school, remember that it's much harder for even the friendliest of your classmates to hit a moving target. Some people may want to talk to you, so you'll have to slow down and give them a chance to meet you. Helen, a forty-year-old student at the University of Wisconsin–Madison, used this method to find a study partner:

> Since I was one of the few students that had a car, I was
> happy to give rides to a couple of girls who had quite a long
> way to their dorms. I guess when you're a mom, you just
> keep on being a mom. It was a nice, friendly way to break
> the ice with all of those students who were so much
> younger. One of these girls is in my sociology class this se-
> mester, and we are now working on a project together.

After so much worry that she wouldn't fit in or might feel "too
old," Helen actually found that her age and situation helped her in
the college milieu.

3. SMILE, OR AT LEAST DON'T SCOWL, EVEN IF YOU FEEL STRESSED.
It's easy to bring a harried morning at the office with you into the
classroom. But if you practice smiling a bit, looking relaxed, and
being open to new acquaintances, you'll be amazed how many interesting people respond by making social overtures. Even if
you're terribly shy, simply maintaining a cheerful expression can
draw people to you like a magnet.

Of course, you don't have to buddy up with everyone who says
hello. But if you look and act approachable, you'll soon make
friends with other students in each class. Then, if you get the flu
and need someone to take notes for you, or if you want to form a
small study group for an exam, you'll know who to call or E-mail.

4. VOLUNTEER FOR ON-CAMPUS EVENTS THAT WILL PUT YOU IN
LEAGUE WITH THE "DOERS." There are plenty of campus activities in
which you can invest just a bit of time and reap big rewards. You
don't have to edit the yearbook to be involved. Simply showing up
for a social event or signing up to staff an information booth can
put you in touch with hundreds of students and give you an easy
excuse to talk to people. As Leon suggests:

> The most common regret for non-traditional-age students is
> that they missed out on so much of the college experience.

Try to make time to attend events on campus, go to Rally Day celebrations and commencement, have lunch with fellow students, initiate study groups with classmates—this is always helpful, and it can be fun. Another way to get involved with life on campus is to volunteer during orientation. I did this last year and thoroughly enjoyed talking with new students, answering questions, and reassuring them that they were not alone and that I knew how excited and scared they were.

By mentoring others, you can also calm your own anxieties. Teaching has always been one of the best ways to learn, so seek out opportunities to participate in this interactive way.

GETTING TO KNOW YOUR PROFESSORS, AND WORKING WITH THE BEST

Now let's consider your relationships with professors. These are the people who can have the most direct bearing on your future, especially if you plan to go to graduate or professional school. Even if you want to stop with a bachelor's degree, they can still help direct your studies, and they are a potential source of guidance and camaraderie.

If your choice of classes is going to be based on what's taught at 7:30 a.m. or which class fulfills which requirement, stop and ask yourself, "Who are the stars here?" Almost every campus has its roster of professors who consistently win teaching awards and who have demonstrated over time just how much they love their profession and how well they perform its duties. Some of them may be nationally famous in their fields. Others may not be so well-known but may have a fine track record for nurturing students. Some of my friends today, a full decade after undergraduate school, are my former professors. We have become professional colleagues now, and they have taken a great deal of pleasure in watching me grow from a nervous twenty-eight-year-old college sophomore into a fellow academic.

Jan enjoyed her relationships with professors as one of the highlights of her college career as a theology student:

> The professors were always more than gracious to the adult students; in fact, I sensed that they often enjoyed, and even preferred, our class discussions. I noted, too, a relationship between us of friendship and partnership in ministry, rather than merely professor-to-student.

At the University of Miami, Jennifer noted that her relationships with professors extended beyond the classroom after the course was over:

> The professors who participate in this program are very accommodating. Long after the class, one of the professors assisted in the planning of a special field trip to our Holocaust Memorial and Jewish Museum in Miami Beach.

Interaction like this just can't be written into a job description. You can only find it when you seek out and study with the professors who want to invest more in their work than simply teaching and grading.

How do you meet the great professors, the ones who have not only made a mark in their fields, but who are also passionately devoted to teaching and research as vital aspects of the intellectual life? You begin by learning the riches of your own university and taking it upon yourself to shop carefully for the scholars under whom you will study.

You will want to choose professors who are outstanding teachers, and also those who have contributed to their fields. This means that you will look for a combination of qualities that will vary from person to person. One professor may be world-famous for her books and lectures, but she may not teach well. In fact, she may relegate all of her teaching duties to her graduate students while she keeps herself hidden from the unwashed masses. Another professor may be a wonderful teacher but may have published very little, or nothing at all. You'll need a combination of known scholars and excellent teachers to have the best possible experience at your university. If you are very lucky, you will find that some of the big names are also great teachers. You should seize the opportunity to work with them as soon as possible. Here are nine suggestions for finding out their names:

1. ASK INDIVIDUAL DEPARTMENTS FOR HELP. If you're thinking about taking an astronomy course, for example, professors and staff in the physics department will undoubtedly know who many of the best teachers are. Don't just ask for a list of accomplishments, though. Dig deeper and ask, "What are the courses that students consistently love? Which professors are known for taking an interest in their students' lives?" Although few administrators will go on record as saying something negative about a professor, most are happy to point you in the direction of the better teachers, simply because it enhances the reputation of their department campus-wide.

2. CHECK THE WEBSITES OF THE VARIOUS DEPARTMENTS THAT INTEREST YOU. Most sites have a listing of all the professors in the department, along with shortened on-line versions of their curricula vitae (résumés, including publications). You can learn which professors hold certain honors, which is important if you ever hope to earn those credentials yourself. For example, only someone who has earned a Phi Beta Kappa key can recommend a student for membership, so you'll need to work with the right professors if you hope to demonstrate your qualifications for that honor.

3. TAKE ADVANTAGE OF QUIET TIMES IN THE SEMESTER TO MEET PROFESSORS AND LEARN WHO'S WHO. During registration week, stu-

dents often stop by during office hours to talk to professors. They ask questions about what the professor will be teaching that semester, they look over the syllabi, and they discuss their goals and interests. I welcome these informal meetings with students before the semester begins as a way of getting to know students without the pressure of the classroom. I have been able to encourage some to take my classes and to suggest to others that they try a different professor instead if their personal goals seem divergent from mine. Many students have chosen (or perhaps not chosen) my classes on the basis of these talks. You should take full advantage of this opportunity to interview your potential teachers in person.

4. TALK TO ALUMNI AND GRADUATE STUDENTS. If your university has a strong alumni association, you may find that certain professors are known for maintaining relationships with former students long after they've left the university gates. Check back issues of the alumni magazine or newsletter for mention of excellent professors. Also, the graduate students usually get to know professors more intimately than undergrads. Visit the grad student lounges in various departments and ask for recommendations. Some student organizations also publish guides to professors and courses based on student evaluations, and these can be quite helpful, even if they are a bit biased toward the easier courses.

5. CONTACT YOUR CAMPUS PRESS OFFICE. Most universities have an office that keeps a list of resident experts in various fields so that journalists can find people to quote in newspaper and magazine articles. It is important to a university's national standing that it keep the names of its best professors in the public consciousness. Let the office know that you are looking for those teachers who have a reputation for sparkling performances in the classroom and for long-term nurturing of students.

6. SCOUR THE COURSE OFFERINGS IN BULLETINS AND CATALOGUES. I followed this plan at George Mason University and soon learned

that it had a well-funded program called the Clarence J. Robinson professorships. These positions went to stars in their fields who had been chosen from top universities nationwide for their combination of teaching and research excellence. Because of the generous terms of their teaching contracts, they were relaxed and available, and had plenty of time to invest in their students.

I began shopping for Robinson Professor courses in my junior year, and this led me to classes I might never have taken, such as "Scientific Literacy" with Dr. James S. Trefil, "Literature and Biology" with Dr. Harold Morowitz, and "Literature and Psychology" with Dr. Thelma Lavine. These courses were among the highlights of my undergraduate experience. One of the professors, Jim Trefil, became a personal friend. He encouraged me in my choice of graduate school, and he has written me some excellent, well-informed letters of recommendation over the years. Only a professor who knows you and your work, and who has followed your progress, can really do this for you. It is one of the most valuable things you will gain in college.

7. AVOID GRADUATE STUDENT INSTRUCTORS. If you go to a big, research-oriented university, many of your freshman and sophomore courses may be taught by graduate students. Known as teaching assistants (TA's), they are generally young, overworked, and often relatively inexperienced teachers. Their quality varies so wildly that I never recommend taking a course from one. The only exception to this rule pertains to science labs, which grad students traditionally run.

Even though many TA's go on to become gifted, caring professors, you're catching them at a weak point in their academic careers. They can't write you letters of recommendation or nominate you for awards. I have known TA's who taught full course loads while preparing for doctoral exams or defenses of dissertations, and the pressure showed by the end of the semester. Although many of these students are quite talented, you should wait until they enter professorial life before working with them. You can find out who the grad students are by checking with the department if you see an unfamiliar name next to a course offering.

Also, try to avoid any course where the professor is "to be announced" (TBA), since you never know who might fill the slot at the last minute.

8. AVOID PART-TIME FACULTY IF THEY ARE TRYING TO MOVE ON TO ANOTHER UNIVERSITY. You will want letters of recommendation from tenured and tenure-track professors who are respected in the university community. Adjunct lecturers and part-timers often have little or no power in their own departments, let alone in the university as a whole. Part-time professors are often actively applying for tenure-track jobs at other universities, so they may not have the clout you need.

There is an exception to this, however. Occasionally universities will bring in writers-in-residence or visiting scholars from other universities. Some professors may teach part-time because they are managing a thriving profession in their field; many attorneys, business leaders, and authors prefer a split schedule as a way to enjoy the best of both worlds. These are fine choices, and you will do well to work with them. Also, there are many tenured professors who are semiretired, but who teach an occasional course from which you may greatly benefit.

9. ONLY TAKE CLASSES FROM THOSE WHO "DO AND TEACH." Before you sign up for any course ask what the professor has done in the field. Drama professors should have experience on the stage, and not just in university productions. Professors teaching advertising and business should have corporate experience in the open market. Anyone who purports to teach writing should be published. You may have an awkward time if you confront professors directly about this, but their departments should know, or you can check their curricula vitae on the departments' websites.

STUDYING ABROAD WITH FELLOW
STUDENTS AND PROFESSORS

One of the most spectacular advantages of a traditional college program is the opportunity to study abroad elegantly and inexpensively. Nearly half of all undergraduate students study abroad. The top destinations are the United Kingdom, Italy, Spain, France, Mexico, Australia, Germany, Costa Rica, and Japan, but students go just about anywhere in the world. Recently opened destinations such as Russia, Eastern Europe, and China are becoming increasingly popular, as are the Caribbean and Africa. If you travel with a university group, someone else will handle all of the arrangements, including your airline tickets, hotels or private accommodations, and food. You will receive academic credit for having fun, and your résumé will look wonderful.

Study and travel abroad is important for your professional development, because it will give you a more balanced international perspective. If you plan a career in law, business, or politics, your overseas experiences will not just change the way you think about global issues, but will also make you appear more qualified to the people who will make hiring decisions about you. By working with a foreign university, you will learn how uniquely American our system is. Even a brief experience living, working, and conducting research in another country will give you a matchless opportunity to see the world differently.

There is also no better way to learn a foreign language. Forget that nonsense you've heard about adults being "unable" to attain fluency in new languages. If you spend a summer or even an academic year immersed in a culture and a language, you'll be chattering away in no time. Dedication beyond this can lead to complete fluency.

I used my university's study-abroad options to complete a language requirement when I was thirty-three. My French was shaky, so I made arrangements to spend six months in Paris taking language classes every day and living with a French family. The monthly cost of my entire program, including accommodations and food, was slightly *less* than what I paid each month to live in the United States! Going abroad and learning French in Paris was cheaper and far more efficient than sitting in my own living room, flipping flash cards and making myself miserable.

Don't think that studying abroad is restricted to rich kids at private schools whose parents have a second home in Madrid. Of the top twenty research institutions that send students abroad, fifteen are major state universities charging affordable tuition. Here is just a small sample of the great study-abroad programs at universities and colleges around the country:

- *Clark Atlanta University* offers a four-week summer journalism and mass communications program in Kingston, Jamaica, at the University of the West Indies. The 6-credit program costs $3,000, which is just $1,130 more than regular tuition and fees for the university. This includes airfare, accommodations, books, food, and expenses. Participant Nneka J. Priestly, writing for *The Black Collegian*, says that she financed her trip through sponsorships offered by community leaders, as well as family contributions. For information on the program, contact Dr. James D. McJinkins, Clark Atlanta University, James P. Brawley Drive and Fair Street, S.W., Atlanta, GA 30314; the phone number is (404) 880-8309.
- *George Mason University* in Fairfax, Virginia, offers a four-week economics program in China every summer. It also has honors semesters at Oxford and direct-exchange programs with colleges in Spain, Australia, Germany, Malta, the Netherlands, Paraguay, and other countries, plus many more programs. Dr. Yehuda Lukacs, the director of the Center for Global Education, says that the program has an exceptionally high number of commuting and nontraditional students who can earn as many as

30 credits abroad. Find out more about the Center at *www.gmu.edu/departments/cge*.

- *Georgetown University* received the estate of Villa Le Balze in Fiesole, Italy, from a granddaughter of John D. Rockefeller. Students live there with professors-in-residence, earning full academic credit. They study the Italian language, Renaissance and art history, literature, government, and even Italian cinema. Then they spend the three-day weekends exploring Italy in groups. Visit the website at *www.georgetown.edu/ssce/villa*.

- *Ball State University* in Muncie, Indiana, offers its education majors a chance to earn their field experience requirement during a summer semester in Monterrey, Mexico, teaching at the American School Foundation of Monterrey. This cultural immersion helps future teachers decide how they feel about bilingual education and immigrant education programs. They work firsthand with students whom these policies may someday affect. Find out more at *www.bsu.edu/teachers/departments/eled/elementaryeduc/study.htm*.

- *Beaver College* in Glenside, Pennsylvania, sends its students on a freshman-year week in London for only $150 above regular tuition and fees, including airfare. Students attend plays in the West End, visit one of England's great universities such as Oxford or Cambridge, and tour historic sites together. They also enjoy time on their own to sightsee and explore. This short trip is designed to introduce students to foreign study and to encourage them to sign up for the college's other travel-abroad programs. Visit them on the Web at *www.beaver.edu/cea*.

Many universities subsidize all or part of their student fees through special funding, including money from the United States Information Agency and other sources. The federal government has a strong interest in changing the foreign perception of Americans as xenophobic and illiterate in foreign languages. Many nationally funded programs exist to get students out of the United States and around the globe.

Most universities and colleges have access to airfare and accommodation discounts that travel agents working privately can't begin to match. Some universities have a swap system whereby a university abroad—say in Prague or Johannesburg—will send its students to a college in the United States and the U.S. college will send its own students to the university abroad at no additional charge to either party apart from airfare. If you travel to a politically sensitive region such as Russia, Eastern Europe, Korea, the Middle East, Southeast Asia, or another area that has delicate relationships with the United States, you may find yourself a partial guest of the foreign government, staying at little or no cost and gaining firsthand experience of a country that you may otherwise know only through newspaper headlines.

You should thoroughly study your university's catalogue, and also its website, to find out about available programs. Then call the study-abroad office on campus. Don't worry about being "too old"; many of the travelers will be professors and graduate students whose ages range from the late twenties to well beyond retirement age. Remember, too, that you don't need to limit yourself to the offerings of your own university. Many campuses welcome special students from other programs, and your university is quite likely to accept the transfer credit toward your degree if you get everything approved ahead of time. I have listed some good books to help you locate programs in Appendix B.

Many adults think that they can't travel overseas because of work and family commitments. If you plan ahead, however, you will be surprised just how cooperative many people are willing to be. One former boss allowed me to take two months off without pay to backpack in Europe. I presented him with a workable proposal, including plans for someone else to cover my workload and my full assumption of responsibility for making up missed work. You never know until you ask just how flexible your employer might be, especially if you plan your trip at least a year ahead of time.

Families are generally even more flexible. You will probably be able to include your partner in your travel for the same cost as another student, or for not much more. Better yet, your partner may be able to enroll in classes at your college through continuing education, earn course credits, and feel like a full participant in your academic journey.

If you want to try an overseas program with your children, I strongly recommend that you read Rick Steve's *Europe Through the Back Door* (John Muir Publications, 1999), which includes firsthand tips for traveling inexpensively with kids (he has three). Rick's guide will save you many thousands of dollars while affording you a better experience than your high-ticket fellow travelers. You may have to do some creative adjusting to take your family along on a study-abroad adventure, but many families have done it before and had a marvelous time.

Lenny has been taking his children to Italy since they were seven and nine; now they are in their twenties, and they travel confidently alone. Children don't mind curling up in sleeping bags on the villa floor or squashing themselves two to a bed, even for a month or more. Remember that you don't have to take your little ones to restaurants every night. There are plenty of grocery stores and open-air markets that sell food at modest prices, often much lower than those you're used to. And you don't have to pack fifteen suitcases full of enough supplies for the whole trip. Stores all over the industrialized world sell diapers, formula, medicine, and anything else you might possibly need. By learning to live like a local person and traveling light, you can keep your budget and your schedule under control, even with children. Ask professors who regularly go abroad with their families for family-friendly options for your particular excursions.

Besides the opportunities listed in this chapter, every college has its own special programs. But you have to search far beyond the bookstore and the registrar's office to find them.

ENJOYING THE BEAUTY OF THE TRADITIONAL COLLEGE CAMPUS

The best way to feel like a part of your university is to enjoy some of its time-honored campus traditions. Lynn found that she felt like part of the academic community when she participated in one of her college's rituals:

> Lantern Night is a Bryn Mawr tradition when freshmen re-
> ceive wrought lanterns that symbolize wisdom and learning.
> It's performed by several hundred people in the pitch dark of
> our cloister. We wear academic robes and sing hymns to
> Athena in Greek. My family came and it was really wonder-
> ful. My lantern is in my home office now.

Other students reported feeling part of it all when they were accepted as members in clubs or honor societies. Carl remembers the candle-lighting ritual at his Alpha Chi Omega induction ceremony as the highlight of his college career: "It even rivaled how great I felt at graduation."

My own academic moment happened a bit more spontaneously. I had gone to a new-student mixer at the University of Virginia, and I still felt awkward and out of place. As I struggled to think of what to say to *anyone* in that room full of strangers, a group of men in blue blazers and khaki trousers, wearing blue-and-orange-striped bow ties, assembled from out of the crowd. One of them hummed, and then they launched into an a capella rendition of "The Good Old Song," U.Va.'s school anthem. Then they sang the more upbeat tunes "On the Street Where You Live" and "Always Something There to Remind Me." They were the Virginia Gentlemen, one of the oldest a capella choral groups in the nation, and this ten-minute concert was a promotion for their upcoming show. I was charmed, as I later learned generations of Virginia students have been.

•   •   •

Becoming part of campus life and developing an intellectual identity aren't things you strive for. They're things that happen to you. As you follow your academic interests and learn *how* to learn, you'll develop an intellectual identity without artifice or pretense. You won't need to worry about arrogance, because you'll have the humility that comes with understanding your limitations as well as your strengths. Understanding both is necessary for scholarly development, and as you adapt to university culture, you'll learn to keep them in proper perspective.

If you embrace the traditional college experience, much of what you have just read about in the previous chapters will occur naturally. Top professors will seek you out because you are hardworking and dedicated. Fellow students who want friends and cohorts will find you. The right major will make itself evident. Your path will begin to open up as you walk it, day by interesting, challenging day.

Banish the idea of the commuter campus. Forget about stripped-down college curricula "tailored to busy lifestyles." Instead, buy yourself a sweatshirt with a university logo and an extra-large coffee mug and resolve to enjoy the best of on-campus culture. You will quickly learn that waiting to get your bachelor's degree just might have been the smartest move you could have made. By earning a degree now, when you're old enough to appreciate it, you'll find out what most people never discover: Learning is fun. College is important. And your education? You already have quite a bit. Now you're ready to use it to help you earn a traditional bachelor's degree.

We'll close with some wisdom from many of the adult students who made this book possible:

- *Sue (University of Minnesota):* "I encourage everyone to work towards their dream. Sometimes, in looking back over the last couple of years, I can't believe I actually accomplished what I set out to do. My husband says I am almost scary because everything worked out as I had planned."

- *Jennifer (University of Wisconsin):* "It is a big commitment. Sometimes the light at the end of the tunnel seems to be 'off,' but the satisfaction I get after a semester of hard work really makes it worthwhile. I've never received that kind of satisfaction from any job I've ever had."
- *Maggie (University of Wisconsin):* "Take advantage of and appreciate the opportunities that higher education provides. Scholarship has infinite meanings. It takes courage and effort and requires dedication and commitment. It is a blessing and an accomplishment."
- *Dave (American River College):* "Gain an understanding of yourself and try to be that person. Look within and listen. Follow your heart and dreams, regardless of how much resistance there is. And when it seems like too much, ask for help."
- *Arlene (Sarah Lawrence College):* "I have much more confidence in myself since I have been here. I feel more competent and much more sure of my opinions . . . This has been the best process for me. I have grown intellectually, emotionally, and spiritually since I have been here. The nature of the courses I have taken has been very enriching. I have met and become friends with some fabulous people, and I would say that I see the world in a different way than I did before."
- *Cyndy (American River College):* "Eight years ago, if you had told me I would be writing this to you, I *never* would have believed you. I am so passionate about the advantages of getting an education that I could probably write a novel about it."
- *Edward (University of Massachusetts):* "I would say follow your dreams, and if I can do it, anyone can. I worked two jobs, am a single parent, and maintained high grades because I wanted to make the most of this last chance."

- *Lenore (Sarah Lawrence College):* "Go to college if it is your goal. It is never too late. Be creative; develop a plan that best suits you."
- *Sharon (American River College):* "School is great at any age, but at my age you realize just how great it is. I'm here to learn, not just to get a grade . . . I think I'll do it forever."
- *Penny (Aquinas College):* "Do yourself a favor, give college a chance. I guarantee it will enhance your life and the way you feel about yourself."
- *Carol (University of Wisconsin):* "Stick with it and graduate, no matter how long it takes, if that is what you really want."
- *Jack (University of Texas):* "By taking a few years to go out into the real world, I gained experience. I knew why I needed to work and study hard. I knew why I had to make the sacrifice, and the rewards for doing it. I had gained the maturity to make myself do it."
- *Angie (University of Wisconsin):* "Don't let your financial situation stop you from pursuing your dream. The rewards that you will receive from college are tremendous. Every one of us is put on this earth with a purpose; it's up to you to find out what that purpose is and then do something about it. It's going to be tough, but you can do it!"
- *Jennifer (University of Miami):* "I can truthfully say that this degree was a wonderful experience. If they had a further degree in this program, I would sign up in a heartbeat."
- *Julie (University of Miami):* "Getting my bachelor's degree seemed like an unreachable goal. With the consistent support and guidance of my counselor and some hard work, I am proud to say that I earned a degree, raised my self-esteem, and helped my career all at the same time."
- *Jay (University of Wisconsin):* "Just go for it. If you really want to, then the obstacles, such as trying to balance fam-

ily responsibilities and studying, will not be overwhelming. I had thought that being away from school for a long time would be a hindrance, but in fact, my life experiences have proven to be valuable."

- *Penny (University of Wisconsin):* "It all comes down to desire. Maybe you are content without a degree. Then fine, no one should tell you that you are less of a person for not having it. But if you wish you could do it, you can, no question about it."

- *Jan (Aquinas College):* "The six years it took me to complete a B.A. in theology while working full-time and raising two teenagers were not easy, but I kept pushing onward because the goal meant so much to me."

- *Ina (Aquinas College):* "What I wish I had known ahead of time was how enjoyable learning is. The stimulation I receive in the classroom continues to motivate me to learn more. My husband is convinced I will not ever stop going to school."

- *Palma (Sarah Lawrence):* "With the exception of raising my children, I have not felt more alive or been more fulfilled than right now as an adult college student."

- *Jorgiana (University of Arizona):* "I am more diligent than a preacher trying to save a soul! Do it, do it, do it! The rewards are unbelievable. The way I see it, if you start thinking about college and returning or attending, you're probably ready."

- *Heather (University of Wisconsin):* "I think the biggest key to success is commitment. If you are committed to going back to college and getting your degree, nothing will be able to stop you."

- *Sally (University of Wisconsin):* "I love what I am doing and look forward to each new day. A framed picture with a quote by George Eliot has been on my desk for the past several years: 'It is never too late to be what you might have been.' "

Appendix A

Some Recommended Campuses for Nontraditional Students

As this book demonstrates, you don't need to find a special program designed for adults in order to go back to college. In fact, you'll be better off if you enjoy undergraduate school in a manner as close to the traditional experience as possible. However, many campuses are working hard to make adults feel welcome. Here are a few of the colleges and universities that contributed information to this book and that offer special programs for nontraditional students.

Some of these colleges state that they specialize in nondegree options. You may start out there, but you will want to transfer into a mainstream undergraduate program after earning a few credits. Be persistent and firm! If you call and someone tries to redirect you to a distance-learning or weekend college division that is separate from the regular undergraduate experience, insist that you are seeking a traditional on-campus degree.

This list is a good place to start, but you will also want to call the colleges in your area that interest you and ask for information about their programs. You will probably find a niche that meets your needs on just about any campus in the country.

Remember that over time, E-mail addresses and website listings will probably change. You can always find updated information about any college's programs on its main website.

ALASKA

UNIVERSITY OF ALASKA (public, coeducational)
Office of Admissions
P.O. Box 757480
Fairbanks, AK, 99775-7480
907-474-7500
800-478-1UAF
E-mail: *fyapply@uaf.edu*

ARIZONA

UNIVERSITY OF ARIZONA (public, coeducational)
Dianna S. Hyland
Coordinator for Commuter Student Affairs
Office of Student Programs
Arizona Student Unions
P.O. Box 210017
Tucson, AZ 85721
520-621-7597
www.sunion.arizona.edu/~sprograms/centerocs/csa/csa.html

ARKANSAS

UNIVERSITY OF ARKANSAS AT LITTLE ROCK (public,
    coeducational)
Dr. Peggy A. Sissel, Interim Director
Center for Research on Teaching and Learning
2801 South University
Little Rock, AR 72204
501-569-8179
www.ualr.edu

CALIFORNIA

AMERICAN RIVER COLLEGE (community college,
  coeducational)
Bonnie Miller, Career Counselor
Re-entry Center
4700 College Oak Drive
Sacramento, CA 95841
916-484-8011
www.arc.losrios.cc.ca.us/stusrvc/reentry.html

UNIVERSITY OF CALIFORNIA, BERKELEY (public, coeducational)
Adult Re-entry Program
260 Cesar E. Chavez Student Center
Berkeley, CA 94720-4260
510-643-8070
www.slc.uga.berkeley.edu/reentryprogram/reentryhp.html

STANFORD UNIVERSITY (private, coeducational)
William Tingley, Director of Transfer Admissions
Undergraduate Admission
Old Union 232, 520 Lasuen Mall
Stanford, CA 94305-3005
650-723-2091
E-mail: *undergrad.admissions@forsythe.stanford.edu*
www.stanford.edu/group/uga

CONNECTICUT

CONNECTICUT COLLEGE (private, coeducational)
E. Whitney Soule, Director, Return-to-College Program
Ann Whitlach, Coordinator of Continuing Education
Office of Admission
270 Mohegan Avenue
New London, CT 06320
860-439-2200
www.conncoll.edu/offices/cont_ed
E-mail: *admit@conncoll.edu*

TRINITY COLLEGE (private, coeducational)
Individualized Degree Program
300 Summit Street
Hartford, CT 06106-3100
860-297-2150
www.trincoll.edu/~idp
E-mail: *idp@trincoll.edu*

DISTRICT OF COLUMBIA

AMERICAN UNIVERSITY (private, coeducational)
4400 Massachusetts Avenue, NW
Washington, DC 20016
202-885-2513
www.american.edu/academic.depts/isp
E-mail: *adults@american.edu*

GEORGETOWN UNIVERSITY (private, coeducational)
Dr. Phyllis O'Callaghan, Director
Anne Ridder, Associate Director
Liberal Studies Degree Program
P.O. Box 571011
Washington, DC 20057-1011
202-687-5746
www.georgetown.edu/ssce/ls/framemain.html
E-mail: *lsp@gunet.georgetown.edu*

HOWARD UNIVERSITY (private, coeducational, historically
   black)
Dr. Peggy A. Berry, Director
Continuing Education
1100 Wayne Avenue, 6th Floor
Silver Spring, MD 20910
301-585-2295
www.con-ed.howard.edu

FLORIDA

UNIVERSITY OF MIAMI (public, coeducational)
Louise Driscoll Sevilla, Director
Bachelor of General Studies
School of Continuing Studies
P.O. Box 248005
Coral Gables, FL 33124-1610
305-284-2727
305-284-6279 (fax)
www.miami.edu/cstudies/bgs/index.html
E-mail: *louise@miami.edu*

IOWA

UNIVERSITY OF NORTHERN IOWA (public, coeducational)
Office of Admissions
120 Gilchrist Hall
Cedar Falls, IA 50614-0018
800-772-2037
www.uni.edu/nontradi
E-mail: *admissions@uni.edu*

KANSAS

WICHITA STATE UNIVERSITY (public, coeducational)
Mary Bulla
Non-Traditional Student Recruitment Coordinator
1845 Fairmount
Wichita, KS 67260-0124
316-978-3638
800-362-2594
www.twsu.edu/~ntpc/ntsa

KENTUCKY

THOMAS MORE COLLEGE (private, coeducational)
Maureen Bensman
Director of Continuing Education
333 Thomas More Parkway
Crestview Hills, KY 41017
606-341-5800
www.thomasmore.edu/admision/admision.html

Morehead State University (public, coeducational)
Jacquelyn H. Scott, Coordinator
Non-Traditional/Commuter Students
150 University Boulevard
Morehead, KY 40351
800-585-6781
E-mail: *j.scott@morehead-st.edu*

Northern Kentucky University (public, coeducational)
Victoria Schwartz
Admissions Counselor, Adult Students
506 John's Hill Road
Highland Heights, KY 41099-5992
606-442-3536
www.nku.edu/~reentry/
E-mail: *schwartzv@nku.edu*

University of Kentucky (public, coeducational)
Office of Admissions
100 W. D. Funkhouser Building
Lexington, KY 40506-0054
606-257-2000
http://www.uky.edu/newhome/submain/nontrad.html

Massachusetts

Harvard University (private, coeducational)
Harvard Extension School
51 Brattle Street
Cambridge, MA 02138-3722
617-495-4024
www.extension.harvard.edu

MOUNT HOLYOKE COLLEGE (private, all-women)
Carolyn Dietel, Associate Director
Frances Perkins Programs
South Hadley, MA 01075
413-538-2077
www.mtholyoke.edu/acad/programs/fp
E-mail: *frances-perkins@mtholyoke.edu*

SMITH COLLEGE (private, all-women)
Ada Comstock Scholars Program
Northampton, MA 01063
413-585-3090
www.smith.edu/admission/ada.html
E-mail: *comstock@smith.edu*

UNIVERSITY OF MASSACHUSETTS–DARTMOUTH
    (public, coeducational)
Division of Continuing Education
285 Old Westport Road
North Dartmouth, MA 02747-2300
508-999-8605
www.umassd.edu/DCE/DCEacademic.html

WELLESLEY COLLEGE (private, all-women)
Dottie Folino
Davis Degree Program
106 Central Street
Wellesley, MA 02481-8203
www.wellesley.edu/DeanStudent/contin.html
E-mail: *dfolino@wellesley.edu*

MICHIGAN

AQUINAS COLLEGE (private, coeducational)
Catharina J. Marshall
Director of Adult Student Recruitment
1607 Robinson Road SE
Grand Rapids, MI 49508
616-459-8281, ext. 5254
800-678-9593
www.aquinas.edu/continuing/index.html
E-mail: *advising@aquinas.edu*

MINNESOTA

UNIVERSITY OF MINNESOTA (public, coeducational)
University College—Student Support Services
101 Wesbrook Hall
77 Pleasant Street, SE
Minneapolis, MN 55455
612-625-3333
800-234-6564

NEW MEXICO

UNIVERSITY OF NEW MEXICO (public, coeducational)
Dr. David E. Stuart
Associate Vice President for Academic Affairs
Dane Smith Hall, Room 220
601 Yale NE
Albuquerque, NM 87131-1001
505-277-0896
www.unm.edu/preview/evening.htm
E-mail: *evening@unm.edu*

NEW YORK

COLUMBIA UNIVERSITY (private, coeducational)
School of General Studies
Mail Code 4101
Lewisohn Hall
2970 Broadway
New York, NY 10027-9829
212-854-5107
www.columbia.edu/cu/gs
E-mail: *gs-admit@columbia.edu*

FORDHAM UNIVERSITY (private, coeducational)
Linda Marsek, Director of Admissions
College of Liberal Studies
Lincoln Center Campus
113 West 60th Street
New York, NY 10023
212-636-6710
www.fordham.edu/fcls/index.htm
E-mail: *ad_cuenca@lars.fordham.edu*

FORDHAM UNIVERSITY (private, coeducational)
Rose Hill Campus, Keating Hall
Bronx, NY 20458
718-817-3720
http://www.fordham.edu/fcls/rh.htm
E-mail: *ad_marsek@lars.fordham.edu*

New York University (private, coeducational)
The Paul McGhee Division
Office of Public Affairs
7 East 12th Street, 11th Floor
New York, NY 10003
212-998-7100
www.scps.nyu.edu/mcghee/html/programs.htm
E-mail: *scps.adultdegree@nyu.edu*

Sarah Lawrence College (private, formerly all-women,
   now coeducational)
Alice Olson, Director
Center for Continuing Education
1 Mead Way
Bronxville, NY 10708
914-395-2205
www.slc.edu/undergrad/cce/index.html
E-mail: *cce@mail.slc.edu*

North Carolina

Meredith College (private, all-women)
Sandra Close, Director
Office of Continuing Education
3800 Hillsborough Street
Raleigh, NC 27607-5298
919-760-8353
www.meredith.edu/academics/23+acad.htm
E-mail: *closes@meredith.edu*

UNIVERSITY OF NORTH CAROLINA AT CHAPEL HILL
  (public, coeducational)
Continuing Studies
CB #1020, The Friday Center
Chapel Hill, NC 27599-1020
919-962-1134
800-862-5669
www.fridaycenter.unc.edu/cs
E-mail: *pubpro@unc.edu*

PENNSYLVANIA

BRYN MAWR COLLEGE (private, all-women)
Rona Pietrzak, Assistant Dean
Director, Katharine E. McBride Scholars Program
101 North Merion Avenue
Bryn Mawr, PA 19010-2899
610-526-5373
www.brynmawr.edu/admissions/McBrideIndex.html

TEMPLE UNIVERSITY (private, coeducational)
1801 North Broad Street
Philadelphia, PA 19122
215-204-7000
www.temple.edu/undergrad/vbgainin.html

SOUTH CAROLINA

COLUMBIA COLLEGE (private, all-women)
1301 Columbia College Drive
Columbia, SC 29203
803-786-3788
800-277-1301
www.colacoll.edu/professional/index.html
E-mail: *admissions@colacoll.edu*

TEXAS

TEXAS A&M UNIVERSITY (public, coeducational)
Adult, Graduate, and Off-Campus Student Services
Department of Student Life
112 John J. Koldus Building
College Station, TX 77843-1257
409-845-1741
stulife.tamu.edu/agss
E-mail: *agss@tamu.edu*

UNIVERSITY OF TEXAS AT AUSTIN (public, coeducational)
2613 Wichita Street
Austin, TX 78705
512-471-3434
www.utexas.edu/student/admissions/
freshman.html#nontraditional

VIRGINIA

GEORGE MASON UNIVERSITY (private, coeducational)
Office of Undergraduate Admissions
4400 University Drive
Fairfax, VA 22030-4444
703-993-2400
www.gmu.edu
E-mail: *admissions@gmu.edu*

WISCONSIN

UNIVERSITY OF WISCONSIN–EAU CLAIRE (public,
   coeducational)
Rita Webb, Director
Adult Opportunity Office
Schofield 226
Eau Claire, WI 54702-4004
715-836-3259
www.uwec.edu/admin/adultop/
E-mail: *webbrl@uwec.edu*

UNIVERSITY OF WISCONSIN–MADISON (public, coeducational)
Pat Fessenden, Assistant Dean
Student Services
Division of Continuing Studies
905 University Avenue, Room 209
Madison, WI 53715
608-263-6960
www.dcs.wisc.edu/ac3

Appendix B

Books, Software, Websites, and Other Helpful Resources

Here is a select list of resources that you might find helpful as you prepare for college. There is much more out there, but there are also a lot of dubious guides, so don't believe everything you find in print.

Resources for Locating Great Schools

As we noted in Chapter 4, a good university is important. However, that doesn't mean you can just look on the annual top-ten list of a major magazine and be done with it. Here are some guides that can expand your thinking about what makes a great campus:

Custard, Edward T.: *Complete Book of Colleges* (Princeton Review, 2000)
——— and John Katzman: *The Best 311 Colleges* (Princeton Review, 1998)
Fiske, Edward B., and Kathleen Blease: *The Fiske Guide to Colleges* (Times Books, 1998)
Pope, Loren: *Colleges That Change Lives: 40 Schools That You Should Know About Even If You're Not a Straight-A Student* (Penguin, 1996)

————: *Looking Beyond the Ivy League: Finding a College That's Right for You* (Penguin, 1996)
Yale Daily News Staff: *The Insider's Guide to Colleges* (St. Martin's, 1997)

BOOKS ABOUT APPLYING FOR ADMISSION

We talked about admissions in Chapter 6, but you may want additional advice from college admissions officers and other experts. Most guidebooks are written with the high school junior or senior in mind. You'll have to adapt much of their advice to fit your particular situation, but generally these offer much in the way of unconventional wisdom.

Bauld, Harry: *On Writing the College Application Essay* (Barnes & Noble, 1987). Long considered a standard in the field, with fine examples of how to catch the attention of admissions officers without turning them off.

Curry, Boykin, and Brian Kasbar: *Essays That Worked: 50 Essays from Successful Applications to the Nation's Top Colleges* (Fawcett Books, 1990)

Fiske, Edward, and Bruce Hammond: *The Fiske Guide for Getting into the Right College: The Complete Guide to Everything You Need to Know to Get into and Pay for College* (Times Books, 1997)

Georges, Christopher J. and Gigi E: *100 Successful College Application Essays* (New American Library, 1991)

Mayher, Bill: *The College Admissions Mystique and What You Can Do About It* (Noonday Press, 1997)

FINANCIAL AID RESOURCES

Here are some of my favorite financial aid resources on-line:

Yahoo! Financial Aid: *www.yahoo.com/Education/Financial_Aid*
FinAid Resource Page: *www.finaid.org*
fastWeb! Search Service: *www.fastweb.com*

SAT PREPARATION COURSES

Your college may not require the SAT for nontraditional students, but I do recommend taking it if you are trying to get in at a competitive campus.

The Princeton Review	Kaplan Educational Centers
2315 Broadway	888 Seventh Avenue
New York, NY 10024	New York, NY 10106
212-874-8282	212-492-5800
800-234-3088	800-234-3088
www.review.com	*www.kaplan.com*

RESEARCH GUIDES

In Chapter 8, I encouraged you to read some books on how to conduct library research. Also be sure to purchase a style manual to guide you in the format of your finished papers. Here are one research book and two style manuals to get you started:

Booth, Wayne C., Gregory G. Colomb, and Joseph M. Williams: *The Craft of Research* (University of Chicago Press, 1995). One of my all-time favorite guides to thinking about your research and conducting it intelligently, without wasting too much of your precious time. This book is well worth reading through once for general ideas and then using as a reference guide.

Gibaldi, Joseph, and Phyllis Franklin: *MLA Handbook for Writers of Research Papers* (Modern Language Association of America, 1995). The standard student handbook for research-paper style in the humanities.

The Chicago Manual of Style: The Essential Guide for Writers, Editors and Publishers (University of Chicago Press, 1993). This is the standard student handbook for research-paper style in the sciences and social sciences. Don't just use it as a reference work; read it for great think-ahead strategies on organizing your papers.

RESOURCES FOR LOCATING STUDY-ABROAD PROGRAMS

Study and travel in other countries can be the most exciting thing about returning to college. You will be surprised at how much more affordable it will be for you and your family to travel with a university-sponsored program. See Chapter 11 for information on how to go abroad with the help of your college or university.

> Tannen, Greg, and Charley Winkler: *The Student's Guide to the Best Study-Abroad Programs* (Pocket Books, 1997)

Also:

- The Online Study Abroad Directory, a service of the International Study and Travel Center at the University of Minnesota–Twin Cities, *www.istc.umn.edu/osad*. Regularly updated free listing of programs at various colleges and universities.
- Council on International Educational Exchange, 800-2-COUNCIL; *www.ciee.org*. Includes information on working abroad, internships, and volunteer opportunities worldwide.
- World Learning, founded in 1932 as the U.S. Experiment in International Living, 802-257-7751; *www.worldlearning.org*. One of the oldest and most respected international study resources.

OTHER RESOURCES

The Web is a wonderful place to look for information about colleges and universities. Campuses have been wired to the Web since the very beginning, so you will find more authoritative and up-to-date information there than in most books.

Just remember to stick to the experts. A college or university's website is the best source of information about itself. Most sites that you have to pay to use aren't worth the money.

You can use a categorized search engine such as Yahoo!, About.Com, Ask.Com, or Northernlight.com to search for free information about colleges and universities. If you feel over-whelmed, go to Yahoo!'s complete listing of colleges and universities by state to limit the search to your own region.

ACKNOWLEDGMENTS

I am happy to say that the list of people to whom I am grateful for help, support, motivation, and friendship grows ever longer.

To my trusted editor, Elisabeth Kallick Dyssegaard, for her consistency, for her gifts, and for those ever-upbeat telephone feedback sessions. To her editorial assistant, Elaine Blair, for patience and creative suggestions. We made it! And to my dearest David Hendin, a faithful friend and agent, who makes me feel like the luckiest writer in the world.

Also to Byron Woods, whose editorial work before I sent drafts of the manuscript to New York saved my proverbial bacon. John F. Edwards called often with bright ideas and suggested more detail on computers. David Chalfant saw to it that a birthday dinner at Citronelle was not just entertaining, but sustaining. Victoria Bosch Murray kept my spirits up through at least two dark nights of the soul. Kevin Braun remembered good ol' Florida State with entertaining anecdotes. Stevan and Sonja Fisher found back-to-college adults for me working at the Smithsonian. Richard B. Smith convinced me that *Good Will Hunting* was appropriate target practice. Keenan and Kristin Dakota reminded me that there were nurturing moments at Twin Oaks in the 1980s. James S. Trefil helped me see myself as a writer in the first place. Betty and Michael Foley loved me through good manuscripts and bad. John, Aaron, Mike, and Jeanette Foley gave me a sense of family and continuity. Ann Rosenbaum Pelberg told me her stories, and cheered me up at manuscript's end. Leona Fisher offered bouquets of professional and emotional support. Peter Blair told Dad-on-campus stories. Vera Schoenbaum Mathews Gebbert said, "Finish it, dear, and let's move on to Mary Frances!" Talia Greenberg encouraged me with visits to the West End Café, Billy Martin's Tavern, the Round Robin Bar, and the theater. Rochelle and Selig Kainer's lovely collection of friends rivaled the grand salons of literary fame. Dennis Quinn regularly checked in on me from across the academic corridor to make certain I was still typing, and kept me supplied with coffee. Greg Gates helped make traditionaldegrees.com its best, and was a long-term cheerleader. Peter Nichols inspired by astonishing example.

To the storytellers in these pages, thank you for having the courage to go back to college when you did. By triumphing in academia, you left a wonderful path for others to follow. Thanks also to the administrators and other professionals who offered comments, stories, and suggestions. Here are just some of the people who graciously responded to my requests for stories and information:

Nancy Adams, Anne Adkins, David Baker, Beth Banta, La Shawn Barnes, Anna Bates, M. Joseph Bauer, Cynthia Bell, Maureen Bensman, Daniel Best, Palma Bingle, Margaret Birdsong, Jane Borgerson, Mary Bulla, Mary Calhoun, Kristin Carskadon, AnneMarie Caruso, Joseph Carver, David Chaplin-Loebell, Li-Heng Chen, Nannette Clark, Barbara Coleman, Sally Cressler, Jennifer Davidson, Doris Davis, Colin D'Elia, Carolyn Dietel, Rich Dikeman, Kathy Donoho, Judi Dooley, Beverly Dorn, Diana Griego Erwin, Bob Ferguson, Pat Fessenden, Dottie Folino, Fionelle Fonseca, Sharon Fowler, Michael Gillan, David Giuliano, Ken Gonsalves, Mary Ann Greenwald, Jim Hanson, Jay Hatcher, Carol Hein, Fern Henley, Mary Ann Hill, Dale Ann Hughes,

Brenda Humberson, Dianna Hyland, Jorgiana Jake, Elizabeth James, Colette Joyce, Theo Karantsalis, Lenore Karo, Karen Kaufmann, Dave Keal, Mary Kwiatkowski, Penny Lecheler, Debbie Ledo-Anderl, Susan Lewan, Lynn Litterine, Carol Lonning, Rose Ann Lovell, Chris Malarkey, Catharina Marshall, Jennifer McCallum, Grace Meyer, Bonnie Miller, Paul Modjeski, Gail Nelsestuen, Jo Nickel, Alice Olson, Suzanne Olson, Steve Payne, Jack Peterson, Rona Pietrzak, Christine Plummer, Angela Pratt, Diane Rainson, Nancy Riley, Robin Ryan, Roxanne Rykal, Kristina Schoenberg, Polly Scholze, Victoria Schwartz, Jacquelyn Scott, Jennifer Senior, Julie Severson, Louise Driscoll Sevilla, Barbara Silaski, Renee Simone, Peggy Sissel, Julieta Skokan, Regenia Smalley, Whitney Soule, Jennifer Spaeth, Steven Steinmetz, Frankie Stevens, Penny Streling, David Stuart, Emily Sudderth, Susan Teates, Heather Tinder, Denise Treankler, Christian Vance, Heather Varga, Cyndy Vaughn, Jan Vile, Rita Webb, Ryan Windows, Jim Yates, Janice Yogis, Dan Zeh, Jin Hong Zhang.

In case I missed anyone (*oops!*), please visit us on the Web, *www.traditionaldegrees.com,* for an ongoing list of contributors and moral supporters and for additional wonderful stories.